PR 4687.3 .P47 1989
Perkin, J. Russell
A reception-history of
 George Eliot's fiction

DEMCO

A Reception-History of
George Eliot's Fiction

Nineteenth-Century Studies

Other Titles in This Series

*Jane Austen's Beginnings:
The Juvenilia and Lady Susan*
J. David Grey, ed.

Reconsidering Aubrey Beardsley
Robert Langenfeld, ed.

*The Theory of the American Romance:
An Ideology in American
Intellectual History*
William Ellis

Dickens and the Concept of Home
Frances Armstrong

*Elizabeth Barrett Browning
and the Poetry of Love*
Glennis Stephenson

*Realism and the Romance:
Nathaniel Hawthorne, Henry James,
and American Fiction*
Elissa Greenwald

A Reception-History of George Eliot's Fiction

by
J. Russell Perkin

UMI Research Press

Ann Arbor / London

Produced and distributed by
UMI Research Press
an imprint of
University Microfilms Inc.
Ann Arbor, Michigan 48106

Library of Congress Cataloging in Publication Data

Perkin, J. Russell (James Russell)
A reception-history of George Eliot's fiction / by J. Russell
Perkin.
p. cm.—(Nineteenth-century studies)
Includes bibliographical references.
ISBN 0-8357-2011-X (alk. paper)
1. Eliot, George, 1819-1880—Criticism and interpretation—
History. I. Title. II. Series: Nineteenth-century studies (Ann
Arbor, Mich.)
PR4687.3.P47   1990
823'.8—dc20   89-20474
                                                                 CIP

The paper used in this publication meets the minimum requirements of
American National Standard for Information Sciences—Permanence of Paper for
Printed Library Materials, ANSI Z39.48-1984. ∞ ™

for deborah

Contents

Acknowledgments

Any work of scholarship bears the traces of countless debts of both an intellectual and a material nature. It is impossible to acknowledge all of these, but I would like in particular to thank the following individuals and institutions.

The University of Toronto and the Social Sciences and Humanities Research Council of Canada provided financial support for my research.

Professor Frederick Flahiff, a dedicated scholar and teacher of literature, read and criticized the early drafts and was generous with his time and his extensive knowledge of Victorian fiction.

The following teachers, friends, examiners, and colleagues read this book in at least one of its draft stages and made valuable suggestions: Royce Nickel, Virginia Lovering, Brian Corman, Henry Auster, Mario Valdés, David Richter, John Baird, Deborah Kennedy, and the anonymous UMI readers. I am particularly grateful to Royce Nickel for many productive discussions about literature and for his advice about translating German texts.

I am grateful to Josefa Kropp and John Leyerle for discussions that helped me to formulate my research topic more precisely.

I would also like to acknowledge the teaching of Brian Corman, who introduced me to literary history before it became fashionable again, and W. David Shaw, who opened my eyes to the philosophical complexity of Victorian literature.

Finally I want to thank my wife, Deborah Kennedy, who assisted me at every stage, both as a skilled editor and as a critic of my ideas, while I endeavoured to repay the debt as a reader of her work on the literature of the 1790s.

Bibliographical Note

Quotations from George Eliot's works will be identified by parenthetical citations in the text, using the following abbreviations. Quotations from the *Letters* are identified by volume and page number; quotations from the fiction by chapter and page. References to reviews contained in *George Eliot: The Critical Heritage* are also given parenthetically in the text.

AB   *Adam Bede*. Ed. Stephen Gill. Harmondsworth: Penguin, 1980.

CH   *George Eliot: The Critical Heritage*. Ed. David Carroll. London: Routledge & Kegan Paul, 1971.

DD   *Daniel Deronda*. Ed. Graham Handley. Oxford: Clarendon Press, 1984.

Essays   *Essays of George Eliot*. Ed. Thomas Pinney. London: Routledge & Kegan Paul, 1963.

FH   *Felix Holt, the Radical*. Ed. Fred C. Thomson. Oxford: Clarendon Press, 1980.

Letters *The George Eliot Letters*. Ed. Gordon S. Haight. 9 vols. New Haven: Yale University Press, 1954–78.

M   *Middlemarch: A Study of Provincial Life*. Ed. David Carroll. Oxford: Clarendon Press, 1986.

MF   *The Mill on the Floss*. Ed. Gordon S. Haight. Oxford: Clarendon Press, 1980.

R   *Romola*. Ed. Andrew Sanders. Harmondsworth: Penguin, 1980.

SCL   *Scenes of Clerical Life*. Ed. Thomas A. Noble. Oxford: Clarendon Press, 1985.

SM   *Silas Marner: The Weaver of Raveloe*. Ed. Q. D. Leavis. Harmondsworth: Penguin, 1967.

But, perhaps, the moment of most diffusive pleasure from public speaking is that in which the speech ceases and the audience can turn to commenting on it. The one speech, sometimes uttered under great responsibility as to missiles and other consequences, has given a text to twenty speakers who are under no responsibility.

Felix Holt, the Radical

1

Introduction

When I first began work on this study of George Eliot, literary history was not an especially popular concept. Literary historians had been sternly told by Paul de Man that "to become good literary historians, we must remember that what we usually call literary history has little or nothing to do with literature and that what we call literary interpretation—provided only it is good interpretation—is in fact literary history."[1] Although my own work sought to use the *Rezeptionsästhetik* of Hans Robert Jauss as the basis of a historical investigation of George Eliot's fiction, I was sufficiently impressed with de Man's injunction that I at first considered using it as the epigraph to this book. But throughout the 1980s literary history has returned to prominence in a way which rebukes my initial lack of confidence. Furthermore, the discovery of Paul de Man's wartime journalism has situated his own career more apparently within a history which transcends the history of literature and literary criticism. One could perhaps further speculate that de Man's attempts to deny the historicity of literature represent a desire to escape from the naive and dangerous—and, to be bluntly accurate, racist—models of literary history which he had employed at the beginning of his career. I mention these facts and speculations not in an attempt to belittle de Man, whose contribution to literary studies seems to me secure, but in order to show that literary history raises complex issues at the levels both of theory and of praxis, and that even a critic as great as de Man could not escape from the complexities of these issues by seeking to deny the historicity of literature. The pages which follow represent my own attempt to think through the relationship of literature and history, drawing primarily although not exclusively on reception theory.

Literary history was reinvigorated somewhat earlier in Germany than in North America. Jauss formulated his approach to literature under the provocation of both Marxist criticism in East Germany and the challenge to established modes of criticism from within the West German universities during the 1960s.[2] Before discussing the reception history of George Eliot's fiction, I think it would be useful to begin with a brief account of Jauss's career and work. I will then consider some of the criticisms of his work, mainly by Marxists, and will suggest ways in which a rapprochement might be effected between the work of the Konstanz school and the other historical approaches which are influential today, some of which are loosely summed up under the name "New Historicism."[3] It seems to me that there is a lot to be gained by the interaction of the "idealist" approach of Jauss and the more materialist approach of a critic like Jerome J. McGann.[4] My aim in all this is not to set up Jauss as a naive straw man. That style of criticism seems to me counterproductive, and only shows that the critic who practices it has mastered a simple technique for attacking and dismissing everything which does not conform to a particular ideological standard. The popularity of such an adversarial style perhaps accounts in part for the fact that Jauss's work has not become widely known in North America, although it addresses many concerns which have become central to literary studies in the last decade, for Jauss avoids attention-getting ideological simplifications. The fact that I draw on his work so extensively is sufficient proof of my regard for Jauss as a theorist. But I am also conscious of having been trained in a different critical tradition, which values both close reading and empirical investigation more than it does the kind of philosophical approach in which Jauss was schooled. Therefore it is only natural for me to try to reconcile reception aesthetics with my own critical training, and the chapters which follow, I hope, will illustrate something of what may be achieved by such a synthesis.

The work of Hans Robert Jauss emphasizes the idea that literary interpretation is unavoidably contingent upon the historical horizon of the interpreter, and regards literary history as the study of the changing horizons of expectation which determine the way that particular literary works are concretized by historical readers. Jauss is distinguished among recent theorists by his willingness to defend the utility of the concept of aesthetic experience, which is his particular emphasis in the essays which comprise his second major theoretical work, translated in English as *Aesthetic Experience and Literary Hermeneutics*. He argues that the aesthetic dimension of literature is that quality which gives pleasure and which is able to resist ideological determination, and he further maintains that it is this which gives literature its socially formative and transformative power.

In a polemical article entitled "Paradigmawechsel in der Literaturwissenschaft" ("Paradigm Change in Literary Studies") Jauss provides his own analysis of the history of literary studies.[5] This self-conscious account of the history which produced the present situation seems an appropriate place to begin to discuss the work of a literary historian, and Jauss's essay, written in the revolutionary years of the late 1960s, provides some useful insights. He begins with some ironic remarks on method, noting that methods are not "value-free" nor "equally valid at all times." Even in the world of literary studies, "methods don't drop from the sky; they have their own historical location" (p. 45). Jauss adopts Thomas S. Kuhn's now well-known concepts of paradigm, paradigm-shift, and scientific revolution in order to sketch a brief history of literary studies.[6] He identifies three principal paradigms:

1. *Classical humanism*, in which literature was judged according to its conformity with the "pattern and normative system" of the classics (p. 47).

2. *Historicism*, in which modern authors were arranged into a canon and in which the story of a nation's literature was a synecdoche for the story of its spiritual development: "Literature came to be the most exalted medium in which the national character could unfold itself from its quasi-mythical beginnings to the fulfilment of a national classicism" (p. 48).

3. *Stylistics and work-immanent aesthetics*, which includes the work of Leo Spitzer, the Russian Formalists, and the American New Critics. This method treated the literary work as "an autonomous object of investigation" (p. 50).

Jauss then considers the present state of literary studies, and concludes "it is above all apparent that one can no longer regard as self-evident the assumption, which was self-evident for the work-immanent method, that one should be concerned neither with the social conditions nor the historical consequences of art." (p. 51). When considered within the institutional context in which it was written, this statement is highly provocative, for Jauss is advocating an approach with many similarities to Marxist criticism. He is therefore careful to distinguish—rather disingenuously—his own approach from Marxism when he discusses what type of approach might constitute a fourth paradigm. Marxism is rejected for its preoccupation with the reflection theory (*Widerspiegelungstheorie*) and the doctrine of base and superstructure, which preclude an investigation into literary effect (*Wirkung*). Northrop Frye's criticism, on the other hand, lacks a "historical hermeneutic" which could mediate between archetypal structures and individual works (p. 53). Structuralism is also inadequate, and it is in fact not a single theory but several different schools of thought, including a delayed French reaction to the sway of the second paradigm. However, the need to reform literary studies is imperative; traditional methods cannot deal with the problems arising in a society dominated by the mass media. The literary humanities must once again be enabled to perform their task, which is "to wrest works of art away from the past by means of constantly new interpretation, to translate them into a new present, to make the experiences preserved in the art of the past available again, or in other words to pose the questions which are reformulated by every generation, to which the art of the past is able to reply and again to give us an answer" (p. 55).

The article concludes with some "requirements" (*Forderungen*) for a new model of literary study: it must mediate between aesthetic-formalist analysis and the study of the historical reception of literature, and it must mediate "art, history, and social reality"; it must bring together the methods of structuralism and hermeneutics; and it must develop an aesthetics of effect and a rhetoric capable of dealing with not only major literature (*Höhenkammliteratur*) but also "subliterature and the phenomena of the mass media" (p. 56). At the time that he expressed these *Forderungen* Jauss had already published his famous "Provocation" essay, which is a manifesto for the kind of new paradigm which he hoped would be sufficient to meet the crisis in literary studies.

The study of literary reception is a fairly recent development, although one can provide a prehistory for reader-oriented literary study by beginning with Plato's concern for the social utility of literature and his critique of its effects, or with Aristotle's discussion of *katharsis*, which is something Jauss returns to in his own consideration of literary effect. The role of the reader is considered in traditional rhetorical criticism, but it is with literary sociology in the twentieth century that we see the beginning of a serious attempt to study the way that literary interpretation is socially determined. Jean-Paul Sartre's *Qu'est-ce que la littérature* (1948) is one influential work of literary criticism which considered both the reader and the writer in their historical situations.[7] As many have noted, reader-oriented criticism has become a central part of literary study in recent years.[8] It would be a vast and not very useful task to locate Jauss in relation to all the other theorists and critics who have addressed similar concerns, so I will be content here to mention a few of the more important relationships. I have already mentioned the affinity between *Rezeptionsästhetik* and various historical approaches to literature. I should add that Jauss also has links with the school of phenomenological hermeneutics. The work of Mario J. Valdés, drawing on Ricoeur, is complementary to that of the Konstanz school, as Valdés himself acknowledges in his recent *Phenomenological Hermeneutics and the Study of Literature*.[9]

An important philosophical source of much phenomenologically oriented criticism is Hans-Georg Gadamer's *Wahrheit und Methode* (*Truth and Method*), first published in 1960. Gadamer describes his work as "an attempt to understand what the human sciences truly are, beyond their methodological self-consciousness, and what connects them with the totality of our experience of the world."[10] Gadamer distinguishes the understanding characteristic of the human sciences from that which typifies natural science, but not in the traditional way of defining art and history by reference to, and insofar as they differ from, natural science. This he sees as the fundamental error of the whole tradition of Kantian aesthetics and its concept of aesthetic differentiation, by which the work of art is distinguished, as a pure aesthetic entity, from everything in which it is rooted (pp. 76–80). Gadamer suggests that the experience of art contains a claim to truth "which is certainly different from that of science, but equally certainly not inferior to it." He maintains that this "can hardly be recognized if, with Kant, one measures the truth of knowledge by the scientific concept of knowledge and the scientific concept of reality" (p. 87). Jauss similarly defends the cognitive function of art and argues in his later work against an aesthetics of negativity.

Gadamer also provides Jauss with the basis of his theory of literary history, which stresses the historicity of all understanding. Building on Heidegger's analysis of *Dasein*, Gadamer argues that "before any differentiation of understanding into different directions of pragmatic or theoretical interest, understanding is There-being's mode of being, in that it is potentiality-for-being and 'possibility'" (*Verstehen ist die Seinsart des Daseins, sofern es Seinkönnen und "Möglichkeit" ist*) (p. 230). Understanding, for Heidegger and Gadamer, is a fundamental existential knowledge, given in the original character of the being of human life. It is bound up with the temporal nature of human existence. Gadamer says that to Heidegger

> the co-ordination of all knowing activity with what is known is not based on the fact that they are essentially the same, but draws its significance from the particular nature of the mode of being that is common to both of them. It consists in the fact that neither the knower nor the known are present-at-hand in an "ontic" way, but in a "historical" one, i.e., they are of the mode of being of historicalness [*von der Seinsart der Geschichtlichkeit*]. (p. 232)

As a result of this analysis Gadamer seeks to rehabilitate the concept of prejudice by arguing that "pre-judgments" form a necessary part of acts of understanding. He also seeks to show the importance of tradition and authority in interpretation.

The notion of "horizon" is crucial to Gadamer's argument. He defines it as "the range of vision that includes everything that can be seen from a particular vantage point" (p. 269). Horizons are not fixed; they are rather that into which one is always moving. Our prejudices constitute the horizon of a particular present, but this horizon is always being formed, because we are continually challenged to test our prejudices. Thus, Gadamer concludes, the horizons of the present cannot be formed without the past: "There is no more an isolated horizon of the present than there are historical horizons. Understanding, rather, is always the fusion of these horizons which we imagine to exist by themselves" (p. 273). The hermeneutic task is not to cover up the tension between the text and the present, but to bring it out. In a passage which is important for Jauss and for reception theory Gadamer says:

> it is part of the hermeneutic approach to project an historical horizon that is different from the horizon of the present. Historical consciousness is aware of its own otherness and hence distinguishes the horizon of tradition from its own. On the other hand, it is itself, as we are trying to show, only something laid over a continuing tradition, and hence it immediately

recombines what it has distinguished in order, in the unity of the historical horizon that it thus acquires, to become one with itself again. (p. 273)

Jauss first outlined his theoretical position in his inaugural lecture at the University of Konstanz in 1967. The title of the lecture was "What Is and for What Purpose Does One Study Literary History?," an adaptation of the title of Friedrich Schiller's inaugural lecture as historian at Jena in the historically significant year of 1789.[11] Schiller's lecture—"Was heisst und zu welchem Ende studiert man Universalsgeschichte?"—asserts that the task of the historian is to bring a philosophical spirit to bear upon his inquiries in order to trace the connections between past and present, and through the understanding of history to illuminate the present and enable present-day students to perceive their place in the spiritual destiny of mankind.[12] Jauss abandons Schiller's idealist teleology, but he retains Schiller's belief in the importance of historical study, and he is as convinced as Schiller that aesthetic education has an emancipatory potential, however differently the two writers conceive of the process of such education.

An expanded version of Jauss's inaugural lecture was published under the title *Literaturgeschichte als Provokation der Literaturwissenschaft* (*Literary History as a Challenge to Literary Studies*),[13] and the published essay is a manifesto of Jauss's theoretical position. He begins with an account of the state of crisis in West German literary studies, which is presented in terms similar to those of the "Paradigmawechsel" article. In a Hegelian manner Jauss briefly expounds and criticizes two theories which have dissociated themselves from the positivist and idealist approaches of historicism and text-immanent studies respectively. These are the Marxist and Formalist (Russian and Czech) schools, which "sought, in opposite ways, to solve the problem of how the isolated literary fact or the seemingly autonomous literary work could be brought back into the historical coherence of literature and once again be productively conceived as evidence of the social process, or as a moment of literary evolution."[14] Jauss criticizes Marxist theory because its doctrine of base and superstructure, expressed in the concept of *Widerspiegelung* (reflection), denies art and religion and other phenomena their own histories. He attacks Marxism for concentrating on literary production, which allies its methods with those of positivist historicism, with the ironic result that the revolutionary character of literature "is foreclosed to Marxist aesthetics" (p. 14). Formalism, on the other hand, is able "to see the work in *its* history, that is, comprehended within literary history defined as 'the succession of systems'"; this "is however not yet the same as to see the work of art in *history*, that is, in the historical horizon of its origination, social function, and historical influence" (p. 18). Thus, "the historicity of literature does not end with the succession of aesthetic-formal systems; the evolution of literature, like that of language, is to be determined not only immanently through its own unique relationship of diachrony and synchrony, but also through its relationship to the general process of history" (p. 18). Although Jauss's early work has been criticized by Marxists for paying insufficient attention to the socially determined nature of both the production and reception of literature, this key statement clearly recognizes both that literature is a relatively autonomous discourse with its own conventions of understanding and laws of development, and that this discourse remains inextricably linked to social praxis and to other discourses. As much as Sartre or Gadamer, Jauss insists on the situatedness of the literary event. In his critical investigations of particular works or topics in medieval and modern literature he gives an important place to specific social and economic determinants, notably in his brilliant analysis of the communication of social norms in the lyric of 1857.[15]

Having outlined the limitations of Marxism and Formalism, Jauss proposes a synthesis which incorporates hermeneutics and which emphasizes literary reception. This synthesis is expounded in seven theses. Jauss's explication of the first of these concludes:

> The coherence of literature as an event is primarily mediated in the horizon of expectations of the literary experience of contemporary and later readers, critics, and authors. Whether it is possible to comprehend and represent [*zu begreifen und darzustellen*] the history of literature in its unique historicity depends on whether this horizon of expectations can be objectified [*von der Objektivierbarkeit dieses Erwartungshorizontes*]. (p. 22)

The phrase "*Von der Objektivierbarkeit*" raises problems, for it implies a form of positivism which Jauss would totally reject. A number of West German scholars have in fact given the phrase a positivist interpretation, for they have sought to objectify the literary horizon of expectations by means of empirical studies.[16] Such an interpretation is not consistent with Jauss's project as a whole, and I would prefer to see the phrase as suggesting that in order to have a genuinely historical understanding of a literary work one must perceive the "alterity" of that work, that is, see its horizon as in some way distinct from one's own.[17] It is clear from Gadamer's account of the interpretive process that the recognition of the work's otherness is a necessary step, or part (for the process does not take place in a temporal sequence), of the whole process of fusion of horizons which constitutes understanding. The projection of otherness is necessary in order to perceive the originally revolutionary nature of a masterpiece, which can be obscured if the work becomes reified as a result of its canonization. In Jauss's terms, it may be necessary to read such a work "against the grain" (*gegen den Strich*) (p. 26). On the other hand, the text may be so alien to the reader's experience that the fusion of horizons cannot take place: "The initial aesthetic pleasure of the text can finally disclose itself as a naive, modernizing preunderstanding, and the first aesthetic judgment of unreadability can also prove to be incapable of being overcome. Then the text, as a document which only retains historical interest, drops out of the canon of contemporary aesthetic experience."[18]

A work which is no longer perceived as a literary work of art, or, in other words, to which readers no longer respond aesthetically, may nevertheless, given further horizonal changes, return to the canon of aesthetic experience. Literary history is full of examples of this: the contrasting reception of medieval literature in the Enlightenment and Romantic periods is one of the most obvious. At this point it may be appropriate to consider how, if at all, reception theory differs from the traditional history of taste represented in most typical form by reputation studies of the type "la fortune de Racine." To René Wellek there is no real difference: he writes that "in practice 'Rezeptionsgeschichte' cannot be anything else than the history of critical interpretation by authors and readers, a history of taste which has always been included in a history of criticism."[19] To Jauss, of course, there is a clear difference, and their differences on this issue expose more fundamental theoretical divergences between them. Jauss takes into account the changes in receptive codes, whereas previous histories of reputation have always assumed, according to Jauss, "a Platonic point of view according to which the work generates its effect unfailingly and consistently, with no respect for the changes in codes that change in every age the perceptor's understanding of art."[20] Wellek would have no problem with the ideas that he had a Platonic conception of art: "I believe that a work of art enjoins upon us 'a duty that must be fulfilled.' If I am on this account accused of a reversion to objectivism or even of a latent Platonism, I can only say *mea culpa*."[21]

Wellek's inability to see the difference between reputation studies and reception theory indeed stems from his "objectivism." Jauss is concerned with far more than the mere historicist detailing of reactions to a text; above all he is concerned to map the different horizons of aesthetic experience, and to use these horizons to interpret past works of literature. At the same time he aims to show the "modernity," the contemporary relevance, of the works he writes about. Works of art are not timeless, but given the interaction of the two horizons, the questions we can ask and the questions which the text can answer, a particular text is able to have a particular meaning for a particular time. The opposing position—that a text has a determinate meaning which persists and is accessible to all readers—is strongly argued by E. D. Hirsch in *Validity in Interpretation*. Hirsch maintains that the author's verbal meaning is determinate and reproducible, and that it is the only means by which one can claim validity for interpretations.[22] Obviously I do not accept Hirsch's arguments, which, as Robert Scholes has pointed out, founder "on the rock of psychic unity, an assumption thoroughly discredited by theoreticians from Freud to Derrida."[23] However, I think that if one rejects Hirsch one faces the challenge of producing a more convincing account of the way in which literary interpretations are validated. This would involve a complex account of literary traditions and institutions, and of the way that they interact with social norms and values. Jauss's work is suggestive here, but by no means adequate.

Literary interpretation must proceed for Jauss, as for Gadamer, through a dialectic of question and answer: "the past work can answer and 'say something' to us only when the present observer has posed the question that draws it back out of its seclusion" (p. 32). Jauss concludes his manifesto by describing three modes in which the historicity of literature must be considered: *diachronically* in the interrelationships of the reception of literary works, *synchronically* in the frame of reference of literature of the same moment, and thirdly in the relationship of the immanent development of literature to the *general processes of history*. The diachronic mode essentially involves a Formalist view of literary history as the "dialectical self-production of new forms," devoid of any teleology (p. 33). Jauss here comes very close to restating the Formalist belief that innovation is what gives art its aesthetic character, allowing it to defamiliarize our perceptions. Although he several times warns against such an oversimplified approach (e.g., "the one-sided canonization of change requires a correction," p. 33), Jauss elsewhere in the manifesto associates artistic character with "negativity" in a manner which suggests the aesthetics of Theodor W. Adorno. Jauss in fact later—belatedly, one might say—acknowledged the influence of Adorno on his work.[24] His later comparative studies do not simply valorize innovation, but rather seek to reveal the different horizons and modes of aesthetic experience involved in an earlier and a later work. In a comparison of Théophile de Viau and Baudelaire he considers the way that temporal difference is mediated by more fundamental shared expectations, and in a comparison of Goethe and Valéry he examines the way writers re-read and re-write their predecessors.

In his discussion of the second, synchronic, mode Jauss refers to the phenomenon of the coexistence of the contemporaneous and the noncontemporaneous—that is, the fact that works originating at the same historical point may be examples of genres which are perceived as virtually outmoded, or may be part of the mainstream literary production of their time, or may be radically innovative. This makes apparent the necessity of discovering the historical dimension of literature in synchronic cross-sections, for "The historicity of literature comes to light at the intersections of diachrony and synchrony" (p. 37). A good illustration of this is found in Jauss's study of lyric poetry published in 1857. The corpus of poetry includes "the canon of the preceding lyric tradition" represented by Victor Hugo's *Les Contemplations*, "the avant-gardist provocation" of *Les Fleurs du Mal*, and "the daily production of lyric pieces in the journals of 1857, poetry that was intended for instant consumption."[25] These works may appear to have very little in common, but were part of a common experience for the reading public of 1857. As Jauss notes in the "Provocation" essay, a "multiplicity of literary phenomena . . . coalesces again for the audience that perceives them and relates them to one another as works of *its* present, in the unity of a common horizon of literary expectations, memories, and anticipations that establishes their significance" (p. 38)

Jauss's third heading concerns the relationship of the "special history" of literature to "general history."[26] In analyzing this relationship Jauss does not stress the fact that literature *represents* social existence in various modes (e.g., realistic, satirical, utopian). Rather he insists on the socially formative and emancipatory function of literature, in which various discourses or modes of thought are put into question:

> The experience of reading can liberate one from adaptations, prejudices, and predicaments of a lived praxis in that it compels one to a new perception of things. The horizon of expectations of literature distinguishes itself before the horizon of expectations of a historical lived praxis in that it not only preserves actual experiences, but also anticipates unrealized possibility, broadens the limited space of social behaviour for new desires, claims, and goals, and thereby opens paths of future experience. (p. 41)

Thus the link between literature and history is not only to be found in the description of the reflection of historical processes in works of art: "The specific achievement of literature in social existence is to be sought exactly where literature is not absorbed into the function of a representational [*darstellenden*] art" (p. 45). To illustrate this mode of inquiry Jauss considers the way in which the formal innovation of *style indirect libre* in Flaubert's *Madame Bovary* was read by its first readers. The lack of an authoritative voice expressing the moral judgments of the community in Flaubert's novel had the effect of forcing the reader to reconsider ethical norms which would have been regarded as beyond question in everyday perception.

Jauss concludes the "Provocation" manifesto with a Schillerian declaration that the gap between literature and historical praxis can be bridged if literary history "discovers in the course of 'literary evolution' that properly *socially formative* function that belongs to literature as it competes with other arts and social forces in the emancipation of mankind from its natural, religious, and social bonds" (p. 45). Jauss's Modernist bias is apparent once again in this discussion of the relationship between literature and history. It seems curious to exclude the notion of mimesis from the socially formative role of literature, as Jauss does when he identifies literary representation with a reflection theory in order to condemn it.[27] Some of his difficulty may be due to his desire to present an account of the potentially revolutionary nature of art without relying on either a Romantic idealism or on Marxism. In fact there is more similarity between the neo-Marxism of the Frankfurt School and reception theory than Jauss acknowledges. In his later work, much of it collected in *Aesthetic Experience and Literary Hermeneutics*, he presents a much more complete and complex picture of aesthetic experience. For example, in an adaptation and critique of Northrop Frye he provides a range of modalities of identification with the hero in literature, ranging from participation in an actual event (e.g., courtly games of love) to the ironic identification with the vanished hero or anti-hero.[28] Identification may be progressive or regressive in each modality. Thus norm-reinforcing identification with a superior figure is not necessarily viewed as a means of ideological oppression. The mode of identification is a neutral category and the criterion of artistic character is no longer solely innovation.

Jauss's early work appeared in the context of a period of extreme political and social unrest in the Federal Republic of Germany. More radical critics were rejecting the literature of the past as a bourgeois inheritance which not only inhibited revolutionary praxis, but which had been tainted by National Socialism.[29] In opposition to this *Ideologiekritik* Jauss attempted to redefine literary studies and to present an approach which would make them relevant to the present. He maintained that within the existing social structures, by means of institutional reform, the literature of the past could be read in a way which would reveal its revolutionary character. This position, which Wlad Godzich rightly terms "liberal-reformist," was radical enough to outrage the conservative academic establishment in West Germany, particularly because Jauss used what seemed to be Marxist concepts.[30] At the same time, the attack on the reflection theory was a direct challenge to the East German literary academy. Jauss questioned the East German claim that its socialist society is the true heir to the values of the classical German literary tradition.

It is worth briefly examining some Marxist responses to reception theory, since they foreground the problems of the theory, some of which Jauss later attempted to rectify. The East German critic Robert Weimann attacked Jauss for attempting to stand above history in his use of the paradigm model, and because the horizon of expectations is derived from purely literary criteria rather than being defined "in terms of the social *Praxis* of the reader."[31] With reference to the former, Weimann is right to expose the weaknesses of the paradigm model, but he speaks in a positivistic way of "the objectivity of history itself," and he asserts that objectivity in historical thought derives "from the process of discovering and associating phenomena within the reality of their movement."[32] Here, in his use of Lukács's favourite word, *reality*, Weimann seems to be attempting to argue that the historian can go beyond empirical facts and remain objective, which is a faith only possible to a scientific socialist or someone with an equally dogmatic understanding of history. Weimann also criticizes Jauss's lack of attention to the mimetic function of literature,[33] and associates his aesthetics with Adorno's: "Both Adorno and Jauss are so much concerned with the symptoms of a false consciousness in the reception of cultural values that a revolutionary renewal of the possibility of their true functioning never occurs to them."[34]

With reference to the horizon of expectations, Weimann suggests that "empirical considerations" are necessary in order to give more specific definition to the abstraction "the reader."[35] This is a valuable criticism, suggesting a means by which reception theory might be enriched by drawing on traditional empirical research into publishing history and the sociology of the reading public. (I will return to this point at the conclusion to my discussion of the objections to reception theory.) In defence of Jauss, however, it is important to remember that he is concerned to identify the way in which literature is socially formative, by which he means, among other things, the way that it enables readers to transcend their socially determined horizons. The danger of sociology of literature is that it can easily assume that readers always read in a completely determined manner. Jauss emphasizes the unpredictable nature, or what he calls the "refractoriness" (*Unbotmässigkeit*), of aesthetic experience.[36] On the other hand, Jauss sometimes seems to assume that reading takes place entirely in the context of literary horizons. Like Weimann, Bernd Jürgen Warneken also criticizes the fact that the experience which makes up the reader's expectations in Jauss's examples is, almost exclusively, specifically literary experience.[37] This is a deficiency that Jauss has to some extent corrected, but more work needs to be done to produce literary history which adequately acknowledges both sides of this issue.

The extent to which a reader's perception of a text is preconditioned became a central issue in the dispute between Jauss and the East German critic Manfred Naumann. Naumann's Marxist theory of literary reception attempts to reconcile a belief in the determined nature of literary reception with the belief that reading a work has a transformative effect. He maintains that

> A decisive role in bridging the gap between produced work and reader is played by *social modes of reception* [*gesellschaftliche Rezeptionsweise*]. By this term we designate the fact that particular modes of thought and canons of evaluation are formed in regard to traditional and contemporary literature, according to the objective social functions transmitted to literature by the material and ideological relationships in a given social formation.[38]

In a response to some of the Marxist criticisms of his work Jauss admitted that he had not sufficiently stressed the way in which one's preunderstanding of a literary work is conditioned, but he nevertheless insists that such a work is not a "catechism," but rather allows for the freedom of a dialogical understanding. He further responds by suggesting that his theory presents difficulties for the Marxist project of appropriating the heritage of the past (*Aneignung des Erbes*).[39] A further response is provided in "The Idealist Embarrassment," in which Jauss attacks the way that Naumann's theory presupposes an ideologically correct mode of perception, so that a writer, in Naumann's view, seeks not only to liberate the reader from prejudices, but also "wishes to compel him to perceive things *correctly*."[40] Jauss's implication is that the East German model presupposes a reader who can be conditioned into accepting a mode of reading that is part of a total ideology, which is furthermore regarded as objectively correct. In "The Idealist Embarrassment" Jauss seeks, through an analysis of passages of the young Marx, to show that Marx himself assumed an idealist aesthetic which is very different from the Marxist-Leninist doctrine of reflection. He begins by quoting the famous question Marx asks in the *Einleitung zur Kritik der politischen Ökonomie* (1857): "But the difficulty is not in grasping the idea that Greek art and epos are bound up with certain forms of social development. It lies rather in understanding why they still constitute for us a source of aesthetic enjoyment and in certain respects prevail as the standard and model beyond attainment."[41] Jauss uses neo-Marxist theories of aesthetics to argue that art is the idealist core of dialectical materialism, and that in the early *Ökonomisch-philosophische Manuskripte* (1844) Marx presents art as the paradigm of nonalienated labour. Jauss's conclusion is that the divisions "bourgeois/ Marxist" and "idealist/materialist" do not apply in aesthetics, "thanks to the idiosyncrasy of aesthetic understanding, which in its nonviolent, nongovernable, and therefore 'subversive' effectiveness again and again has eluded all ideological jurisdiction and domination by society's regulatory establishments."[42]

Another objection to reception theory is stated succinctly by Robert Holub: "Without a model of society or history, non-Marxist advocates of reception have trouble steering a course between a complete relativity and an uncritical legitimation of tradition."[43] Reception theory, it is true, presupposes a particular philosophical understanding of history, but not a specific theory of historical change or sociological model. In fact, from the point of view of their philosophical assumptions, Naumann and Jauss share a very similar notion of literary reception. Naumann's theory is given a greater appearance of cohesiveness by its allegiance to a Marxist conception of society which it regards as objectively true. Jauss is less clear on his social model, but I would argue that this gives his approach greater scope for investigating the many ways in which literary interpretations have been formulated and validated. If used carefully, his approach is no more likely to uphold tradition than Marxism is; indeed, Marxist criticism is itself capable of legitimating tradition powerfully, by providing persuasive and deterministic explanations of how literary phenomena were produced.

Jauss avoids a historicist relativism by his dialectical awareness of both the alterity of past art and the necessary modernity of works of the past which are part of the canon of contemporary aesthetic experience, that is, which have more than an antiquarian interest. The literary historian's task is not only conditioned by but also enabled by the historicity of the interpreter himself or herself. Nor can Jauss be said to legitimate tradition uncritically, as Gadamer is often charged with doing. Jauss criticizes Gadamer's elevation of the classic, claiming that in responding to a work which has gained the "self-evident character of the so-called 'masterwork'" it is necessary to relocate the work in the dialectic of question and answer.[44] Whatever the veneration it enjoys as a "classic," a literary work only remains important if it can provide answers to questions which are posed by the present moment. Obviously some form of tradition plays a part in determining this, but there are always competing traditions, and traditions are revised, rewritten, abandoned, and created all the time. While the works of the classics such as Goethe and Shakespeare have a central role in many traditions, there are traditions in which these writers have a marginal relevance, although even there they will exert some sort of influence, probably largely negative.

Some further reservations about reception theory are expressed by John Frow in *Marxism and Literary History*:

> The problem with the concept of a horizon of expectations, however, is that it appeals to a phenomenology of consciousness rather than a theory of signifying systems and practices, and so remains vague about the structuring of *discursive* authority. In any case the "horizon" is described as an accumulation of quite heterogeneous values . . . and Jauss offers no explanation of the mediations between them. In particular it is unclear in what relation the literary system stands to other discursive formations.[45]

In making these charges, Frow is essentially repeating the criticisms already outlined, but his language implies a way of resolving the problem of connecting literature to other historical phenomena. Here I will briefly sketch the manner in which I think an accommodation between the Konstanz school and current Anglo-American historical approaches might be effected.

Notwithstanding its somewhat problematic status, Jauss's concept of the horizon of expectations remains useful because it is a means of exploring the interrelationships between literature and other discourses, and because it can include a variety of social norms and values, in addition to the specifically literary expectations which readers bring to a text. However, to answer Frow's understandable reservations, more work needs to be done on showing *how* literary form is related to social practices. Such work seems to me more likely to be persuasive if it takes the shape of historical investigation rather than theoretical argument. Both Frow himself and Fredric Jameson, among others, have presented these connections in a theoretical context, using textual examples but relegating them to a secondary status.[46] What is necessary now is more specific study of particular horizons, and in particular of the way that they are made up of conflicting values involving contradictions and repressions.

Both Jauss and some of the critics now termed "New Historicists" have a deep suspicion of the value of empirical evidence. During the "East-West" debate with Naumann, Weimann, and others, Jauss acknowledged some weaknesses in his earlier theoretical work, and indicated that he thought that the debate was a productive one for both sides.[47] But although he has modified his original position, Jauss remains far more interested in what Frow calls the "phenomenology of consciousness" than in material practices. Similarly, the new historicists seem preoccupied with criticism that employs transhistorical abstractions such as power and hegemony, to the exclusion of investigation of particular historical situations. There have been several recent critiques of new historicism which make this point. Marjorie Perloff attacks a Marxist reading of a Blake poem which "ignores the poem's actual mode of production and distribution as well as its reception."[48] Edward Pechter suggests that new historicists tend to see literature in simple terms, as a reproduction of power relations, sacrificing "the potential power of the text—the power to open up new areas of experience, unfamiliar ways of being in the world."[49] He suggests that despite the "theoretical richness" of Fredric Jameson's writing, his "actual interpretations—of Milton and Conrad, for example—revive an old-left political allegorization that embarrasses even those critics who are themselves most deeply committed to the historicization or politicization of the text."[50] Finally, David Simpson also finds problems with Jameson's work, asking, "in his commendable reluctance to concede anything to what he calls "vulgar materialism" . . . has he perhaps gone too far in the other direction, to the point where no empirical constraints can be recognized to disturb the autonomous clarity of the theoretical model?"[51]

Simpson has the same problems with reception theory that Frow does, and as an alternative to Jauss he proposes research which provides "a more thoroughly materialist dimension," calling for criticism which takes far more account of the sociology of literature and also of the often-ignored field of textual bibliography.[52] He suggests (like Perloff invoking the impressive work of McGann) that "useful beginnings may be found in the small and intransigent details that are least susceptible to hermeneutic instability: the cost and format of books, the size of imprints, and the relations between authors, editors, and printers."[53] Such inquiries are already well underway in the study of Romantic poetry. New critical editions of Wordsworth and Hölderlin, for example, have begun to change perceptions of those poets. The texts of many of the great Romantic poets can now be seen as far more complex and fragmented works, incorporating in their own histories much more of their historical context than was previously recognized. Earlier editions had imposed a great deal of editorial ordering and rationalization upon the unruly manuscripts of poets like Wordsworth and Hölderlin, presenting them as self-contained artifacts and repressing the conditions of their production. It seems likely that the study of the history of fiction will turn in a similar direction in coming years. Some signs of this are John Sutherland's call for greater attention to publishing history,[54] and Michael McKeon's monumental work, *The Origins of the English Novel*

1600–1740, which takes account of both the ideological and material circumstances of the production and reception of early English fiction.[55] McKeon's book is likely to have a major influence on subsequent historical criticism of English fiction. In the field of the history and criticism of nineteenth-century English fiction, N. N. Feltes has made a significant contribution to the development of a materialist approach.[56] His book contains much valuable information and many insights into the way that literary production is socially determined. However, it is also weakened at times by an overly literal application of Althusserian concepts and by an excessively reverent attitude to the Marxist texts Feltes is fond of quoting from.

In spite of the criticisms I have summarized and the modifications I have suggested, I would nevertheless affirm the usefulness of reception theory as the most comprehensive and flexible among the various approaches which are currently reinvigorating literary history. But I do not think that one should feel forced to choose between reception theory and the materialist history advocated by Simpson and others. Rather there is a need to find a dialectical synthesis which will preserve the insights of both and hold them together in a creative way. The history which follows is intended as a modest contribution in this direction.

I will conclude this introduction with some comments on the relationship of the preceding theoretical outline to the study of George Eliot which follows. Jauss's many studies of French and German literature from the Middle Ages to the twentieth century imply various directions in which his theoretical work may be utilized for the study of literature. In his investigation of the motif of "la douceur du foyer" in the lyric of 1857, Jauss undertook a synchronic investigation into a large corpus of poetry. In the discussion of *Madame Bovary* at the end of the "Provocation" manifesto, and at greater length in a study of Baudelaire's "Spleen II," he examines individual works of 1857 in order to place them within the changes of the horizons of reading. In the latter study Jauss interprets the poem "Spleen" in three moments or stages, based on traditional hermeneutic practice: (1) an aesthetically perceptual reading (*intelligere*); (2) a retrospectively interpretive reading (*interpretare*); and (3) a historical reading (*applicare*) that begins with the reconstruction of the horizon of expectations "in which the poem 'Spleen' inscribed itself [*in den das Gedicht eintrat*] with the appearance of the *Fleurs du mal*," and which follows the history of its reception up to "the most recent one," Jauss's own.[57] The present investigation is primarily concerned with the third stage of interpretation, although obviously what I say presupposes and at many places incorporates my own understanding and interpretation of Eliot's fiction. Jauss acknowledges, following Gadamer, that the three steps cannot really be separated in an act of interpretation, but it is possible as a heuristic exercise to focus on one or another.[58] My study emphasizes the horizonal changes which take place in the reception-history of George Eliot's fiction, but as a history of reception it is also inevitably (and consciously) an interpretation of that fiction.

George Eliot's fiction raises a problem of particular interest for reception history. After becoming the object of virtual cult status during her lifetime, Eliot's novels fell into disrepute shortly after her death, at about the time that literary studies was being formulated as a discipline in British universities. (The fact that they were still frequently reprinted during that period suggests that her work still enjoyed a relatively wide popular readership.) Eliot was not fully rehabilitated by critics until the mid-twentieth century, whereupon *Middlemarch* became one of the staple classics of undergraduate courses. To judge by recent citations in the *MLA Bibliography*, the advent of feminist and post-structuralist criticism increased the volume of writing about George Eliot still further. Therefore a reception-history of Eliot's fiction is, even more than such a study of most authors, an investigation into the social goals and methodological premises of the discipline of English studies. As a corollary to this observation, it is interesting to observe how much the valorization, by Leavis and his followers, of a particular kind of literature, and especially of a certain mode of "realism" in fiction, has conditioned our understanding of Eliot and thus of the history of English fiction. However much it may have fallen out of favour now, it seems to me that it would be difficult to overestimate the influence of *The Great Tradition* in determining our sense of what "the English novel" is. One of my goals in this history is to synthesize some of the excellent recent work on Eliot, and to suggest an account of her fiction which is very different from that of the generation of New Critics. Much of the strength of Eliot's fiction comes from her adaptation of nonliterary sources, or of literatures other than English, and she is thus a very different kind of novelist from the other canonical Victorian novelists. They can more successfully be taught without reference to literatures other than English, or reference to various intellectual disciplines; it is not surprising that a pedagogy which concentrated on autonomous works of English fiction and the interrelationship among them did not value Eliot as highly as her contemporaries did, or as we do at present.

Another of my aims in undertaking a reception-history is to find a way of reading Eliot "against the grain" of the accumulated critical tradition, by showing how interpretive acts are the product of particular historical horizons. This approach can enable one to have a more creative encounter with a text from the past than is possible if one merely reads it through the lenses of the particular method in which one has been schooled. I do not, however, mean to suggest that one can "restore" a text as one restores a painting, as though the critical tradition were so many layers of varnish which need only to be cleaned away for access to an ontologically pure work of art. Rather, I hope, by undertaking a reception-history, to make myself and other readers aware of the historical nature of our own interpretations. By seeing some of the factors that condition those readings, we may be able to become aware of other possibilities, and thus participate in the emancipatory process which Jauss persuasively argues that literature makes possible. In this way, among others, literary study may offer a source of cultural criticism.

My investigation will take the form of a series of studies of selected concretizations or critical receptions of Eliot's fiction, beginning with the reviews of her early fiction and proceeding to some recent criticism. Obviously, to do justice to any of these receptions it has been necessary to be highly selective. While it would be very interesting to employ reception theory to trace the relationship of Eliot's fiction to the fiction of Hardy or James, or to subsequent women writers, I have ruled out any consideration of reception in the work of other writers of fiction. This has partly been done for reasons of space, but also because the consideration of fiction would require a very different approach from the study of criticism, which is my main concern here.

I have selected from among the available critical responses those whose importance seemed to me apparent, both by what I perceived as their intrinsic "quality" or "significance"—and here my own "pre-judgments" are operative in an obvious way—and because they have been frequently cited and discussed by subsequent critics and thus have been influential in the institutions of literary study and interpretation. I have assumed that, because a whole range of cultural codes and social norms are inevitably inscribed in these critical writings, a critically aware reading of this criticism, and of its moments of blindness and insight, can tell us a great deal about the relationship of Eliot's fiction to general historical processes. I also hope that this history will imply some conclusions about the history of criticism of fiction and about English studies. At this point it may be appropriate to add that I am writing as an academic literary historian and critic, and that I am writing from the context of a Canadian university. This means that for much of the time I write as a member of a North American academic community. However, there are certain to be points where, as a Canadian, I may make assumptions that appear unusual to an American reader. For example, in the Canadian academy British traditions and practices have had much more of an influence, and therefore are viewed as being more significant, than is usually the case in the United States.

I seek to illustrate, by what I hope are representative examples, the dialectic of question and answer which has taken place between Eliot's fiction and her critics through the horizonal changes from 1860 to the present. My primary concern is with the specific history of criticism and the academy, but, like all institutions, criticism is involved with other historical processes. Therefore, I will also attempt to connect the reception-history of Eliot's fiction to the histories of the other discourses, institutions, and social groups which collectively make up what Jauss calls "general history." Sometimes such connections are made by the critics I cite, and it is interesting to view from our present vantage point the way that they saw the historicity of literature manifesting itself.

My history takes account of the reception of all of Eliot's novels, but I will discuss in detail only those works or aspects which illustrate what I consider to be important issues for different schools or particular moments of criticism. The works I discuss will also, according to the presuppositions which I have set out, reflect the questions and the concerns of the present time. Thus it is not surprising that *Felix Holt* and *Daniel Deronda* emerge as more significant, and *Middlemarch* as less, than they would have been fifteen years ago.

A particular theme or problem which emerges from Eliot's fiction was neatly formulated by U. C. Knoepflmacher, who said that there are in Eliot's work two conflicting impulses: "She wanted to unfold before her readers the temporal actuality she believed in; yet she also wanted to assure them—and herself—that man's inescapable subjection to the flux of time did not invalidate a trust in justice, perfectibility, and order."[59] This opposition is formulated in many related ways in the criticism: for example, as the tension between realism and idealism, or between a nostalgic (or realistic) portrayal of the past and a project oriented towards the future that allies Eliot with the Victorian sages, or as a split between Eliot the novelist (or "artist") and Eliot the philosopher or intellectual. Most critics in some way allude to this issue, with some seeing a serious defect in Eliot's inability to reconcile Wordsworthian recollection with positivist didacticism, and others admiring a powerful synthesis of mind and heart, and an art which is truly philosophical. Tracing this problem as a leitmotif will reveal much, both about changes in the reception of Eliot's fiction and changes within the literary horizon of expectations with regard to the question of the generic definition of the novel.

George Eliot in the 1850s

George Eliot's first novel, *Adam Bede*, was a great success both critically and commercially, and it therefore is a good text for a case study of the Victorian reception of Eliot's fiction. Before dealing with this novel, however, it would be useful to sketch a brief account of Eliot's aesthetic of fiction in relation to the prevailing norms of the 1850s regarding both the nature and purpose of fiction. This will involve some consideration of the issue of "realism" in fiction.

It is important from the outset to be aware of how different Eliot was from many of her novel-writing contemporaries; her intellectual interests ally her more with the poets and the writers of nonfiction prose.[1] She was extraordinarily widely read in the thought of her time, and had affinities to both the Enlightenment tradition of Philosophical Radicalism and the central tradition of German idealist aesthetics—she read Kant, Schiller, and almost certainly Hegel.[2] In assessing George Eliot's aesthetics one must bear these affinities in mind. She is, like many Victorians, both a Romantic and a rationalist. Like the Romantic poets she stresses the importance of the imagination. Her theory of poetry is an expressive one, and she is heir to much of the Romantic thought which is now described as "organic," in her view both of artistic form and of society. At the same time she was deeply involved in rationalist projects of biblical criticism, she edited and wrote for the radical *Westminster Review*, and she was aware of the latest scientific developments through George Henry Lewes and a circle of friends which included Charles Darwin, John Tyndall, and W. K. Clifford. A similar contradiction is to be found in John Stuart Mill, but Eliot claimed a larger scope for literature than did Mill. She did not see literature as purely the product of imaginative expression; Eliot's novels have complex intellectual structures, and rational cognition plays an important part in reading them, whereas, as she and George Henry Lewes recognized, scientific work also requires imagination.[3]

The expressive component of Eliot's thought is, of course, something that she shared with almost all of her contemporaries. M. H. Abrams, in *The Mirror and the Lamp*, has very ably documented the shift in the late eighteenth century from a mimetic to an expressive theory of poetry. According to the mimetic tradition, "poetry departs from fact principally because it reflects a nature which has been reassembled to make a composite beauty, or filtered to reveal a central form or the common denominator of a type."[4] For the Romantic, however, poetry is to be distinguished not from prose, but rather from scientific discourse. Poetry is differentiated from rational discourse by the fact that it conveys the emotional attitude of the poet to its subject matter, and because it works primarily on the imagination, or the feelings of the reader, not on his or her rational faculties: "it incorporates objects of sense which have already been acted on and transformed by the feelings of the poet."[5]

For Abrams, as was the case for Matthew Arnold and George Eliot, the central figure of English Romantic poetry and the most influential exponent of an expressive theory of poetry is William Wordsworth. Eliot purchased a six-volume edition of Wordsworth in 1839, and reported to her friend Maria Lewis that "I never before met with so many of my own feelings, expressed just as I could like them" (*Letters* 1:34). Whereas she abandoned some of the literary enthusiasms of her Evangelical days along with her faith, Eliot never abandoned her love for Wordsworth.[6] Her early novels are full of Wordsworthian quotations and echoes, and there are larger structural parallels as well, notably between Wordsworth's "The Thorn" and Eliot's *Adam Bede*.[7] For Eliot, as for many Victorians, Wordsworth provided a means of dealing with various forms of religious and epistemological crisis; his work thus forms an important component in the aesthetic horizon in which Eliot thought about her own literary work.

In the famous formulation of the Preface to *Lyrical Ballads* (1800) Wordsworth says that "all good poetry is the spontaneous overflow of powerful feelings" produced by a poet "who, being possessed of more than usual organic sensibility, had also thought long and deeply."[8] Wordsworth says that his poems are distinguished from the popular poetry of the day because "the feeling therein developed gives importance to the action and situation, and not the action and situation to the feeling."[9] George Eliot made a strikingly similar statement in an explanation of her artistic principles made to John Blackwood, who was at the time publishing her *Scenes of Clerical Life* in serial form in *Blackwood's Magazine*. She wrote: "I undertake to exhibit nothing as it should be; I only try to exhibit some things as they have been or are, seen through such a medium as my own nature gives me. The moral effect of the stories of course depends on my power of seeing truly and feeling justly" (*Letters* 2:362). This passage implies that the moral effect of the stories depends on the moral sensitivity and awareness of the author herself; Eliot is still firmly in the tradition—to be reversed at the latter end of the nineteenth century by at least some writers—which held that it is impossible to become a good poet unless one has previously become a good person.[10] She later put it more emphatically, in a letter to

Edward Burne-Jones (20 March 1873): "A nasty mind makes nasty art, whether for art or any other sake" (*Letters* 5:391).

Eliot's assertion, in the letter to Blackwood, that she undertakes to exhibit nothing as it should be, only things as they are or have been, suggests a commitment to a type of literary realism which also has some of its roots in Wordsworth. In the preface Wordsworth says that:

> The principal object, then, proposed in these Poems was to choose incidents and situations from common life, and to relate or describe them, throughout, as far as was possible in a selection of language really used by men, and, at the same time, to throw over them a certain colouring of imagination, whereby ordinary things should be presented to the mind in an unusual aspect; and, further, and above all, to make these incidents and situations interesting by tracing in them, truly though not ostentatiously, the primary laws of our nature: chiefly, as far as regards the manner in which we associate ideas in a state of excitement. Humble and rustic life was generally chosen.[11]

The interest, and the poetry, are to come from the poet's feelings as he presents the material, rather than from either the action described of itself, or the use of rhetoric as traditionally conceived. There are overtones of primitivism in this theory, as Abrams points out,[12] and these are reinforced by the choice of "humble and rustic life" as closer to the essential passions and elementary feelings of all humankind. George Eliot's own realism similarly attempts to elevate the commonplace and to locate its poetry in the manner of telling. Her early works focus on unprepossessing figures like the incompetent curate Amos Barton, or the irascible miller Edward Tulliver, and even approach naturalism in the depiction of the brutal lawyer Dempster and his alcoholic wife. Like Wordsworth she chooses rural or provincial subject matter in her early novels. Wordsworth overturned the traditional hierarchy of genres by his valorization of the lyric; Eliot makes us see the tragedy and the epic quality in the lives of commonplace figures who had hitherto been regarded as subjects for comedy or burlesque. Her references to the traditional high genres suggest that they still exerted a major influence on literary thinking, and we shall see that the hierarchy of genres affected G. H. Lewes's evaluation of Jane Austen. But Eliot is also seeking to exalt the novel by raising it to the status of these genres while at the same time writing works with a different frame of social reference from the tradition of "high literature," and even from the tradition of the novel.

In "Amos Barton," the first of her *Scenes of Clerical Life*, she writes: "The Rev. Amos Barton, whose sad fortunes I have undertaken to relate, was, you perceive, in no respect an ideal or exceptional character, and perhaps I am doing a bold thing to bespeak your sympathy on behalf of a man who was so very far from remarkable" (*SCL* 1:5;41). However, she continues, after addressing the reader in a rather clumsy imitation of Thackeray:

these commonplace people—many of them—bear a conscience, and have felt the sublime prompting to do the painful right; they have their unspoken sorrows, and their sacred joys; their hearts have perhaps gone out towards their first-born, and they have mourned over the irreclaimable dead. Nay, is there not a pathos in their very insignificance,—in our comparison of their dim and narrow existence with the glorious possibilities of that human nature which they share? (*SCL* 1:5;42)

Eliot's exalted language, bordering on the religious, suggests the seriousness which she is intending to infuse into the genre of the domestic novel. The "prompting to do the painful right" and the mourning "over the irreclaimable dead" suggest the world of classical tragedy. The pathos which in such tragedy results when one sees the powerlessness of even the most heroic man or woman in the face of ineluctable laws of destiny becomes for George Eliot the pathos resulting from the possession of the "glorious possibilities" of human nature in the limiting and constraining conditions of a commonplace existence. The theme of much of Eliot's later fiction is here in embryo—the theme, articulated in the prelude to *Middlemarch*, of the difficulty of attempting to live a heroic or a noble life in an unheroic time, when much of one's thinking and acting is determined by material, social, and economic constraints. Beginning with *Romola*, she seeks to dramatize for her characters a way of being which is able to overcome these constraints by acknowledging, accepting, and yet transforming them. This involves more of an attempt to acknowledge the social dimension of existence than one finds in Wordsworth, and it is therefore necessary to turn to other aspects of literary realism than the Wordsworthian tradition.

There has been considerable debate as to the relationship between George Eliot's theory of realism and the criticism of George Henry Lewes.[13] I do not intend to become sidetracked by attempting to judge the extent of their mutual indebtedness, but it is worth noting that there is considerable similarity between the early views of Eliot and those of Lewes on the subject of realism, and furthermore that their theories both resemble those of John Ruskin. But Eliot, as might be expected, is a more flexible and subtle thinker on this question than Lewes. Lewes had a rather narrow view of what constituted truly great literature, as he demonstrates several times in his *Life of Goethe*, and he remained far more committed to a classical hierarchy of genres than Eliot was.

The word *realism* was originally a philosophical term, which early in the nineteenth century came into use in criticism of painting. It is interesting to note that its first application to literature occurred in a French study of Flemish and Dutch painting, in which *réalisme* was used to refer to Mérimée and Balzac. Thackeray was described as "the chief of the Realist school" by a writer in *Fraser's Magazine* (1851), while the word *realism* first occurs in English in a literary context in an article on "Balzac and His Writings" (*Westminster Review*, 1853).[14] We now tend to think of the English realist novelists as, among others, George Eliot, Elizabeth Gaskell, and Anthony Trollope, but in the 1850s Thackeray was seen as both the preeminent contemporary novelist and the initiator of a new realism, or fidelity to the details of real life.[15] Eliot shared the general enthusiasm for Thackeray's work, describing him to Blackwood as "on the whole the most powerful of living novelists," although she said she was "not conscious of being in any way a disciple of his" (11 June 1857; *Letters* 2:349). It is, however, clear that Thackeray is a strong presence in the early fiction of George Eliot, and it must be remembered that the disavowal of discipleship was prompted by Blackwood's critical references to the "harsher Thackerayan view of human nature" revealed by the first part of "Janet's Repentance" (*Letters* 2:344).

It is less surprising to find Thackeray considered a realist if realism is thought of as an attempt to modify the conventions of literature, and to attack conventions which hamper the presentation of an author's true perceptions and feelings. But, as George Levine points out, such a commitment makes literary realism highly self-conscious, in a manner initiated in *Don Quixote*.[16] Levine quotes a series of addresses to the reader from nineteenth-century novels, all of which exemplify one of the realist novel's techniques for attempting to claim the special authenticity of allegiance to experience over art, namely the assertion of the superiority of the ordinary experience represented to the kind of experience described in other works of literature.[17] The passage from *Scenes of Clerical Life* quoted above is the last in Levine's list of examples, and it therefore relates at least as much to a Thackerayan tradition as to a Wordsworthian one.

George Henry Lewes defines *realism* in terms of faithfulness to the artist's own perceptions. In a review of a number of German novels he wrote:

> A distinction is drawn between Art and Reality, and an antithesis established between Realism and Idealism, which would never have gained acceptance had not men in general lost sight of the fact that Art is a Representation of Reality—a Representation which, inasmuch as it is not the thing itself, but only represents it, must necessarily be limited by the nature of its medium . . . but while thus limited, while thus regulated by the necessities imposed on it by each medium of expression, Art always aims at the representation of Reality, i.e. of Truth; and no departure from Truth is permissible, except such as inevitably lies in the nature of the medium itself. Realism is thus the basis of all Art, and its antithesis is not Idealism, but *Falsism*.[18]

Unlike those Victorian critics who talked about realism as a "copy," "transcript," or "daguerreotype,"[19] Lewes recognizes that there are epistemological and ontological problems involved in a theory of realism. A work of art is not and cannot be "reality" itself; it is something which has its own mode of being. The relationship of that mode of being to "reality" is complex, particularly because of the philosophical disagreements about the very nature of that reality. But Lewes is committed to some kind of representational theory, and it is interesting to see that when he goes on to give examples of "Falsism" they are of the sort of banal literary formulas which Thackeray parodied in some of his early works, such as milkmaids who appear in picturesque costumes which are never old or dirty. Lewes repeats these canons of realism in his essay on Jane Austen, and a number of times throughout the *Life of Goethe*. In the former he also insists on the hierarchy of literary forms with an almost neoclassical rigidity, saying that Jane Austen is a genius, but not the highest *kind* of genius because of the nature of her subject matter.[20] Similarly, in his review of Freitag's *Soll und Haben* he says that the book endeavours to represent the life of the German bourgeoisie "and although it may not be so great an achievement to represent such a form of life as to represent the life of a poet, an artist, a thinker, or a statesman, it would be a greater achievement to represent the ordinary life truly than the extraordinary life inconsistently."[21] There is an interesting mixture of social and aesthetic categories here, which shows how completely the two were mingled and muddled in discussions of this nature, and which also shows that there was a progressive social dimension to the experiments of Wordsworth and Eliot with the traditional genres. Lewes was much more traditional in this respect than Eliot. It was Lewes who originally suggested that Eliot should write *The Spanish Gypsy*, the neoclassical failure on which she expended so much time and energy, and which, conforming to an abstract notion of "high art," took her far away from the true sources of her genius.

The *Life of Goethe* is a rather one-sided appreciation of Goethe's achievement, and it includes a number of attacks on symbolic and philosophical art. Lewes does not appreciate or value Goethe's more symbolic works such as the second part of *Faust* or *Die Wahlverwandtschaften*. Goethe is praised for his "strong feeling for the real, the concrete, the living" and for his constant striving to study Nature "so as to see her *directly*, and not through the mists of fancy, or through the distortions of prejudice,—to look at men, and *into* them,—to apprehend things as they were."[22] The strongly moral tone of this passage, with its injunctions to see the real nature of things, reminds one of the tone of Arnold and Ruskin, but it also reminds one that Lewes had strong links with Positivism.[23] Although he was aware of the problems involved in perception he nevertheless here indicates a faith in the ability of genius to achieve artistic perception with virtually a scientific exactitude.

Like Thackeray and Lewes, Eliot attacked the falsely literary in the name of realism. Her most sustained commentary on literary conventionalism is the famous essay "Silly Novels by Lady Novelists" (1856), which amusingly classifies various types of novel: the mind-and-millinery species, the oracular, the white neck-cloth novel, and the modern-antique species. The essay is a plea for a reviewing practice which would treat all novels, whether by men or women, in the same manner, and not make an exception of the frivolous lady novelist, who, Eliot claims, is exempted from the standards which are applied both to men and to "serious" women writers. In effect, Eliot is mapping the literary horizons of her own time, and championing the kind of writing by women which displayed culture instead of merely parading information, and which portrayed reality instead of spinning fantasies: "No educational restrictions can shut women out from the materials of fiction, and there is no species of art which is so free from rigid requirements. Like crystalline masses, it may take any form, and yet be beautiful; we have only to pour in the right elements—genuine observation, humour, and passion" (*Essays* 324). Eliot also tries to dissociate herself from the ordinary lady novelists, who write for the vulgar marketplace. They lack, Eliot charges, "an appreciation of the sacredness of the writer's art" (*Essays* 323). George Eliot would later be horrified when a French article called her a rival of the novelist Dinah Mulock, author of *John Halifax, Gentleman* (by no means a silly novelist, even if not a writer who is highly regarded today). In Eliot's view, Mulock was "read only by novel readers, pure and simple, never by people of high culture. A very excellent woman she is, I believe—but we belong to an entirely different order of writers" (*Letters* 3:302). There was a practical reason for Eliot's scorn for the lady novelist. As Nigel Cross has shown, a stereotype of the frivolous fashionable authoress had evolved in the era of the "silver-fork novel," and all female novelists were in danger of being identified with the stereotype.[24] Eliot's aggressive attacks are attempts to obtain recognition for serious women's writing, and to avoid being herself identified as a "lady novelist."[25] It was the income from her fiction which allowed George Eliot to move from the rather Bohemian existence of her early years in London to the bourgeois respectability which she cultivated at the Priory, but she nevertheless wanted to be considered as something more than a mere novelist. In one way, at least, she was different: she did not take much interest in the fiction of her contemporaries; instead, her letters record wide reading, in several languages, in the great literature of the past and in all the chief areas of intellectual activity of her own time: philosophy, history, science, Homeric scholarship, and sociology. She describes herself to Barbara Bodichon in 1863: "I sit in another room taking deep draughts of reading—Politique positive, Euripides, Latin Christianity and so forth, and remaining in glorious ignorance of 'the current literature'" (*Letters* 4:119). As Cross's study shows, however, this was as much the product of Eliot's good fortune as of her intellectual inclination. The average popular novelist did not make much money from her writing, and could not afford to ignore the fashions of literary taste; she was the slave of her publisher and had to produce a large number of novels in order to remain solvent. She would not have had the time for "deep draughts of reading." While Eliot was offered £10,000 for *Romola*, a well-known novelist like Julia Pardoe regularly sold her copyrights for a few hundred pounds at a time.[26]

Janice Carlisle, in a discussion of *Scenes of Clerical Life*, has shown that Eliot uses a persona in that work which owes something to Thackeray, and that the effect of this persona is to transform the fictional conventions satirized in the "Silly Novels" essay in such a way that to contemporary readers the *Scenes* appeared to be a remarkably fresh and unliterary work.[27] For example, Mr. Tryan in "Janet's Repentance" is at times uncomfortably close to the hero of a "white neck-cloth" or Evangelical novel. However, in the description of the "Tryanites" gathered in Mrs. Linnet's parlour (chapter 3), we are made aware, through the sometimes heavy-handed satirical tone of the narrator, that the quasi-sexual devotion of the women to Mr. Tryan is not viewed without irony by the author. To this extent George Eliot is a disciple of Thackeray; in this incident and in a number of other places in the *Scenes* Eliot's realism is determined by a critical relationship to the conventions of popular fiction. However, her subject matter is very different from Thackeray's, and in *Adam Bede* Eliot wrote what Thackeray thought was inconceivable, a "real rustical history."[28]

The *Scenes of Clerical Life* is the work in which Eliot is most committed to a programmatic realism. David Lodge, in his introduction to the Penguin edition of the *Scenes*, argues provocatively that "Amos Barton," the first story, "was in some respects the most original (though not, of course, the greatest) work of fiction George Eliot ever wrote."[29] While this is an eccentric judgment which ignores, for example, the originality of the structure and the modernity of *Daniel Deronda*, Lodge nevertheless goes on to make a perceptive point about "Amos Barton": "In no other novel or story did she carry out so uncompromisingly her own programme of making the commonplace and unglamorous figure the centre of attention, or allow her narrative such freedom to follow its own inner logic, assuming a shape that seems given by experience rather than dictated by art or moral purpose."[30] A brief look at Eliot's own theory of realism in relation to Ruskin will help to make evident exactly why she never again carried out so uncompromisingly the programme Lodge identifies. Ruskin shared with Wordsworth and Eliot the desire to substitute a sincere and carefully cultivated perception for literary and artistic *idées reçues*. Thus Eliot reacted warmly to volume 3 of *Modern Painters*, writing in the *Westminster Review*:

> The truth of infinite value that he teaches is *realism*—the doctrine that all truth and beauty are to be obtained by a humble and faithful study of nature, and not by substituting vague forms, bred by imagination on the mists of feeling, in place of definite, substantial reality. The thorough acceptance of this doctrine would remould our life; and he who teaches its application to any one department of human activity with such power as Mr. Ruskin's, is a prophet for his generation. It is not enough simply to teach truth; that may be done, as we all know, to empty walls, and within the covers of unsaleable books; we want it to be so taught as to compel men's attention and sympathy.[31]

Eliot here emphasizes the need for a *study* of nature in order to be able to create an effective work of art, but there is no simple notion of transcription or photography. Truth and beauty are to be "obtained by" the study of nature, but this does not suggest that they are equivalent to an unmediated reproduction of nature, even if George Eliot had been naive enough to believe that such a thing was possible. In fact, no major critic has ever suggested that it was. Even Georg Lukács, during his most programmatic commitment to a socialist dogma of realism, clearly said that realism

> is the recognition of the fact that a work of literature can rest neither on a lifeless average, as the naturalists suppose, nor on an individual principle which dissolves its own self into nothing. The central category and criterion of realist literature is the type, a peculiar synthesis which organically binds together the general and the particular both in characters and situations.[32]

Perhaps the only real examples of a naive theory of realism are to be found in the works of literary journalists, or in the views attributed by structuralist and post-structuralist critics to straw figures of their own devising.

The passage from Eliot's review of Ruskin emphasizes that the crucial factor in evaluating work is the extent to which it compels "men's attention and sympathy" for what is true. Thus realism is not an end in itself, but rather a doctrine valued because it stresses sincerity, for a sincere author is able to create the sympathy necessary for a work to have a moral effect. Eliot's aim, increasingly as her fiction became more ambitious, was to evoke in her readers the emotions which moved her when writing, and what she wanted from her readers was a sympathetic openness to her aims.[33] She wrote in "The Natural History of German Life," "The greatest benefit we owe to the artist, whether painter, poet, or novelist, is the extension of our sympathies" (*Essays* 270).

Eliot's attitude is in fact very similar to Ruskin's. Darrel Mansell, Jr., has shown that Ruskin did not mean that art should imitate nature, any more than Eliot did: "He means the very opposite: that the artist should begin by humbly and faithfully studying nature, and then should produce art which is distinctly different from nature in that the artist's imagination is evident in his treatment of the subject."[34] This is Eliot's position not only in her review of Ruskin, but in the much-quoted passage on realism in *Adam Bede*, which in its context is a defence of the portrayal of Mr. Irwine as a man with failings, rather than as the all-knowing cleric of a "Silly Novel." In the passage the narrator says that he[35] has no aspiration to represent "things as they never have been and never will be," but

> I aspire to give no more than a faithful account of men and things as they have mirrored themselves in my mind. The mirror is doubtless defective; the outlines will sometimes be disturbed; the reflection faint or confused; but I feel as much bound to tell you, as precisely as I can, what that reflection is, as if I were in the witness-box narrating my experience on oath. (*AB* 17;221)

He goes on to praise Dutch paintings for their "rare, precious quality of truthfulness" (*AB* 17;223), and declares: "Paint us an angel, if you can, with a floating violet robe, and a face paled by the celestial light; paint us yet oftener a Madonna, turning her mild face upward and opening her arms to welcome the divine glory; but do not impose on us any aesthetic rules which shall banish from the region of Art those old women scraping carrots with their work-worn hands" (*AB* 17;224). There are several things to note about this passage. The first is that the image of the mirror once again stresses the importance of the perceiver in any act of perception. It is a phenomenological theory, concerned with the contents of consciousness, since for Eliot this is all we can be certain of knowing. Secondly, in addition to the traditional image of the mirror, the passage uses the forensic metaphor of the witness-box, which brings to mind the close connection between early novels and criminal biographies or confessions. Works like Defoe's novels relied on the forensic metaphor to ground their appeal to truth.[36] In her review of Ruskin, Eliot had commented that it was not enough simply to teach the truth if no one is listening. The analogy with the courtroom suggests that the truth needs to be given some kind of legitimacy to compel attention. Furthermore, one must not be misled into thinking, as a superficial reading might suggest, and as casual critical comments on the passage often imply, that Eliot is using the Dutch realists as an image for the kind of art she is practising.[37] She is rather using the comparison to assert the dignity of what was conventionally regarded as "low" subject matter. She is not saying, any more than Ruskin did, that Dutch painting is the highest form of art; she is only asking that it be recognized *as* art.[38] In *The Principles of Success in Literature* Lewes cautions against the confusion of "realism" with "detailism," or an undue attention to the familiar and unessential: "There are other truths besides coats and waistcoats, pots and pans, drawing-rooms and suburban villas."[39] Eliot to some extent shared this notion, for it is clear in the passage in *Adam Bede* that a Madonna is a more dignified subject than the old woman scraping carrots. There are limits to the extent of George Eliot's democratic sympathies.

Eliot's own position with regard to decorum and genre is more complex, and an interesting analogy for it may be found in the Dutch art she mentions in *Adam Bede*. Modern art historians have argued that many of the Dutch paintings which were once regarded as realistic genre pieces are in fact moral allegories, full of religious iconography which refers to scriptural types or which implies a moral judgment on the scene being presented. From the beginning, Eliot infused her fiction with similar complexities, although she was probably not aware of this view of the Dutch school of painting. Thus, although she attacked certain literary conventions and stock situations she used much more venerable literary topoi and types to create the moral effect which she sought. In her later novels, beginning with *Romola*, she began to employ overtly heroic characters and actions, but less obtrusive effects are apparent even amidst the commonplace "Scenes" with which she began. They serve to elevate and dignify the commonplace, the "emmet-like Dodsons and Tullivers" (*MF* 4,1;238). By this technique Lewes's neat scheme of classification is confounded. If, for example, a poor housewife is treated seriously as a Madonna-figure, as well as being portrayed realistically in the poverty of her material circumstances, where is the distinction between Raphael and Teniers, or Homer and Jane Austen? This is precisely how Milly Barton is treated in "Amos Barton" (*SCL* 1:2;19), and the technique is repeated with greater subtlety in the works which follow. Thus when Janet Dempster is saved by Mr. Tryan she becomes linked to a whole history of conversion stories and Christian allegories; she does not degenerate into total degradation, unlike the heroine of a naturalist novel such as George Moore's *The Mummer's Wife*.

George Eliot's literary technique may further be illuminated by analogies with the visual arts, for her work has affinities with the realism of the very literary painters of the Pre-Raphaelite Brotherhood. M. H. Abrams has suggested that the conventional use of painting as a metaphor to illustrate the nature of poetry—*ut pictura poesis*—almost disappears during the Romantic period, with music becoming the art most frequently linked with poetry.[40] However true this may be for poetry, painting remains an important image in criticism of prose fiction and in self-referential passages in works of fiction. I have already cited several references to Dutch and Flemish art, and Richard Stang comments that "the pictorial metaphor seems omnipresent in Victorian criticism of fiction."[41] Hugh Witemeyer, in his very useful monograph *George Eliot and the Visual Arts*, shows that painterly analogies were a significant part of Eliot's fictional technique, and he sets her work in the context of a general tendency towards both pictorial writing and literary painting. Witemeyer summarizes the purpose of his work in the following way:

> Even the critics who recognize Eliot's pictorialism are often uncomfortable with it and characterize its effect as either sentimental and escapist, or distancing and alienating. We have, then, nearly lost sight of a dimension of George Eliot's art which she and her first readers valued highly. To recover that unseen dimension is the primary aim of this study and its illustrations.[42]

A brief discussion of *Adam Bede* in the light of Eliot's pictorial and other symbolic techniques will illustrate the complexity of Eliot's "realism," and the extent to which it is qualified by other literary devices and modes. The overall effect may nevertheless, after these qualifications, be considered "realist" in the light of the collection of theories I have outlined by means of Wordsworth, Thackeray, Ruskin, and Lewes. The novel contains a mixture of styles, which treat the events narrated with varying degrees of involvement, detachment, sympathy, or irony.[43]

In her essay "The Natural History of German Life" (1856), Eliot had mocked the pastoral conventions used to represent rural scenes in art and literature, and contrasted the peaceful and happy impression which haymaking presents in the distance with the appearance the same scene makes when one approaches nearer:

> Observe a company of haymakers. When you see them at a distance, tossing up the forkfuls of hay in the golden light, while the wagon creeps slowly with its increasing burthen over the meadow, and the bright green space which tells of work done gets larger and larger, you pronounce the scene "smiling," and you think these companions in labour must be as bright and cheerful as the picture to which they give animation. Approach nearer, and you will certainly find that haymaking is a time for joking, especially if there are women among the labourers; but the coarse laugh that bursts out every now and then, and expresses the triumphant taunt, is as far as possible from your conception of idyllic merriment. (*Essays* 269)

The way that one perceives a scene is determined not only by the presence of conventions of varying degrees of flexibility and usefulness, but also by one's perspective. Thus a variety of attitudes may be taken to a particular scene and each attitude has its own claim to valorization as "realistic," since the differences are a matter of distance, whether physical, social, or moral—the latter measured by the perceiver's sympathy or lack of sympathy with the object of perception.

In the early work, the narrator and the allegorical and symbolic patterns and details combine to place the reader in relation to what is being presented. For instance, in the passage quoted above there is clearly a moral advantage to knowing the true nature of haymaking, for one will not then make the mistake of idealizing conventionalized representations of landscape and rural scene, devoid of their human and moral—and perhaps political—dimension. In *Adam Bede* Eliot uses pastoral conventions herself in order to preserve the reader's sympathy for Adam and the Poyser family. The farm workers are a background presence, never allowed to become significant enough to create an unwanted perspective on the central figures. Hetty's actions put her outside of the pastoral world of the novel, and she is therefore transported to a premature death. We must sympathize with her, but only up to a point, because Adam is to be the central figure at the end. Because of its use of "spatial distance," Michael Squires has described *Adam Bede* as a pastoral novel.[44] One of Squires's most interesting observations is that chapters 12 and 13 of the novel, in which after a struggle with his conscience Arthur meets Hetty in the wood, make use of the literary topos of the *locus amoenus*.[45] This gives their sexual union overtones of the first sin in the Garden of Eden, which is appropriate in a novel in which the hero will become a secular modern equivalent of Christ.

In addition to the pastoral, Eliot embellishes the realism of *Adam Bede* by the use of typological symbolism. Witemeyer argues that Eliot uses a technique of "pictorial idealization" that redefines typological symbolism in order to preserve its usefulness for dignifying representations of phenomenal experience with spiritual meaning, but without dogmatically asserting an orthodox Christian reading of human experience. Witemeyer uses the word *typology* in a loose sense, as he maintains the Victorians did, "to denote any exemplary or religious norm which finds successive incarnations in history."[46] Eliot's hero Adam Bede, although described as "by no means a marvellous man," is also "not an average man" (*AB* 19;258). His first name suggests that he is Everyman, and several scenes link him via pictorial typology, and also by allusions to Ludwig Feuerbach, to Jesus Christ, the "Suffering God" (*AB* 35;410) of Feuerbach's *Das Wesen des Christentums*, which Eliot had translated in 1854.

Adam Bede opens with a detailed description of a carpenter's workshop, precisely located for us "in the village of Hayslope, as it appeared on the eighteenth of June, in the year of our Lord 1799" (*AB* 1;49). However, the narrator's drop of ink at the tip of his pen is like the magic of an "Egyptian sorcerer," and this image makes us alert to the way in which the description of this very prosaic workshop relates to "far-reaching visions of the past" (*AB* 1;49). The vivid pictorial imagery used to depict the workshop recalls the detail of a Victorian genre painting, and Witemeyer relates the scene to such paintings on the theme of duty and work as Ford Madox Brown's *Work* (1852–65).[47] The words of the hymn which Adam sings could easily have been painted on the frame of this kind of painting. As the tallest and strongest workman Adam is obviously a Carlylean worker-hero, but because the scene is set in a carpenter's shop, because he is named Adam, and because he is singing a hymn, the scene takes on typological overtones. Thus the description blurs the boundary between the realistic genre scene and the sacred history painting in a manner typical of Victorian painting.[48] For example, John Everett Millais caused an outrage when he painted *Christ in the House of His Parents* (1850), a realistic treatment of the subject which became known by the title given to it by its detractors, *The Carpenter's Shop*.[49]

Adam Bede is also connected to Christ by allusions to the Christ of Feuerbach, who embodies the highest aspirations of humanity. Feuerbach had written in *The Essence of Christianity*: "God suffers—suffering is the predicate—but for men, for others, not for himself. What does that mean in plain speech? Nothing else than this: to suffer for others is divine; he who suffers for others, who lays down his life for them, acts divinely, is a God to men."[50] Similarly, the narrator of *Adam Bede* comments that "Deep, unspeakable suffering may well be called a baptism, a regeneration, the initiation into a new state" (*AB* 42;471). Adam's suffering softens his hardness and makes him more indulgent to his brother Seth, for sorrow "lives in us as an indestructible force, only changing its form, as forces do, and passing from pain into sympathy" (*AB* 50;531). Another typological genre scene emphasizes the way that suffering transforms in George Eliot's "religion of humanity." Adam is sitting in his rented room while Hetty's trial takes place, and Bartle Massey comes to bring him news. The references to Adam "haggard and unshaven" (*AB* 42;475) and to Bartle Massey taking off his hat and spectacles (*AB* 42;472) help us to particularize the scene in the shabby room and to imagine it as one of the popular Victorian pictures of betrayed spouses or lovers, the most famous of which is Augustus Egg's series *Past and Present* (1858). However, the scene takes place in an "upper room" (*AB* 42;471), and the shared meal of bread and wine is obviously a secular eucharist, with Eliot's language even echoing the liturgy.[51]

I have attempted, in the first part of this chapter, to sketch some of the critical assumptions and aesthetic ideas which were part of the horizon against which Eliot defined her own fictional project. But to formulate a more precise account of the reception of her first fiction it is necessary to turn to the documentary evidence of the early reviews and other recorded comments of contemporary readers, and to consider that evidence in the light of both the literary horizons sketched above and of the historical situation of which both the readers and the fiction are a part.

Adam Bede (1859) was George Eliot's first full-length novel, appearing just over a year after the publication in book form of the *Scenes of Clerical Life*. In spite of the fact that the *Scenes* had attracted relatively little attention, *Adam Bede* was a remarkable success. While it was not a runaway best-seller if compared with works such as *Uncle Tom's Cabin* or the novels of Dickens and Charles Reade, it still sold 3,350 copies in the three-volume format and 11,000 copies in two volumes within a year of its first publication.[52] It is also interesting to note that the novel was reviewed by twenty of the twenty-five periodicals which Michael Wolff chose as representative of the spectrum of Victorian culture in a study focussing on the year 1859.[53] (This compares with twenty-two reviews for Darwin's *Origin of Species* and Tennyson's *Idylls of the King* and sixteen for Mill's *On Liberty*). Wolff says that "*Adam Bede* . . . was the novel of 1859 acclaimed by its contemporary reviews as enlarging the scope of fiction and bringing the novel to readers who ordinarily could not be bothered with such a plebeian form."[54] By considering *Adam Bede* in the literary-historical context of the prevailing assumptions about fiction in 1859, and by considering the critical reception of the novel against the background of the larger historical situation of which it was a part, I will try to consider both some of the causes and some of the implications of *Adam Bede*'s success. Following Jauss's statement that "the historicity of literature comes to light at the intersections of diachrony and synchrony,"[55] I will attempt to situate *Adam Bede* not only in relation to the range of contemporary views of fiction, but also will contrast its reception, in the next chapter, with the reception of *Daniel Deronda*. The contrast between these two "synchronic cross-sections" will have implications for the history of the novel in general in the nineteenth century, as it separated towards the end of the century into largely distinct "serious" and "popular" manifestations. I will also develop, in opposition to the readings of some of the more influential Victorian critics of *Adam Bede* (and with the assistance of other Victorian and modern readings) my own critical account of the novel. By means of this oppositional technique I will suggest some of the nonliterary factors which led the Victorians to read *Adam Bede* as they did, and I will thereby attempt to link my account of the reception of the novel to what Jauss calls the experience of "general history."

Before examining the periodical reviews and other evidence of the reception of *Adam Bede*, I will provide a sketch of the literary horizon of expectations of the English reading public with respect to fiction during the years immediately prior to 1859. The evidence shows a narrower range of levels or modes of literary discourse than those identified by Jauss in his examinations of French literature of the year 1857. There is certainly no English equivalent to avantgarde writers like Baudelaire or Flaubert. However, a spectrum may be mapped, and it includes the following positions:

1. Those who for religious or utilitarian reasons disapproved of all fictional writing (Evangelicals and extreme Benthamites);

2. The conservative publishers, booksellers, and library proprietors (I will take John Blackwood as an example), who made a living from the marketing of literature as a commodity, but who also had certain ethical and political aims in their selection of books to sell. They were suspicious of anything which would unduly startle or outrage their reader's sensibilities, and thus encouraged the production of works which reproduced already "automatized" literary forms.[56] However, as the example of Blackwood shows, they did have their own aesthetic standards;

3. The less reputable publishers, who published the work of the poorly paid "common writers" of the time, and who treated literature completely as a commodity. Even more than the figures in the second category, they encouraged the production of automatized forms. This class of publishers and their writers in fact established the beginnings of what we now call "genre fiction." Publishers like Henry Colburn and the much-maligned T. C. Newby (who nevertheless published Trollope and Emily Brontë) would fall into this category;[57]

4. Innovators such as Thackeray, with his parodies of the "Newgate" or "silver-fork" and other schools, and his new "realism" in his own fiction, or Charlotte Brontë, who introduced new subject matter, and who examined the life of women in nineteenth-century England from a radically personal—and female—perspective.

The presence of the first attitude to fiction may be seen in the defensive tone which some of the favourable reviews of *Adam Bede* adopt. They make it clear that the aesthetic value of any prose fiction, even the very best, was far from self-evident in 1859; on the contrary, those who praised Eliot's novel felt compelled to begin by meeting ethical and epistemological objections to the writing of novels. The second position I have identified may be illustrated by a brief look at the correspondence between Eliot and Blackwood about the *Scenes of Clerical Life*, which leads conveniently into a consideration of the perception of Thackeray in the 1850s. The third position represents the view of fiction that Eliot was most anxious to distance herself from, while the fourth undoubtedly helped her to work out her own formal innovations.

In an entry in her journal entitled "How I Came to Write Fiction" (written 6 December 1857), George Eliot describes how Lewes encouraged her to write a novel after hearing her read a fragment which she had once written, "an introductory chapter describing a Staffordshire village and the life of the neighbouring farm houses" (*Letters* 2:406). In their early years together Eliot and Lewes had been making a precarious living from literary journalism, and it is probable that Lewes encouraged her to write a novel in the hopes of increasing their income. The market for fiction was a lucrative and a growing one, but Lewes's own attempts to take advantage of it had not been very successful. This motive would explain why Lewes planned to send the story to *Blackwood's* if it "turned out good enough" (*Letters* 2:407). *Blackwood's* was a conservative monthly, and was certainly not sympathetic to the Philosophical Radicalism of the *Westminster Review*, to which Eliot had contributed a number of articles immediately before writing the *Scenes*. However, *Blackwood's* had a firmly established reputation for publishing fiction, and Lewes had already contributed a number of popular articles to the magazine.

Eliot describes in her journal entry how she had mentioned to Lewes "that I had thought of the plan of writing a series of stories containing sketches drawn from my own observation of the Clergy, and calling them 'Scenes from Clerical Life' opening with 'Amos Barton'" (*Letters* 2:407–8). It is interesting to note the artistic metaphor of "sketches," which is also implied in the title "Scenes." The metaphor occurs in the titles of several other well-known works, and it suggests a rather more impressionistic type of writing than that of the typical novel of the time, which tended to pose as a "History," "Life," or "Memoir." Two works by famous authors which identify themselves as "sketches" are in fact collections of journalistic essays in which the persona of the essayist features strongly: Dickens's *Sketches by Boz* (1836) and Thackeray's *Paris Sketch Book* (1840). The original subtitle of *Vanity Fair*, in the edition published in monthly parts in 1847–48, was "Pen and Pencil Sketches of English Society." (The only other use of the word "scenes" in a work of this period which I have been able to trace is in Francis Smedley's obscure novel of 1850, *Frank*

Fairleigh, or Scenes from the Life of a Private Pupil). Eliot's title and conception of her first work of fiction thus suggest its affinities with Thackerayan
realism, and further suggest that it is to be conceived of as a journalistic explora-
tion of clerical life by an educated and urbane writer.

When he sent the manuscript of "Amos Barton" to John Blackwood, Lewes
compared Eliot's treatment of the clergy "in its *human* and *not at all* in its
theological aspect" with Goldsmith's *Vicar of Wakefield* and the novels of Jane
Austen, and he further reassured Blackwood that "the tone throughout will be
sympathetic and not at all antagonistic" (*Letters* 2:269). Blackwood approved
of the story on the whole, although he found a number of faults and commented
that "his clergymen with one exception are not very attractive specimens of the
body" (*Letters* 2:272). This is the first instance of a recurring objection Blackwood made to Eliot's writing. He did not accept the "realistic" theory of fiction
which Eliot had developed, and he continually sought to make her tone down
the descriptions of the failings of her characters and the satirical commentary
she made on the society in which she portrayed the characters. He also tried to
encourage Eliot to create the kind of ideal clergymen and heroines she had
described in "Silly Novels by Lady Novelists." She attempted to explain to him
that his objections were based on a different notion of art from her own, and
that she did not intend to allow Blackwood's conservative aesthetic views or his
nervousness about the sensitivities of the reading public to influence her way
of writing fiction. Early in their correspondence about the *Scenes* she commented that "in reference to artistic presentation, much adverse opinion will of
course arise from a dislike to the *order* of art rather than from a critical estimate
of the execution. Anyone who detests the Dutch school in general will hardly
appreciate fairly the merits of a particular Dutch painting" (*Letters* 2:291–92).

Blackwood was particularly discomfited by "Janet's Repentance," and said
that the first part "rather puzzles me." He thought that "the colours are rather
harsh for a sketch of English County Town life only 25 years ago" (*Letters*
2:344). He concluded his response to the first instalment of the story with some
advice and a question:

> For the meantime I feel certain that I am right in advising you to *soften* your picture as much
> as you can. Your sketches this time are all written in the harsher Thackerayan view of human
> nature, and I should have liked to have seen some of the good which at page 10 you so neatly
> indicate as existing at Milby. When are you going to give us a really good active working
> clergyman, neither absurdly evangelical nor absurdly High Church? (*Letters* 2:344–45)

George Eliot encountered further objections from Blackwood, not only to the
remainder of "Janet's Repentance," but also to the first volume of *Adam Bede*,
where she may well have thought that she was providing a portrait of "a really
good active working clergyman." Blackwood, however, wrote that "the Vicar

is a capital fellow and the visit to the sick room is very touching, but I wish for the sake of my Church of England friends he had more of the 'root of the matter in him'" (*Letters* 2:445). It seems likely that, as Roland F. Anderson argues, this letter of Blackwood's was the provocation which led George Eliot to write chapter 17 of *Adam Bede*, "In which the Story Pauses a Little," where she defends the depiction of characters who are not perfectly virtuous by using the famous Dutch painter analogy.[58]

Since it is evident that Blackwood had a conservative attitude to fiction, which he himself contrasted with Thackeray's approach, it may be helpful at this point to mention two important mid-decade reviews of Thackeray, both of which discuss *The Newcomes* (1853–55) along with other works. In a very sympathetic review in the *Quarterly*, the editor and essayist Whitwell Elwin declared that *The Newcomes*

> is Mr. Thackeray's masterpiece, as it is undoubtedly one of the masterpieces of English fiction, if fiction is the proper term to apply to the most minute and faithful transcript of actual life which is anywhere to be found. The ordinary resource of novelists is to describe characters under exceptional circumstances, to show them influenced by passions which seldom operate in their excess with each individual, and to make them actors in adventures which in their aggregate happen to few or none. . . . Mr. Thackeray looks at life under its ordinary aspects, and copies it with a fidelity and artistic skill which are surprising. Men, women, and children talk, act, and think in his pages exactly as they are talking, acting, and thinking at every hour of the day.[59]

It is immediately apparent from this extract that Eliot's programme for realism was not as original as she sometimes implies in her comments on the practice of other novelists. In fact, the ground was well-prepared, and, as we shall see, what was most original in her early fiction was the choice of subject matter rather than her tone or mode of presentation. Elwin's review further argues that although Thackeray "disclaims the assumption of the preacher's office" his work is nevertheless highly moral in nature, for "a writer who depicts life with perfect fidelity, and indulges in no corrupting descriptions of vice, must, whether he designs it or not, be a powerful moralist."[60] The review also implies that the comprehensive nature of Thackeray's satire, and the balance of satire and "benevolence, honour, and disinterestedness" make the novel a just representation of the world, giving it a fundamental unity of purpose.[61]

A less sympathetic but very interesting and perceptive account of Thackeray is found in a review by William Caldwell Roscoe, whom Richard Stang describes as "one of the finest and least known of Victorian critics."[62] For Roscoe, Thackeray is to be commended for his accurate delineation of character, but he lacks "deeper insight." He is "a daguerreotypist of the world about us."[63] Thackeray lacks a spiritual dimension, and this is his most serious shortcoming: "He professes to paint human life; and he who does so, and who does not base his conception on that religious substructure which alone makes it other than shreds of flying dreams, is an incomplete artist and a false moralist."[64] The artist's duty is to raise people out of failings, not simply to rail at those failings. Roscoe concludes with a rather surprising comparison of Thackeray and Goethe. Thackeray is like Goethe, he says, "not only in his mode of depicting characters as they live, instead of reproducing their depths and entirety from the conception of a penetrative imagination, but also in his patient and tolerant acceptance of all existing phenomena, and his shrinking not merely from moral judgment but from moral estimate."[65] The Ruskinian term "penetrative imagination" further suggests the lack in Thackeray of a spiritual dimension, for in Ruskin the term refers to the form of imagination which is able to penetrate beneath the phenomenal forms of things and ascertain a more essential and spiritual truth.[66]

Thus for Roscoe, as for John Blackwood, Thackeray has a harsh view of reality, unrelieved by spiritual affirmation. Furthermore, his novels focus on the drawingrooms of the upper-middle class and aristocracy, and although they are to be commended for their accurate and biting representation of the life of this part of society they do not, for these readers, reach below the superficies of that life. Such readers wanted fiction which they could feel was "healthy," "wholesome," or "improving" (commenting on only a slightly later period, 1865–80, Kenneth Graham says that the reviewers' adjectives make the novel "sound like a seaside-resort for the soul").[67] Eliot's fiction must have seemed like a miraculous answer to the prayers of these readers. It preserved the realism of Thackeray's fictional enterprise, but moved it to a very different social and geographical setting, which provided the charm of novelty (and a certain degree of social daring in describing such "low" subject matter). Eliot was also perceived by most readers as being more sympathetic than Thackeray, and until her real identity was revealed she was praised for her religious insight and her moral analysis.

In *The Virginians* Thackeray had written that "the real business of life, I fancy, can form but little portion of the novel's budget," for, he asks, "Would a real rustical history of hobnails and eighteenpence a day be endurable?"[68] This, of course, is the kind of novel which Eliot was to write in *Adam Bede*. However much she admired Thackeray's power as a novelist, she did not treat his usual subject matter of the upper classes until her last novel. Eliot's undertaking in *Adam Bede* demanded considerable daring, for even in Scott, her most obvious fictional precursor in this respect, the peasants and fishermen who speak in dialect are not the central figures; the centre is occupied by the person described by Lukács as "a more or less mediocre, average English gentleman."[69] As a woman, Eliot had not had the standardizing conventional education of the English gentleman. This fact, combined with her experience of growing up in the countryside and serving for a time as her father's housekeeper, and with her absorption in the poetry of Wordsworth, enabled her successfully to make a rural carpenter and a Methodist factoryworker the central figures in her novel, while the squire and the vicar are relegated to the status of secondary characters. The focal points in the novel, the homes at whose hearths the novel's moral heart is located, are the Hall Farm and Adam's cottage, not the Chase or the Rectory.

Eliot at least once in the novel implies a distinction between her work and that of Thackeray. Thackeray's debunking of the notions of heroism and honour was celebrated and controversial. He had given *Vanity Fair* the subtitle "A Novel without a Hero" when it was published in book form (1848). In *Henry Esmond* he satirizes the idealizing school of historians:

> I wonder shall History ever pull off her periwig and cease to be court-ridden? Shall we see something of France and England besides Versailles and Windsor? I saw Queen Anne at the latter place tearing after her staghounds, and driving her one-horse chaise—a hot, red-faced woman, not in the least resembling that statue of her which turns its stone back upon St. Paul's and faces the coaches struggling up Ludgate Hill. She was neither better bred nor wiser than you and me, though we knelt to hand her a letter or a washhand-basin.[70]

Eliot was more concerned with creating new models of heroism than with debunking old ones. We are clearly meant to see both Adam and Dinah as exemplary figures. Eliot says that her depiction of Adam's admiration for Mr. Irwine will doubtless be

> despised as a weakness by that lofty order of minds who pant after the ideal, and are oppressed by a general sense that their emotions are of too exquisite a character to find fit objects among their everyday fellow-men. I have often been favoured with the confidence of these select natures, and find they concur in the experience that great men are over-estimated and small men are insupportable. (*AB* 17;228–29)

This aside is made, ironically enough, in a Thackerayan tone, and it concludes with the amusing exemplum of the landlord Mr. Gedge, who moves from the Royal Oak to a neighbouring town in the hopes of finding customers worthy of him, and decides that the inhabitants of both town and country are equally "a poor lot, sir, big and little" (*AB* 17;230). It is tempting to regard Mr. Gedge as a representative of the Thackerayan type of writer. In this little fable Eliot is declaring her agreement with Roscoe's fictional aesthetic, in which the writer is expected to raise readers out of the atmosphere of their failings by eliciting sympathy for human imperfections. She is perhaps also explicitly telling Blackwood and any reader who shares his views that her avowal of "realism" does not mean that she shares Thackeray's "harsh" view of human nature.

Eliot's *Scenes of Clerical Life* (1858) attracted little critical notice on first publication, but two reviewers did note that George Eliot's voice was a fresh and original one, which was distinct from that of any living novelist. Samuel Lucas in the *Times* compared Eliot with Galt, Lockhart, and Crabbe, and said that a "closer resemblance than usual" is established in the stories "between the conceptions of fiction and the realities of the world" (*CH* 62).[71] The *Saturday Review* noted that "George Eliot is a new novelist, who to rare culture adds rare faculty, who can paint homely every-day life and ordinary characters with great humour and pathos, and is content to rely on the truth of his pictures for effect" (*CH* 67). Eliot's first work established her in the minds of her early readers as an author who depicted the homely and the domestic in a realistic manner. These qualities are also abundantly present in *Adam Bede*, thus satisfying the expectations of her first readers, but there is the added surprise and pleasure of the Wordsworthian rural setting. Eliot seemed to have been aware of the novelty of the subject matter of *Adam Bede*. She wrote to Blackwood, "My new story haunts me a good deal, and I shall set about it without delay. It will be a country story, full of the breath of cows and the scent of hay. But I shall not ask you to look at it until I have written a volume or more" (*Letters* 2:387). She clearly did not want to have to deal with Blackwood's quibbling objections to each small instalment of the story, but rather intended to confront him with a large portion of the work all at once, in the hope of making a more favourable impression, and also overcoming any resistance he might have had to the subject matter.

Adam Bede was published 1 February 1859, and Eliot had a presentation copy sent to Mrs. Jane Carlyle (along with copies to Dickens, Thackeray, and several others).[72] Mrs. Carlyle's response to the work was enthusiastic, and stressed both the setting and the uplifting effect the book had had on her, which seems in part to derive from its rural subject matter. The passage strikingly parallels the way in which the urban Victorian "literary proletariat" read Wordsworth:

> It was as good as *going into the country for one's health*, the reading of that Book was!—Like a visit to Scotland *minus* the fatigues of the long journey, and the grief of seeing friends grown old, and Places that knew me knowing me no more! I could fancy in reading it, to be seeing and hearing once again a crystal-clear, musical, Scotch stream, such as I long to lie down beside and—*cry* at (!) for gladness and sadness; after long stifling sojourn in the South; where there [is] no *water* but what is stagnant and muddy.
>
> In truth, it is a beautiful most *human* Book! Every *Dog* in it, not to say every man woman and child in it, is brought home to one's "business and bosom," an individual fellow-creature. I found myself in charity with the whole human race when I laid it down. (*Letters* 3:17–18)

Eliot asked Blackwood to give a message to Mrs. Carlyle: "Will you tell her that the sort of effect she declares herself to have felt from 'Adam Bede' is just what I desire to produce—gentle thoughts and happy remembrances; and I thank her heartily for telling me so warmly and generously what she has felt" (*Letters* 3:24). Similarly, in a letter to Charles Bray, Eliot comments that "praise is so much less gratifying than comprehension and sympathy," referring to two reviews she had read of *Adam Bede* (*Letters* 3:148).

Several reviewers emphasized the peaceful rural aspects of the novel. For example, the *Atlantic Monthly* said, "We do not know where to look, in the whole range of contemporary fictitious literature, for pictures in which the sober and brilliant tones of Nature blend with more exquisite harmony than in those which are set in every chapter in 'Adam Bede.' "[73] The reviewer mentions none of the violent or tragic incidents in the novel. Anne Mozley, writing in *Bentley's Quarterly Review*, recognized the other dimensions of the novel, but like the *Atlantic Monthly* reviewer she focuses on the depiction of rural life: "We do not know whether our literature anywhere possesses such a closely true picture of purely rural life as *Adam Bede* presents. Every class that makes up a village community has its representative; and not only is the dialect of the locality given but the distinct inflection of each order" (*CH* 97).

Eliot is continually compared with Thackeray in the reviews, but generally she is thought to present a happier world, and also a world in which religious or ethical values are more apparent. For example, a review in the *Edinburgh Review* says that "Mr. Eliot has been compared to Thackeray; but Thackeray's chief power lies in describing the sort of world we live in, and the author of Adam Bede leads us into the world we do *not* live in."[74] W. L. Collins in *Blackwood's* also praised the balanced view Eliot took of humanity: "We have here no morbid dwelling upon evil, nor yet an unreal optimism which dresses out life in hues of rose-colour; but a hearty manly sympathy with weakness, not inconsistent with a hatred of vice."[75]

Almost all the reviews of *Adam Bede* single out Mrs. Poyser for special praise, and many of them discuss several of the other characters as individuals, divorced from the context of the novel. The most extreme example of this form of criticism comes in the surprising statement in the *Edinburgh Review* that, although Mrs. Poyser is not the heroine of the novel, "yet we feel her to be of more importance to us than all the other characters: they retire into the background while we listen to the vigorous good sense of her conversation; their destinies are interesting to us chiefly because they are Mrs. Poyser's neighbours."[76] Many of Eliot's readers would open each subsequent novel with the hope of finding another Mrs. Poyser, a hope which must have become increasingly desperate in the later novels. This response testifies to Eliot's ability to create character, and the Victorian habit of reading aloud undoubtedly gave readers a greater susceptibility to the lively idiom of a character like Mrs. Poyser, but it would distress Eliot more and more that readers of her novels often did not treat the work as a whole, as an artifact with a significant purpose, but rather responded to their favourite characters and ignored all types of design. The ubiquitous Victorian metaphors of the "crowded canvas" or the "portrait gallery of sketches" show both that the novel was not expected to have the same kind of unity as the drama or the narrative poem, and that—for most, although not all, critics—it was also not expected to have an underlying and unifying theme or purpose. Rather, it was a story which portrayed characters who had some kind of relationship to one another, and who should be presented in a way which was both entertaining and morally beneficial.

Although the emphasis on characters, abstracted from the work, shows that most critics were not equipped with the critical concepts to talk about the thematic or philosophical structures of Eliot's work, they were nevertheless generally able to recognize that *Adam Bede* was different from most contemporary fiction. A number of them comment on the amount of fiction currently being produced, and then say that *Adam Bede* is something very different from the average work. The tone of these remarks is often defensive, showing that the reviewers were not confident that the novel deserved to be considered a serious literary genre. Some of the reviewers explicitly addressed the objections of those who, for ideological reasons, disapproved of all prose fiction.[77] The *Saturday Review* recommends *Adam Bede* to persons who only read one novel a year (*CH* 73), while the *Literary Gazette* expresses itself more colourfully: "a certain amount of rubbish has to be shot from the cart of Mr. Mudie, and a very liberal allowance it is, for every novel that establishes a fair claim to live, and to teach the generations yet unborn. Adam Bede is one of these."[78]

Several reviewers commented on the religious dimension in the novel. The *Literary Gazette* reviewer tried to speculate about which part of the Church of England the author belonged to,[79] and the *Saturday Review* was sure that George Eliot was a country clergyman (*CH* 73). Frances M. Taylor, writing for the Catholic *Dublin Review*, thought that she could detect signs of the author's sympathy for Catholicism, and she also used the story as a means of recommending the establishment in England of institutions like the French "Enfans Trouvé" as a means "of doing something to avert the progress of that frightful crime of infanticide which is spreading like a plague-spot over our land."[80] R. H. Hutton, in a lengthy review article of George Eliot's first three works, published in 1860, treated Eliot's religious subject matter in some detail and asserted that she had far more understanding of religious faith than other English novelists: "she sees far more clearly than any of them the actual space occupied by spiritual motives in human life,—the depth, beauty, and significance which they, and they alone, give to human action."[81] The only reviewer to realize that Eliot was presenting different forms of religious belief as poetic expressions of a "religion of humanity" was John Chapman, who almost certainly was taking advantage of inside information as to the true identity of George Eliot.[82] Chapman says of Eliot:

> He nowhere obtrudes his own convictions; but, hazarding a conjecture, we think we see indications that he regards the numerous theological creeds, about which the clerical mind has so long disputed, as being only shells of different shape and colour, enclosing the fruit of the religious spirit common to the human race, or as so many mental structures which in less successive metamorphoses man forms and afterwards cuts off.[83]

Once it became known that George Eliot was the same person as the translator of Strauss and Feuerbach, it became more common to read philosophical significance into her works (usually not in a sympathetic manner). One of the earliest such treatments was Richard Simpson's essay on "George Eliot's Novels" in 1863. Simpson identifies the purpose of Eliot's works as the promotion of "positivist beliefs." For her the religion of Positivism "must claim to be founded on Christianity; it must be exhibited as the inner substance, which, having ever existed as a germ within the shell of Christianity, will be displayed in all its fresh ripeness when the dead husk drops away" (*CH* 224). However, Simpson, who was himself a Roman Catholic associated with Lord Acton and the Liberal Catholic movement, concludes that "the positive good of George Eliot's sensible ethics outweighs the negative evil of her atheistic theology" (*CH* 249–50). Simpson's ability to appreciate the value of works which undermined the authority of his own religious affiliation is unusual among Victorian critics. An example of more typical commentary is a review of *Adam Bede* which appeared in the Methodist *London Quarterly Review* in 1861, after George Eliot's identity became public knowledge. It describes the book's literary qualities as "the artistic skill which hides its evil beneath its good" (*CH* 105). Simpson's essay, which is one of the best pieces of Victorian writing on George Eliot, typifies the way that, from early in the 1860s, writers sought to place her among the intellectual positions of the mid-Victorian period. This caused her works to be read for their social, religious, and moral "argument" rather than for the more elemental pleasure of reading a good story. For this reason Eliot began to be distinguished from writers like Dickens and Thackeray, who, for all their power, were regarded as "mere novelists." Eliot was treated more seriously, as a "Victorian sage" like Carlyle or Ruskin or Arnold.[84] Herbert Spencer's opinion of her novels is often referred to: he disapproved of fiction on principle, and when he was a member of the London Library Committee he objected to the purchase of all novels but those of George Eliot.[85]

In addition to placing Eliot among the competing intellectual systems of the day, writers began soon after the publication of *Adam Bede* to attempt to place her among the English writers of the past and present, in order to determine exactly how she was to be read. Whereas the earliest reviews emphasized her originality, later and more substantial review essays place her in what was becoming a definite tradition in English fiction. In his 1860 review essay Hutton constructs a model of the history of the novel in which Eliot is seen as a writer who inherited and combined within herself two schools of fiction, which she sublimated into something uniquely her own. The first consists of the social novelists, who are "of a very light intellectual soil." These writers include Jane Austen, Thackeray, and Trollope, and they all disappoint, whatever their skill at social depiction, "in not giving more insight into those deeper roots of character which lie beneath the social surface."[86] The other type is represented by

Charlotte Brontë, who penetrates beneath the drawing-room surfaces of the world of the social novelist; her charm "lies in the Rembrandt-like distinctness with which the mind conceived is brought into the full blaze of light, and the direct vigour with which all its prominent features are marked out."[87] For Hutton, Eliot combines aspects of both of these schools, and also has affinities with Sir Walter Scott.

Both Hutton and Simpson remark on the affinities between George Eliot and Goethe. Simpson suggests that Goethe may be the source of Eliot's emphasis on renunciation and self-sacrifice. Hutton remarks on the similarity between the *schöne Seele* of Goethe's *Wilhelm Meister* and Eliot's depiction of Dinah Morris. He also comments that scenes of idyllic beauty such as Adam finding Hetty picking currants in the garden remind us "of the soft poetic touch with which Goethe delineated a situation that had sunk deep into his mind."[88] One obvious passage which comes to mind, and which Hutton may have been thinking of when he made his comparison, is the description of Lotte cutting bread for her brothers and sisters in *Die Leiden des jungen Werthers*. In reviews of *The Mill on the Floss* the influence of Goethe is viewed less favourably. Geraldine Jewsbury in the *Athenaeum*[89] and the very hostile reviewer for the *Dublin University Magazine* (*CH* 150) link the presentation of love in the third volume of the *Mill* with the notion of "elective affinities" in Goethe's novel *Die Wahlverwandtschaften*. These comments are all significant in that they show that a knowledge of Goethe was part of the horizon of the educated reader of the 1860s, and that Victorian readers naturally thought of Goethe when they read Eliot's fiction. In this respect we have lost a valuable perspective on Eliot's work, for it was seen by its earliest readers as part of a European movement of fiction. The works of Thackeray and Dickens seem provincial by comparison, and we perhaps do Eliot a disservice by studying her along with them rather than with Goethe and Balzac, or Flaubert and Keller.[90] The fact that Goethe was widely regarded as an immoral novelist—George Eliot attempted to defend him against this charge in "The Morality of *Wilhelm Meister*" (*Essays* 143–47)—further implies that Eliot was in the avant-garde of English literary figures during her early career, a fact to which the very hostile and outraged reception of the third volume of the *Mill* attests.

One reason that *Adam Bede* had been so well received is that readers tended to assume that the author was not only a Christian gentleman, but probably also a clergyman. Once her real identity was exposed, however, Eliot had to contend with the perception of herself as not only a woman, but also a fallen woman, and furthermore the translator of atheistical works of German philosophy and the associate of the somewhat Bohemian group of which John Chapman, the editor of the *Westminster Review*, was a focal point. This may explain why Eliot strongly repudiated E. S. Dallas's claim in the *Times* that *The Mill on the Floss* may be read as suggesting "that it is a grand thing to lead a Bohemian life, and that respectability and the payment of one's debts is necessarily mean and uninteresting" (*CH* 137).[91]

The responses to *The Mill on the Floss* were the low point in Eliot's relationship with contemporary reviewers. Few had commented on the sexual misconduct in *Adam Bede*, although the *Saturday Review* did object to the detailed description of Hetty's pregnancy, which it said read "like the rough notes of a midwife's conversations with a bride" (*CH* 76). However, with their knowledge of the real identity of George Eliot, reviewers scoured the *Mill* for passages which would reveal the presence of a heretical and perverted sensibility, and they found ample evidence in the third volume. The *Dublin University Magazine* summarizes the plot of *The Mill on the Floss* in a way which makes it sound completely ridiculous, and concludes, "A life of pervading selfishness, ill-nature, stupidity, narrow culture, lit by stray and few gleams of high or holy feeling, is the poor result of this microscopic inquiry, this pretentious striving after truth" (*CH* 148). The Rev. J. C. Robertson took the occasion of the publication of *The Mill* to write a long and hostile review of Eliot's first three works. According to Robertson, Eliot "delights in unpleasant subjects—in the representation of things which are repulsive, coarse, and degrading."[92] She is a dangerous writer, because she is cultivated and gifted, but she does not provide anything to "soothe, to elevate, or to purify."[93] Robertson suggests that for her the various forms of the Christian faith are merely mythical shells, as they are for the disciples of Dr. Strauss. Eliot had clearly polarized her readers by writing *The Mill on the Floss*. She had not lived up to their expectations by creating a second Mrs. Poyser; she had dwelt at length on the experience of children, which had formerly been largely the preserve of moralistic Evangelical tales; and she had moved from the gentle pastoral scenes of Loamshire to the stifling atmosphere of the provincial petit-bourgeoisie in and around a not particularly pleasant town. Moreover, the novel presents a rather bleak view of history and of the possibilities for individual aspirations to be fulfilled if they surpass the horizon of the average Philistine consciousness, and readers were now alerted to look out for the unsound moral teaching which would certainly emanate from a woman who had lived with another woman's husband and who had translated Feuerbach.

However, it is unlikely that there could have been a total reversal in George Eliot's mind between two novels written so close together. This suggests that the Victorian enthusiasm for *Adam Bede* missed certain features of the novel, which, when they reappeared in starker form in *The Mill on the Floss*, were seized on by readers who were now predisposed to be hostile. I have tried in the preceding pages to delineate the expectations which governed the reading of *Adam Bede*. I will now turn to a reading of that novel which, drawing on recent criticism, reads the work against the grain of the Victorian view of it, although it takes some comments by Victorian reviewers as starting points to be developed or questioned. This, I think, is a particularly interesting exercise because *Adam Bede* is not for modern readers the most immediately appealing of George Eliot's novels, and we tend to dislike it for all the same reasons that the Victorians liked it. However, I think it can be shown that Eliot does not succeed in her nostalgic attempt to create a totalizing *Gemeinschaftswelt* of pastoral, from which disruptive elements have been purged, and which has been strengthened and purified in the process. By concentrating on inconsistencies in the novel's social analysis and by closely reading its rhetoric, particularly the figurative language referring to nature and to the antitheses of earth and sky, presence and absence, and openness and concealment, one can get a very different view of the novel from the serene impression Jane Carlyle took away with her and see that it is not merely a pastoral idyll which displaces the tensions of 1857 by projecting an idealized world of 1799; rather it may be read as a complex reenactment of precisely those tensions, along with the tensions of Eliot's own life. This makes the harsh tone and the bleakness of the sociology in *The Mill on the Floss* less surprising. *Adam Bede* also produces a powerful dialectic between nature and the human existent, between the striving for transcendence and the fall into facticity, which interestingly repeats the central movement which post-structuralist critics have identified within the rhetoric of romantic poetry.[94]

In her book *George Eliot and Community* Suzanne Graver discusses George Eliot's works in relation to the typology of Ferdinand Tönnies, who formulated as an ideal construct a division of societies into two types: *Gemeinschaft*, or "local, organic, agricultural communities that are modelled on the family and rooted in the traditional and the sacred"; and *Gesellschaft*, or "urban, heterogeneous, industrial societies that are culturally sophisticated and shaped by the rational pursuit of self-interest in a capitalistic and secular environment."[95] Obviously *Adam Bede* depicts a society which tends towards the pole of *Gemeinschaft* rather than *Gesellschaft*. It portrays a world in which everyone has a well-defined place and role, and in which ritual and tradition dominate over innovation and deviation. There are innumerable examples of this in the novel, from Adam's deference "to every one who had more advantages than himself" (*AB* 16;208) to details such as Mr. Poyser's joke to Kester, "not a new, unseasoned joke, but a good old one, that had been tried many times before, and had worn well" (*AB* 53;562). However, the notion of community which George Eliot's totalizing vision at times seems to be urging is one which would impose on human life an ahistorical stasis; it is, in other words, an idealized myth of community, which is constructed for specific ideological reasons, and yet which is deconstructed in the novel because Eliot's radical sympathies and intellectual honesty did not allow her to participate fully in the kind of romantic-conservative political discourse necessary to project a coherent myth of organic community.

A nineteenth-century reviewer gives us an insight into the reasons for the enthusiastic reception of *Adam Bede* as a harmonious idyll of *Gemeinschaft*. Writing in the *Dublin Review*, Frances Taylor betrays a nostalgia for the time George Eliot depicts so evocatively, when "war kept the population under, and men were thankful to stay in their own homes, and die in the place in which they had been born."[96] Taylor clearly views the period of the late eighteenth century as an ideal moment when the lower orders were content to know their place, and before they had begun to demand their share of Victorian prosperity. This idealization was no doubt produced by the common Victorian fear of social anarchy and revolution which was prominent during the 1840s, and which lurked in the background until the events surrounding the Second Reform Bill once again brought it to prominence. With its sparsely populated rural settings, *Adam Bede* does not feature any of the unruly crowds or mobs which are so prominent elsewhere in Eliot's fiction.[97] Indeed, the only large gathering of people (apart from the crowd at the melodramatic scene of Hetty's near-execution) is the festivity to celebrate the young squire's coming of age, which takes up the whole of Book Third. However, Eliot did not succeed in resolving the tensions she had created in the novel, and by carefully reading the reviews one can find hints that this disturbed some of her contemporary readers, even if they accepted in large part the closure she employed.

As critics have often observed, *Adam Bede* presents an idealized community that is not without its dangerous weaknesses, and it dramatizes the reassertion of continuity and *Gemeinschaft* after the interruption which results when Hetty loves above her station and Arthur betrays the code of gentlemanly honour. Murray Krieger sees the work as the assertion of a "classic" vision, which overcomes the more extreme, "tragic" vision of the hero for whom the novel is named:

> For all her admiration of him, the novelist and her work seem at war with their hero, struggling with him to dominate not only the story but the consequences of its central catastrophe. Adam's stony morality, planted in Loamshire, struggles to subvert Loamshire's (and Eliot's) insistence on using its classic continuity to convert even catastrophe into comedy. But of course the paradox is seeming only: Eliot has well arranged matters to assure the conversion of Adam and his puritanical intent rather than his subversion of Loamshire's (and her) absorptive and restorative continuity.[98]

However, by seeing *Adam Bede* in personalized existentialist categories, Krieger misses the real tensions involved in the novel, for he too-easily identifies Eliot, by way of a neat parenthetical equivalence, with the totalizing aims of the novel's depiction of community, and by using the image of Eliot as a benevolent deity who "has well arranged matters" he imposes a univocal and determinate structure—"But of course the paradox is seeming only"—on a text which deconstructs its own claims to authority.

In order to undo the view of *Adam Bede* suggested in this quotation from Krieger, one can begin with the uneasy comment made by a perceptive anonymous reviewer in the liberal *North British Review*. This reviewer was made uncomfortable by George Eliot's portrayal of Hetty Sorrel, about whose experiences of alienation and confrontation with imminent death the existentialist Krieger has surprisingly little to say. According to *North British Review*, "Hetty is the dark shadow lying athwart the tale. The prominence given to her sin we regard as a drawback to these delightful volumes."[99] Hetty's fate indeed disturbs the happy, sun-drenched scenery of the novel, and it does so because we feel that it is disproportionate, arising from the ordering of society and not from the natural order. Unlike the work of previous novelists, as Raymond Williams has shown, George Eliot's early fiction lays bare the social and economic relationships which are elements in the determination of human conduct.[100] Williams uses the scene in which Squire Donnithorne visits Mrs. Poyser's kitchen to illustrate Eliot's depiction of the imbalance of power in the social relationships of Hayslope. One can also apply this analysis to Arthur Donnithorne's relations with Hetty. In the first scene in which we see them together the social anatomy is precise. Hetty responds admiringly to the signs of wealth and power which Arthur manifests: his white hands, gold chain, and militia commission; but "the poor child no more conceived at present the idea that the young squire could be her lover, than a baker's pretty daughter in the crowd, whom a young emperor distinguishes by an imperial but admiring smile, conceives that she shall be made empress" (*AB* 9;144–45). Later, when they meet in the wood, Eliot's figurative language enacts in miniature the rhetorical strategy of the entire novel. The narrator laments:

> Poor things! It was a pity they were not in that golden age of childhood when they would have stood face to face, eyeing each other with timid liking, then given each other a little butterfly kiss, and toddled off to play together. Arthur would have gone home to his silk-curtained cot, and Hetty to her home-spun pillow, and both would have slept without dreams, and to-morrow would have been a life hardly conscious of a yesterday. (*AB* 12;175–76)

The effect of this long digression into the subjunctive mood is that the reader's sense of the social distinction between Hetty and Arthur is blurred precisely by the figure in which it is asserted. The picture of the two as little children is so graphic that it becomes as real as the actual encounter which is taking place. This blurring of the social realities is reinforced in the chapter "Evening in the Wood" by the classical references which transform Arthur and Hetty—as do the more general resonances of the *locus amoenus* topos—out of the realm of history and into that of the timeless "classics": "He may be a shepherd in Arcadia for aught he knows, he may be the first youth kissing the first maiden, he may be Eros himself, sipping the lips of Psyche—it is all one" (*AB* 13;182). But "it is all one" only because we are seeing the meeting from Arthur's point of view; it is only the mind of a classically educated gentleman that is able to make the kind of literary allusions which attempt to conceal the social exploitation involved in Arthur's seduction of Hetty. (The relationship between Arthur's "classics" and the "classic" view of Krieger's essay is perhaps not fortuitous.)

With this perspective on the classical allusions in mind we can return to the earlier quotation in which Arthur and Hetty figure as little children. The passage is a remarkably accurate microcosm of the novel as a whole. Arthur and Hetty meet, have a sexual relationship, and return to their old positions. After his purgatorial suffering Arthur returns to his ancestral home to take up the duties of being the squire again. Hetty remains in her own class in spite of her fantasy of being a lady, and after contemplating committing suicide, and being sentenced to death and transported after a reprieve, she at last achieves a sleep without dreams. The passage also functions as a synecdoche for the entire novel in its desire for a tomorrow "hardly conscious of a yesterday." Both in the wish expressed in the quotation and in the overall pastoral mode which so appealed to Frances Taylor in her review, the narrative seeks the timeless static present of the classic. The inauthenticity of this yearning is pointed to, however, by a crucial absence in the childish encounter quoted above. What is missing is Hetty's suffering, the "dark shadow athwart the tale" which disturbed the reviewer in the *North British Review*.

Hetty, as critics often point out, is a very limited character. However, this serves to magnify the gulf between her and Arthur, a gulf which both the classic discourse mentioned above and the figure of Hetty and Arthur as children attempt to conceal. For Hetty, Arthur is virtually a deity, but her sexuality is a means by which she can aspire to an equal immortality, to be rewarded with the fine things which she pathetically desires. Sexuality is thus a potentially subversive force, and must be rigidly controlled by social difference. Adam Bede, who, unlike Hetty, accepts his place in Hayslope, nevertheless sees the seduction of Hetty by Arthur in class terms, as an abuse of power. He refuses, initially, to forgive Arthur, saying that he is the one who is truly to blame. This potentially revolutionary sentiment, which threatens to extend the democracy of divine judgment to the English rural social hierarchy, must be tamed in order to maintain that hierarchy, and to this end Mr. Irwine—who is "everybody's friend in this business" (*AB* 40;465)—persuades Adam to moderate his judgment. John Goode notes that Irwine's refusal to allow Adam to blame Arthur "shows quite clearly how the ideological pattern of the novel prevents us from carrying the limits of moral enquiry beyond the merely individual to the social."[101] According to Sally Shuttleworth, "the initial recognition that Hetty's plight was, in part, a direct consequence of social stratification is later suppressed."[102] However, these comments are not entirely accurate, for Eliot provides enough evidence as to the social difference between Arthur and Hetty, the differences in their levels of consciousness, and the social power relations in the society of Hayslope that the reader does not entirely accept the static view of community that the novel emphasizes. The intense concentration on Hetty's experience during the two chapters "The Journey in Hope" and "The Journey in Despair" creates a sympathetic identification with her which is not dispelled by Eliot's insistence throughout the novel on her vanity and materialism. Vanity and materialism are shown in this novel to be class privileges; such behaviour has severe consequences for those of the lower orders who adopt it.

The injustice which Hetty suffers is foregrounded by the resolution of the plot of *Adam Bede*. Hetty is punished with transportation and ultimately dies overseas because she dreamed of changing her social rank. Adam, who eventually is persuaded once again to accept the demarcations of class society and to forgive his employer for abusing the privileges of his rank, is rewarded by becoming a small-scale entrepreneur in his own right. The novel enacts the tensions of an ideology which, on the one hand, is concerned to control the aspiration of the proletarian class, and which, on the other, preaches a gospel of fulfilment through work, in which every man is expected to find satisfaction in the work appropriate to his own station, but can also aspire to self-betterment through hard work and the exercise of his native skills. At the end of the novel Adam's social status has changed, but on another level nothing has changed. Adam and Seth are still together in their old home, and Dinah has replaced Lisbeth (whose name is repeated in one of the children) as the maternal figure. Arthur has returned to his estate, and the community appears to have weathered the storm. It is only the "dark shadow" of Hetty's fate which suggests another perspective.

There is another way in which *Adam Bede* presents an ordering myth which disintegrates once it is closely examined, and once again a perceptive Victorian critic offers us a clue as to how to re-read and deconstruct a reading popularized by other Victorian critics. I noted above that for many early readers *Adam Bede* presented a comforting picture of the influence of religion in rustic life. However, as soon became known, Eliot was not a believing Christian. As Richard Simpson implies, there is a fundamental intellectual dishonesty in the Positivist or religious humanist practice of using religious language and forms to command authority for a system of thought which rejected the metaphysical grounds for religion. (This practice reached its absurd conclusion in Comte's institutionalized parody of Catholicism.) Simpson writes of Eliot:

> She knows that the master of superstition is the people, and that here wise men must follow fools; and that it is only by sympathy, and by entering other people's minds, that we can gradually reconcile their thoughts to our own; while, on the other hand, if we wish to secure a lasting existence to our own thought, we must make it popular. It is no small victory to show that the godless humanitarianism of Strauss and Feuerbach can be made to appear the living centre of all the popular religions. (*CH* 225)

In her attempt to portray effectively in *Adam Bede* the operation of a secular religion of humanity, Eliot is forced to use language implying a divine inspiration and divine presence at work in Dinah Morris. In other words, the secular myth is set in a time of faith in order to make it believable. Eliot also, in order to project the "healing myth" of the novel, makes assumptions about nature which are severely questioned elsewhere in the text. If one reads carefully the figurative language pertaining to nature and divine presence, a much more tragic vision appears than most Victorian readers realized, and the classic resolution advanced by the epilogue appears as an arbitrary imposition which in no way resolves the oppositions the novel generates. In order to conclude this discussion of *Adam Bede* I will examine a few significant passages which are concerned with nature and presence.[103]

The epigraph to the novel (from Wordsworth's *Excursion*, 651ff.) suggests that the work will speak "Of nature's unambitious underwood, / And flowers that prosper in the shade," and the narrative frequently implies that Loamshire is a privileged garden-county where nature and men and women live in a happy unity. This aspect of nature is first intimated in the long panoramic description of the village of Hayslope, a "rich undulating district of Loamshire" which "lies close to a grim outskirt of Stonyshire, overlooked by its barren hills as a pretty blooming sister may sometimes be seen linked in the arm of a rugged, tall, swarthy brother" (*AB* 2;61). However, even in Loamshire nature may bear a stony aspect, as will be seen in two incidents in the novel: the death of Thias Bede, and the plight of Hetty Sorrel. My reading of these episodes will suggest that Eliot's view of nature in this apparently Wordsworthian novel is a less benevolent one than Wordsworth's.

While Thias Bede stumbles home and drowns in the brook, Adam is working late in the workshop. At twelve o'clock he looks out the door and "the only motion seemed to be in the glowing, twinkling stars; every blade of grass was asleep" (*AB* 4;91). In other words, there seems to be no sympathetic response from nature, except in the stars whose very distance from Adam signifies separateness. When he hears the knock, "as if with a willow wand," Adam looks outside again, but "the leaves were motionless, and the light of the stars showed the placid fields on both sides of the brook quite empty of visible life" (*AB* 4;93). Once again the stillness of nature emphasizes the indifference of natural objects to the suffering of humanity, and this time the light of the stars points to an absence, not to an animating Wordsworthian presence. However, the mysterious knock of the willow wand must also be taken into account. George Eliot was too much of a rationalist to allow the supernatural sign to stand as an index of nature's sympathetic presence, but neither does she want to demystify the occurrence completely. In the third edition of *Adam Bede* she added a sentence to her description of Adam's reaction to the sound he hears: "I tell it as he told it, not attempting to reduce it to its natural elements: in our eagerness to explain impressions, we often lose our hold of the sympathy that comprehends them" (*AB* p. 596n.). Here Eliot is doing precisely what Simpson describes Positivists in general as doing. The Positivist, he says, "may have a hearty sympathy with the orthodoxy of the uneducated, or, what comes to the same thing, of past generations of educated men" (*CH* 225). She is attempting to use Adam's uneducated sensibility to import into her novel a notion of nature which is not elsewhere supported by the text. Soon afterwards, the description of Thias Bede's funeral presents a different type of relationship between humankind and nature. It comes after a long passage describing the leisurely walk of the Poyser family to church, on a day when the natural world itself seems to observe the Sabbath, and "the sunshine seemed to call all things to rest and not to labour" (*AB* 18;232). Lisbeth Bede is looking back on her husband's grave, and her consciousness is presented in indirect discourse: "Ah! there was nothing now but the brown earth under the white thorn" (*AB* 18;241). This suggests that human beings are only truly one with the Loamshire countryside when they are part of its loamy substance, when they cease to be conscious and become natural objects that decay in the earth. The thorn which grows by Thias Bede's grave becomes a recurring motif for the suffering of humanity in the novel (as well as calling to mind Wordsworth's poem "The Thorn"). The enchanted grove in which Hetty meets Arthur is for Dinah "a thorny thicket of sin and sorrow, in which she saw the poor thing struggling torn and bleeding, looking with tears for rescue and finding none" (*AB* 15;203).

In chapter 35 the narrator recalls travelling in Europe and seeing crucifixes amidst pleasant country scenes, and the sign of the cross becomes the sign of the separation of culture and nature: "It has stood perhaps by the clustering apple-blossoms, or in the broad sunshine by the cornfield, or at a turning by the wood where a clear brook was gurgling below; and surely, if there came a traveller to this world who knew nothing of the story of man's life upon it, this image of agony would seem to him strangely out of place in the midst of this joyous nature" (*AB* 35;409–10). Hetty's experiences similarly point to a concept of nature at odds with the benevolent Wordsworthian view. Her journey away from home, and her experience amidst the rich fields of Warwickshire, show that her place in the world is a precarious one, and that it was maintained in Hayslope by the many small rituals of family and village life. Instead of finding a refuge she comes to feel that she has "reached the borders of a new wilderness" (*AB* 37;424); and she loses her way and finds herself in a dark night of the soul which leads to no illumination in the morning (*AB* 37;431). Alone in the hostile landscape by a pool, she nevertheless eats her bread and, conscious of "the horror of this cold, and darkness, and solitude—out of all human reach" (*AB* 37;432), she feels "a strange contradictory wretchedness and exultation" (*AB* 37;432). Her wretchedness arises because, unlike Thias Bede, she does not drown and so cannot be absorbed by nature, but instead must face nature as an adversary; her exultation arises from the human quest for transcendence, which drives her to resist the hostile landscape and the disturbing apparition of the elderly man, and to form new plans and a new destination. Hetty is gradually reduced to a more and more degraded state of animality in her physical being, but she strives to transcend this through the intentional acts of her consciousness. In this she resembles—however unlikely the comparison may seem at first sight—the heroes of Samuel Beckett's fiction.

If Hetty points to the separation of culture from nature, Dinah Morris is an example of how a woman can live a good life in the world. In her we see the positive embodiment of a humanistic religion, but it depends upon a metaphysic which Eliot herself rejected. An interesting place to begin a discussion of Dinah is with a hymn which Seth Bede sings in a passage immediately following the description of Hetty's night by the pond:

> Dark and cheerless is the morn
> Unaccompanied by thee:
> . . . .
> Visit, then, this soul of mine,
>   Pierce the gloom of sin and grief—
> Fill me Radiancy Divine
>   Scatter all my unbelief. (*AB* 38;437)

For Seth, Dinah herself is a divine presence, and earlier in the novel he has applied the words of a hymn to the expression of his love for Dinah. For Dinah, however, the words of such a hymn apply to the presence of the Holy Spirit within her. Hetty is continually compared with natural objects in the novel, whereas Dinah exists *as* a natural object obeying the immanent laws of the divine presence within her. The rector Mr. Irwine is described as fitting in well with his natural surroundings: "however ill he harmonised with sound theories of the clerical office, he somehow harmonised extremely well with that peaceful landscape" (*AB* 5;113). When Irwine has spoken to Dinah, however, he asserts that she is even closer to nature, saying, "He must be a miserable prig who would act the pedagogue here: one might as well go and lecture the trees for growing in their own shape" (*AB* 8;136).

Hetty remains close to the earth of Loamshire, and it seeks to claim her in a hostile and watery embrace; Dinah aspires to the airy heights, above the treeless hills of Stonyshire, where apocalyptic fires will devour all earthly objects. The contrast between the two is neatly made in a comparison of both women to birds: "Hetty looked at her much in the same way as one might imagine a little perching bird that could only flutter from bough to bough, to look at the swoop of the swallow or the mounting of the lark" (*AB* 14;186–87). In another contrast which is significant in the novel, Hetty continually attempts acts of concealment: of her earrings, her pregnancy, her baby. Dinah opens herself to divine action and speaks openly to others, whether to individuals or the congregation who assemble to hear her preach.

Dinah's religion is based, like Adam's, on the text of the Bible, but unlike him she sees herself as a channel of divine power. Her inward light is something which is brightest when the outward light is failing. In her letter to Seth she writes: "I sit on my chair in the dark room and close my eyes, and it is as if I was out of the body and could feel no want for evermore" (*AB* 30;373–74). Another significant description of Dinah's religious experience comes in the chapter "The Two Bed-Chambers": "She closed her eyes, that she might feel more intensely the presence of a Love and Sympathy deeper and more tender than was breathed from the earth and sky. That was often Dinah's mode of praying in solitude. Simple to close her eyes, and to feel herself enclosed by the Divine Presence" (*AB* 15;202). Here Dinah has gone even beyond the remote sky (location of the stars which twinkled indifferently as Thias Bede drowned). She experiences a presence which fuels the love and pity she pours out for others. Nature is obliterated, and when it appears later in the chapter it is as the thorny thicket which threatens to destroy Hetty.

Elsewhere in the novel, however, there are more rationalistic explanations for Dinah's piety. After explaining that Dinah and Seth believed in miracles and instant conversions, the narrator comments: "it is impossible for me to represent their diction as correct, or their instruction as liberal. Still—if I have read religious history aright—faith, hope, and charity have not always been found in a direct ratio with sensibility to the three concords; and it is possible, thank Heaven! to have very erroneous theories and very sublime feelings" (*AB* 3;82). Similarly, Irwine attributes Dinah's influence over her auditors to her beauty rather than to the content or mode of inspiration of her preaching (*AB* 25;320). The narrator also directly comments on Dinah's feeling of divine guidance:

> As Dinah expressed it, "She was never left to herself; but it was always given her when to keep silence and when to speak." And do we not all agree to call rapid thought and noble impulse by the name of inspiration? After our subtlest analysis of the mental process, we must still say, as Dinah did, that our highest thoughts and our best deeds are all given to us. (*AB* 10;158–59)

Dinah is thus paradoxically presented as a *schöne Seele* who lacks a transcendent source for the beauty which shines out of her; sometimes the narrator seems to toy with physiological explanations for the operation of human sympathy, but clearly he is not satisfied with these. However, for the novel to close satisfactorily the paradoxical presentation of Dinah must be resolved in some way. This is accomplished when Adam falls in love with Dinah and she with him. She is afraid that by loving him she would be turning her back on the light which has shone upon her (*AB* 52;552), so that darkness and doubt could take hold of her. Yet when Adam goes to meet her at the hilltop, where there is "no presence but the still lights and the shadows, and the great embracing sky" (*AB* 54;575), she consents to marry him. In the absence of any spiritual presence in the sky, Dinah expresses her belief in the divine will by accepting human love. In the epilogue Dinah is, as Lisbeth was before her, a housewife waiting for Adam to come home, and she has been barred from preaching and thereby silenced.

It is interesting that when Dinah's sense of presence is banished by her acceptance of earthly love, a romantic mystification of nature reasserts itself. At this point in the novel the extreme visions of both Dinah and Hetty have been purged. Hetty, who in her dark night had a vision of nature as pure immanence, leaves England and disappears from the text. Dinah, whose transcendent vision of the presence of God annihilated the phenomenal forms of nature, diminishes into an ordinary housewife. Through Hetty, Eliot suggested that nature has no transcendent meaning. Through Dinah, she created a vision of transcendental meaning which turned out to be a rationalistic parable. The epilogue is an attempt to piece together the jagged edges of the story, and to show the restored Edenic happiness of Loamshire. However, just as Adam's social advancement reminds us of the social oppression which was Hetty's downfall, so there are traces in the epilogue of the disturbing insights Eliot explored through Dinah and Hetty. The reference to Hetty's death brings back memories of her suffering, and of the pitilessness of nature. Seth's comment about Dinah being barred from preaching suggests that, however misguided Dinah's sense of divine presence might have been from a rationalistic point of view, it nevertheless has not been fully compensated by her present role. The epilogue imposes an uneasy and unconvincing stasis on the dialectical movements *Adam Bede* generates. It is interesting to note that in *Romola* George Eliot tries to resolve the problems of writing a secular story of sanctity by having Romola grow into her saintly role, and attain it by losing a husband, which is precisely the reverse of the pattern in *Adam Bede*. *Romola* also concludes with a family genre-piece, but unlike *Adam Bede* the family in *Romola* does not have a father figure. However, *Adam Bede* does not fully reinforce the Victorian ideology of the patriarchal family. Dinah is most an "angel in the house"[104] when she has no ties to any man and when even earthly objects at times lose their reality for her.

I should emphasize in conclusion that my reading of *Adam Bede* is not intended to falsify the Victorians' readings of the work, but rather to supplement them by introducing new contexts and frames in which to place it. As Jauss notes in his essay on Baudelaire's "Spleen II":

> Questions left unposed are opportunities for the subsequent interpreter. They must not lead to the point of completely abolishing the answer that the predecessor found in the text to his questions. The coherence of question and answer in the history of an interpretation is primarily determined by categories of the enrichment of understanding (be they supplementation or

development, a reaccenting or a new elucidation), and only secondarily by the logic of falsifi-
ability.[105]

The tensions and discontinuities which my interpretation focuses on are already
evident in some of the incidental and uneasy comments of Victorian readers.
The horizonal changes which make my interpretation possible have the effect
of moving these tensions out of their incidental and marginal position in the
discourse of those readers. My reading of *Adam Bede* has also served to reveal
the relationship between the novel and the experience of general history, by
demonstrating the way that the novel thematizes or attempts to repress concerns
of Victorians about class conflict, the grounds of religious belief, and sexual
politics, and by showing how the horizons of the Victorian readers largely forbid
them from perceiving such textual operations, although in a number of cases
they are aware of them as troubling adumbrations. The present concerns of
literary criticism have foregrounded these aspects of Eliot's text for me, but in
due course my own reading will certainly be revealed as equally temporally
bound, and equally blind to things which seem self-evident to future readers of
the *Adam Bede*.

The Reception of *Daniel Deronda*

George Eliot's fiction seeks to present the psychological, historical, and philosophical grounds of an ideal community of humanity and to dramatize the realization of that ideal in the consciousness of one or more characters. She pursued her fictional aims through a series of different "experiments in life," as she once termed her novels (*Letters* 6:216). In *Adam Bede* she had nostalgically depicted a historical-pastoral rural community where *Gemeinschaft* predominated; in her last novel she deals with the *Gesellschaft* of contemporary life for the first time, but draws on the most ancient part of the Western cultural tradition to give her novel a prophetic, if not apocalyptic, quality. *Daniel Deronda* is a new beginning for George Eliot in a number of ways.[1] She is more obviously critical of English society than she had been in her earlier fiction, and she addresses more fundamental social and political questions, even if, as I will suggest, the novel ultimately reaches an ideological impasse similar to that of her previous works, and retreats in a manner similar to them from these wider questions into an interior and personalized world. By dealing with Jewish life in realistic detail Eliot also moves away from the traditional subject matter of the English novel, and challenges the stereotypical presentation of Jews in English literature. For these and other reasons *Daniel Deronda* evoked a deeply divided response, in which one can trace the origins of the split which developed in the late Victorian reading public into what would become known as "highbrow" and "middlebrow" culture.

By the time she wrote *Daniel Deronda* George Eliot was generally seen by the reading public as England's preeminent literary figure. The deaths of Thackeray (1863) and Dickens (1870) left her without a serious rival for supremacy in the realm of fiction. She was also regarded more and more as a moral teacher, and her works were read by some with an almost religious fervour. Paradoxically, the moral analysis for which Eliot was so praised derives from the "atheistical" doctrines for which she was attacked. Her rejection of orthodox Christianity and her anguished quest for a new basis of morality meant that her novels did not—as did the novels of many of her contemporaries—fall back on conventional morality in an unthinking way. She was seen to sympathize with individual moral dilemmas, yet she was rigorous in her treatment of transgressors. She thus appealed to those who desired moral certainty but who were skeptical of the claims of social institutions to provide it; following Feuerbach, Eliot personalized the sources of moral action, locating them in human feelings. Her fiction was widely praised for its "sympathy," as in R. H. Hutton's comment—in a review of book 1 of *Middlemarch*—that "one of George Eliot's great charms consists in her large friendly way of letting the light fall on human weakness" (*CH* 289). In 1866, before the publication of *Middlemarch*, John Morley wrote an article for *Macmillan's*, praising her fiction as an outstanding example of literature, whose end he declared to be "nothing but *a criticism of life*."[2] Eliot was so pleased with Morley's article that she asked Lewes to thank Alexander Macmillan for it (*Letters* 4:309n.). Morley said that if a novel has any purpose beyond "the idlest diversion and time-killing" then it must lie in

> those reflections . . . which lead people to work out for themselves notions of what is graceful and seemly, to teach themselves a more exquisite intellectual sensibility, and to enlarge their own scope of affection and intensity of passion. These are the rightful fruits of that pleasure which is the first aim of the novel-reader, and which he too often takes to be the only aim, and to be itself the fruit when in truth it is only the blossom.[3]

Morley's comments are typical of the seriously intellectual critical expectations which the best Victorian reviewers brought to bear on works of fiction. However, even these standards did not enable the reviewers to come to terms fully with *Middlemarch*, which appeared in part form in 1871–72. They found its tone "sad" and "melancholy."[4] There was wide divergence in their accounts of the theme of the novel: some saw it as primarily an analytical and psychological study of the individual consciousness of the central characters, while others saw it as a statement of social determinism.[5] The novel also disturbed readers because it confounded their expectations of the conventionally happy ending of a marriage between Dorothea and Lydgate.[6] (Eliot would more daringly shatter such expectations in *Daniel Deronda*.) In spite of these objections, however, *Middlemarch* consolidated Eliot's hold on the reading public, which had never quite regained its original strength after *Adam Bede* was followed by the revelation of her identity, the harsh reception of *The Mill on the Floss*, and the relative failure of *Romola*. In addition, *Middlemarch* strongly reinforced the view of George Eliot as a writer of great intellectual power and learning. Even those critics who were doubtful about *Middlemarch* tended to recognize its literary merit. The reviews often question the tone and the philosophy underlying the novel while acknowledging George Eliot to be among the great English writers. R. H. Hutton, for instance, begins his review of book 6 by saying that "*Middlemarch* bids more than fair to be one of the great books of the world" (*CH* 302), and he concludes his review of the complete work with the comment that "it is not too much to say that George Eliot will take her stand amongst the stars of the second magnitude, with the cluster which contains Scott and Fielding, and indeed all but Shakespeare, on a level of comparative equality with them" (*CH* 314).

Although the reviews were not enthusiastic, *Middlemarch* was a commercial success, and this owes something to the format in which it was published. John Blackwood had been disappointed by the fact that *Felix Holt* had not sold well, in spite of the generally positive critical response it received. He was also determined to try to defy Mudie's Select Library, for Mudie had been exacting large discounts, because of his stranglehold on the distribution of three-volume novels, which at the standard price of a guinea and a half were rarely sold to individuals.[7] Blackwood therefore willingly accepted Lewes's suggestion (*Letters* 5:145–46) that they should market the work in eight parts, at a price of 5s. a part. This avoided the need for a risky four-volume edition, and yet it was not a traditional serial publication either. As John Sutherland notes:

> *Middlemarch* should have the stiff covers and narrative wholeness associated with the library volume; at the same time it should have the reduced price and deferred payment associated with the serial. It would thus be both bought and hired. The scheme certainly had a certain novelty though, paradoxically, it would also appeal to the more traditional kind of reader who felt that standards should be kept up in a world where fiction was increasingly becoming the property of the newspapermen.[8]

The novel appeared at two-month intervals, beginning in December 1871, with the last two numbers being accelerated to monthly intervals. N. N. Feltes argues that the format of *Middlemarch* is an assertion of Eliot's professional status as a writer, "displaying publicly her own control not only over the terms, conditions, and content, but over the setting in which she performs her work."[9] The new format thus is another assertion of her unique status among contemporary writers. It allowed her the freedom of writing a very long novel, but also the scope of large individual parts to develop her text in relatively organized units. She and Blackwood were able to assert their independence of Mudie, who had threatened not to take the novel, but ended up taking about 1,500 copies of each of the parts.[10] The novel was a commercial success, selling about 5,000 copies in part form, and it probably would have sold more if Blackwood had not been cautious in his printing, following his own instincts instead of Lewes's more optimistic projection.[11]

Like *Middlemarch*, *Daniel Deronda* was published in eight parts, but this time monthly, at the beginning of each month from February to September 1876. Three journals—*The Athenaeum*, *The Spectator*, and *The Examiner*—reviewed several or all of the parts of *Daniel Deronda* as they appeared, and they did so in full consciousness that they were participating in a major public event. This event—the enthusiastic public reception of George Eliot's new novel—was itself a topic of interest for several of the reviewers who waited to write until the entire novel had appeared. Sidney Colvin noted in the *Fortnightly Review* that the characters of the novel

> have been among the public personages whose doings and motives have been most warmly canvassed in newspapers and in common talk. . . . We have all had our say, and if to many the book has seemed not easy, and to some not agreeable, the interest of all is the great tribute to its power; find what faults we please, it is certain that no other writer living is able thus to arrest, occupy, and nourish our thoughts.[12]

The review in the *Edinburgh Review* begins with a long passage which is part panegyric and part analysis of George Eliot's prominent position in contemporary English literature. The article starts by noting that Eliot's career as a novelist has been an unusual one, with no preliminary struggle to be endured before acceptance was gained. In fact, the unidentified writer says,

> A more unanimous and a more enthusiastic verdict has rarely been got by any competitor for the prizes of literature. She has outstripped even those who hold the highest place among the kindred writers who were a little way before her in the race. There are many, to whom Bulwer Lytton is nauseous, and Thackeray cynical, and Dickens vulgar, who have nothing but unbounded admiration to give to the author of "Adam Bede" and "Silas Marner."[13]

Although "a fame more thoroughly deserved has seldom existed," the reviewer laments that Eliot has also become fashionable,[14] which may be part of the reason for the unprecedented reception of *Daniel Deronda*, a work more eagerly awaited than any piece of fiction since the days of Scott:

> The eagerness with which this work has been looked for, the wide and general reception it has met with, the anxiety of critics who have not even waited for its completion, but have discussed it piecemeal as an object of national interest, if perhaps somewhat discouraging to those calmer observers upon whom the cumulative force does not tell, is perfectly natural and reasonable.[15]

George Eliot had never been restricted by the demands of the literary marketplace to the same extent as most novelists of her time. Her relatively secure financial position saved her from the fate of the hack who had to turn out at least one three-volume novel a year; she had an unusually sympathetic publisher; and she also saw her writing career in terms of a vocation.[16] Sutherland notes that "once an author had made his name he would experience the surrounding urge for stability as an insidious coercion to turn out recurrent bestsellers according to a proven successful formula," a pressure which affected the careers of even Dickens and Thackeray.[17] George Eliot would have felt this pressure in the constant harking back to the early success of *Adam Bede* and the praise for her humour and depiction of provincial life. But she was determined to resist the pressures of the marketplace as much as was compatible with her continuing career as a novelist. During the composition of *Romola* she wrote:

> Of necessity, the book is addressed to fewer readers than my previous works, and I myself have never expected—I might rather say *intended*—that the book should be as "popular" in the same sense as the others. If one is to have freedom to write out one's own varying unfolding self, and not be a machine always grinding out the same material or spinning the same sort of web, one cannot always write for the same public. (*Letters* 4:49)

Eliot was sufficiently committed to an idea of artistic integrity that she gave up £3,000 of George Smith's original offer of £10,000 for *Romola*, rather than have to print the work in smaller portions than she thought appropriate.[18]

This relative artistic autonomy allowed Eliot to see her writing as something higher than that of a "mere novelist" like Dinah Mulock. Her mature attitude to her own fiction is expressed in a well-known letter to Frederic Harrison, who had been trying to persuade her to write a Positivist utopia. She replied:

> That is a tremendously difficult problem which you have laid before me, and I think you see its difficulties, though they can hardly press upon you as they do on me, who have gone through again and again the severe effort of trying to make certain ideas thoroughly incarnate, as if they had revealed themselves to me first in the flesh and not in the spirit. I think aesthetic teaching is the highest of all teaching because it deals with life in its highest complexity. But if it ceases to be purely aesthetic—if it lapses anywhere from the picture to the diagram—it becomes the most offensive of all teaching. (*Letters* 4:300)

Eliot may well have gained the confidence necessary to experiment with a radically new type of novel in *Daniel Deronda* from the popularity and moral authority she enjoyed following the appearance of *Middlemarch*. In addition, the literary horizon of the 1870s was favourable to attempts to teach by aesthetic means. As Kenneth Graham notes in *English Criticism of the Novel 1865–1900*, an insistence on moral teaching in fiction was "at its crudest and most vigorous" between 1865 and 1880.[19] Even Anthony Trollope, who was not the most intellectually inclined of authors (he commented that in reading Eliot's later works "one feels oneself to be in company with some philosopher rather than with a novelist"),[20] felt the need to assert the didactic purpose of his vocation. He wrote in his *Autobiography*:

> There are many who would laugh at the idea of a novelist teaching either virtue or nobility,— those, for instance, who regard the reading of novels as a sin, and those also who think it simply an idle pastime. . . . I have regarded my art from so different a point of view that I have ever thought of myself as a preacher of sermons, and my pulpit as one which I could make both salutary and agreeable to my audience.[21]

Eliot's most unequivocal statement about the didactic nature of authorship comes in a brief note entitled "Authorship," which was published after her death by Charles Lee Lewes as part of a collection of fragmentary essays he called "Leaves from a Notebook." Lewes dates these pieces "some time between the appearance of 'Middlemarch' and that of 'Theophrastus Such'" (*Essays* 437). In the piece called "Authorship" Eliot wrote that a "man or woman who publishes writings inevitably assumes the office of teacher or influencer of the public mind" (*Essays* 440). As Eliot more consciously assumed this office she evolved her so-called sibylline manner, which was a persona created to convey moral truths as effectively as possible. This manner was probably best illustrated in her Sunday afternoon receptions at the Priory, but it is also evident in *Impressions of Theophrastus Such* (1879), her last published work. The *Impressions* are an uneasy amalgam of the autobiographical essay, the moral essay, fiction, and journalism, although by the time one reaches the final essay the fictional persona and the fictional mode have all but disappeared as Eliot presents her views on nationalism and race, providing in effect a gloss on *Daniel Deronda*. Another example of Eliot's tendency to adopt the role of the sibylline moral sage is her correspondence with Alexander Main, a fervent admirer whose devotion she and George Henry Lewes did little to discourage. In fact, Main was allowed to compile, and Blackwood published, a collection of extracts from Eliot's works entitled *Wise, Witty, and Tender Sayings in Prose and Verse* (1872)— this in spite of Eliot's many statements about artistic form and her famous strictures about the nature of aesthetic teaching in her letter to Frederic Harrison.

The perception of Eliot as an earnest Victorian sibyl was to be disastrous for her reputation during the latter part of the nineteenth century and well on into the twentieth, but in the last decade of her life she utilized its power boldly to attempt in *Daniel Deronda* to make a social critique, an examination of the metaphorical bases of English culture, and an attack on anti-Semitism. Eliot may have consciously decided, after the rather muted conclusion of *Middlemarch*, to write a more external and heroic "epic" work, reworking the theme of *The Spanish Gypsy* in a novel. While *Middlemarch* makes social criticism on a small scale, focussing on a provincial town before the first Reform Bill, *Daniel Deronda* is a scathing indictment of the state of English society in the 1860s, presenting it as a decadent civilization whose culture has atrophied even as it embarks on its imperialistic venture. The novel uses the idea of national unity to present an alternative that combines a rationalistic view of the universe with a faith in the possibility of human community. As in her tragic poem, Eliot somewhat disturbingly uses ideas about racial inheritance in *Daniel Deronda* in order to suggest that the protagonist's acceptance of a national mission does not seem merely an arbitrary choice, but rather is seen as the necessary outcome of his or her preceding life and heritage. In "Notes on the Spanish Gypsy and Tragedy in General," George Eliot had written of the heroine of her verse drama:

A young maiden, believing herself to be on the eve of the chief event of her life—marriage—about to share in the ordinary lot of womanhood, full of young hope, has suddenly announced to her that she is chosen to fulfil a great destiny, entailing a terribly different experience from that of ordinary womanhood. She is chosen, not by any momentary arbitrariness, *but as the result of foregoing hereditary conditions*: she obeys.[22]

Daniel Deronda is like *The Spanish Gypsy* and unlike most of Eliot's other works in that it attempts to go beyond the depiction of community either as existing in the past (*Romola, Adam Bede, Silas Marner*), or merely existing in potential, in the microcosm of the social totality to be found in the bonds between individual characters (*The Mill on the Floss, Middlemarch*). Both *Deronda* and *The Spanish Gypsy* attempt to fuse the bourgeois liberalism of the *Westminster Review* circle with a romantic organic view of society, and to use biological theories to effect the fusion.

Eliot's first mention of *Deronda*, when she was in the early stages of planning the work—"simmering towards another big book" is the phrase she uses—is already defensive: "people seem so bent on giving supremacy to Middlemarch that they are sure not to like any future book so well" (*Letters* 5:454). Blackwood responded favourably to the novel when he received the first instalment of manuscript. He had by this time learned that George Eliot's sensitivity to criticism meant that even small objections had a paralyzing effect on her creativity. But he did suggest that he should arrange for a "gossiping paragraph" in order to reassure the public, when the title *Daniel Deronda* was announced, that in spite of the foreign name the book would be a picture of English life (*Letters* 6:186–87). Blackwood arranged for a paragraph to be printed in the "Literary Gossip" column of the *Athenaeum*: "A report is going the round of the papers that 'George Eliot has a new novel in preparation, illustrating American Life.' The first part of the statement is, we believe, true; the second part is undoubtedly incorrect."[23] Later, on Lewes's suggestion (*Letters* 6:193), another paragraph was inserted in the *Athenaeum* in an attempt to mitigate the effect it was feared that the Jewish subject matter would have, and also, no doubt, to capitalize on the popularity of *Middlemarch*: "George Eliot's new work is, we have reason to know, like 'Middlemarch,' a story of English life, but of our own day, and dealing for the most part with a higher sphere of society."[24]

Eliot seems to have become more and more disillusioned with English life in the early 1870s. Her letters reveal a growing conservatism (e.g., *Letters* 7:46–47), combined with an intolerance for the productions of the popular press and for popular culture in general. In a letter to François D'Albert-Durade, written while she was in the midst of writing *Daniel Deronda*, she comments on changes she had observed in the cultural life of European towns:

Everywhere there is a prosperous crowd to be amused, and the tastes of the crowd are not yet refined, so that Art must condescend to please the low average. This condescension is painfully marked in our huge rich London; but of late we have been a little cheered by a revived interest in the Shakespearean drama to counterbalance Offenbach. (*Letters* 6:174).

A similar tone infuses *Theophrastus Such*, which includes several essays on the vanity of authors and the false motivations of scholars. The essay "Debasing the Moral Currency" conjures up a vision of a civilization being destroyed by a burlesque tone which can only be held in check by "the spiritual police of sentiments or ideal feelings."[25] Eliot's attitudes to culture thus reflect the split which was developing between high bourgeois culture and the general society of late Victorian England. The reception of *Daniel Deronda* provides further evidence of this split, and shows George Eliot being championed, ironically enough, by the forerunners of Modernism, the movement which would repudiate her as the embodiment of everything it disliked about the Victorian bourgeoisie.

Daniel Deronda is very much concerned with the importance of the liberating potential of ideas and of the exercise of rationality to overcome reified structures of thinking and feeling, such as the prejudice of anti-Semitism. In these concerns Eliot allies herself with the spirit of Heinrich Heine, for no one was better at ridiculing the consequences of unthinking prejudices and outdated structures than he was. Heine's brilliant satire had made him the object of considerable suspicion in England in the early part of the nineteenth century. He was initially viewed as a blasphemous and dangerous revolutionary by the English press, but later in the century George Eliot and Matthew Arnold were instrumental in bringing him to the fore in English literary circles.[26] In her *Westminster Review* article "German Wit: Heinrich Heine," Eliot described him as "one of the most remarkable men of this age" and "an artist in prose literature, who has shown even more completely than Goethe the possibilities of German prose; and—in spite of all the charges against him, true as well as false—a lover of freedom, who has spoken wise and brave words on behalf of his fellow-men" (*Essays* 223). Eliot read Heine again intensively in the period 1869–70, as notebook and journal entries attest.[27] Matthew Arnold also had acclaimed Heine in an 1863 Oxford lecture, calling him the successor of Goethe in the war of liberation of humanity.[28] Arnold notes that Heine recognized and attacked the English inaccessibility to ideas, and that he was particularly enraged by what he called the "*ächt britische Beschränktheit*," the genuine British narrowness.[29] In *Daniel Deronda* the presence of three chapter epigraphs from Heine (chapters 34, 62, 63) is a hint of his influence on the novel. Eliot's use of Heine constitutes a link between her analysis of English society and Arnold's. For both writers, Heine is on the side of culture, a soldier in the war against the Philistines.

The presence of Heine in *Daniel Deronda* is just one example of Eliot's impatience with both popular culture and the increasingly imperialistic society in which she lived. Her politics, as they developed during the 1870s and as they are expressed in that novel, are an example of the kind of Romantic cultural conservatism which developed towards the latter part of the nineteenth century in both England and Germany, and which criticized capitalism not in the name of social revolution but in the interests of preserving "culture." These questions were topical when Eliot wrote *Daniel Deronda*. A few years earlier Matthew Arnold had articulated his concern about the possible consequences of the Second Reform Act in *Culture and Anarchy* (1869). Various of Arnold's key phrases and terms are frequently employed in Eliot's novel, for example, "culture," "doing as one likes," and "Philistine." Similarly, the contemporary concerns about education in general and women's education in particular find expression in the descriptions of Deronda's dissatisfaction with English education and his difficulty in choosing a career, and of Gwendolen's woefully inadequate schooling.

Daniel Deronda also takes issue with late Victorian society on the question of ethnic minorities. For a person of her class and her time, Eliot had an unusually tolerant attitude towards Judaism. In 1848, writing to John Sibree about Disraeli, she had commented that "everything *specifically* Jewish is of a low grade" (*Letters* 1:247), but by the time she wrote *Daniel Deronda* her own experience of the intolerant hypocrisy of English society had made her more sympathetic. On 29 October 1876 she wrote to Harriet Beecher Stowe, in words which come as an enlightened relief from the typical anti-Semitism of other Victorian writers:

> Precisely because I felt the usual attitude of Christians towards Jews is—I hardly know whether to say more impious or more stupid when viewed in the light of their professed principles, I therefore felt urged to treat Jews with such sympathy and understanding as my nature could attain to. Moreover, not only towards the Jews, but towards all oriental peoples with whom we English come into contact, a spirit of arrogance and contemptuous dictatorialness is observable which has become a national disgrace to us. There is nothing I should care more to do, if it were possible, than to rouse the imagination of men and women to a vision of human claims in those races of their fellow-men who most differ from them in customs and beliefs. (*Letters* 6:301)

Before he becomes involved with Mordecai's ideas, Daniel Deronda is described as having regarded Judaism "as a sort of eccentric fossilized form" (*DD* 32;334), but this is more obviously true of the class in which he was reared. *Daniel Deronda* depicts the upper class as a group of people who spend their time in pointless riding, hunting, and "visiting and receiving of visits" (*DD* 44;509). In place of the finely woven texture of *Gemeinschaft* we are presented with a world in which Gwendolen's credo of "doing as she likes" is the rule. Grandcourt treats his dogs and fellow human beings with equal imperiousness. He and Sir Hugo Mallinger utilize the unwholesome emissary Lush for their own material ends. Culture for this class is perverted into drawing-room entertainment, or a display of books to be abstained from (*DD* 28;292). Mrs. Arrowpoint regards Tasso as a splendid romantic subject, but, like Klesmer, Tasso is not thought to have any bearing on the disposition of property or one's thoughts about society and right and wrong. Truly talented artists like Klesmer and Mirah are condescended to by those with the power and wealth to patronize them, and Gwendolen, whose sensitive nature, rootlessness, and experience of the insecurity of her class position might be expected to make her aware of other perspectives, is unable to see her future from Klesmer's point of view in their interview.

Part of Gwendolen's problem is clearly her inadequate education which has provided her with ambition and self-confidence without the development of the intellectual faculties and awareness of moral issues which Arnold saw as the essence of culture:

> She felt well equipped for the mastery of life. With regard to much in her lot hitherto, she held herself rather hardly dealt with, but as to her "education" she would have admitted that it left her under no disadvantages. In the schoolroom her quick mind had taken readily that strong starch of unexplained rules and disconnected facts which saves ignorance from any painful sense of limpness; and what remained of all things knowable, she was conscious of being sufficiently acquainted with through novels, plays, and poems. (*DD* 4;34).

Deronda, on the other hand, is well-educated, even having the benefit of study in Germany, of which Arnold would have approved. But his education has only prepared him for a life to which his birth does not entitle him. This, together with the "three or five per cent on capital which somebody has battled for," produces in Deronda the kind of mood of indecision which characterizes the poetry of Arnold and Clough, a "sort of contemplative mood perhaps more common in the young men of our day—that of questioning whether it were worth while to take part in the battle of the world" (*DD* 17;169).

Many of the first readers of *Daniel Deronda* were dismayed by the satirical tone and the absence of the richly textured rural description of the earlier works. Even this late in Eliot's career some were still hoping for another *Adam Bede*. In its review of book 1, *The Examiner* compared Eliot's new work to a recent work by Thomas Hardy, a younger novelist who seemed more in the tradition of *Adam Bede* than Eliot herself now was:

> "George Eliot's" characters have not the flexibility and variety which, for example, the author of "Far from the Madding Crowd," whose first chapters were mistaken for her work, succeeds in imparting to his men and women. She always grasps and places clearly before the eye the individuality of her characters, but fails to invest them with those attributes of our common humanity which only the very highest art is able to make us feel running through the strongest of personalities. No amount of mere intellect, however great, can compass that highest achievement of art.[30]

The suggestion that Eliot had forsaken the true sources of her art for an artificial and intellectualized artifice was often made. A. V. Dicey, writing in *The Nation*, suggested that there was something disappointing about the way Eliot's genius had developed, and that the proportions of the qualities which made it up had altered so that reflection prevailed over description (*CH* 399). Dicey concludes the review with the lament that "admiration for the result of labor and meditation cannot banish regret for the abundant life of *Adam Bede* or the unbroken harmony of *Silas Marner*" (*CH* 404). Similarly, R. H. Hutton complained in the *Spectator* that, although *Daniel Deronda* contains more true grandeur than perhaps any other work of George Eliot, "there is much less equality of execution and richness of conception" (*CH* 367–68). In Sidney Colvin's review the sources of dissatisfaction are more plainly expressed. The novel "is not for those who set private happiness in the first place"; rather it is concerned with the way external, universal, and social forces determine human life.[31] Another very unsympathetic critic, writing in the *Saturday Review*, suggests that Eliot seems to be driving at something foreign to her habits of thought. The reviewer also suggests that Eliot is not gifted with "a fertile imagination" and that she has inevitably begun to exhaust the stores of her memory, so that her novels show "more and more effort" (*CH* 377–78).

In general, the reviewers are unhappy first because Eliot has not stayed within the rural and lower middle-class provincial scenes of her earlier work, and second because, having moved into the world of the fashionable drawing room, she does not treat that world with the same affectionate tolerance which she lavished on her less-fashionable characters. This is most clear in her refusal of the conventional happy ending of a wedding of Gwendolen and Deronda, which in the traditional plot of this kind would undoubtedly have been accompanied by the revelation that Deronda was after all the rightful heir of Sir Hugo's estate. In *Middlemarch* the marriage of Lydgate and Dorothea is a faintly adumbrated possibility which could have delivered both characters from the bondage of an unfulfilling life, but they rarely meet in the novel, and remain in different worlds within Middlemarch society. Deronda and Gwendolen, on the other hand, have in effect a Platonic love affair, which ends abruptly with Deronda's rejection of Gwendolen. Eliot's refusal of the conventional form of closure is thus much more striking in her last novel, and it infuriated readers like Sidney Colvin, who complained that there "is no triumphant or satisfying issue to a career which we have followed and realised as we have Gwendolen's. The whole book seems thrown out of balance and harmony when the plot which chiefly interests us ends thus, while happiness and fulfilment crown the other, in which we interest ourselves little by comparison."[32]

The reaction of the reviewers to Eliot's portrayal of English society is well illustrated by their comments on Grandcourt, whom most modern readers agree is the most unequivocally unredeemed and unredeemable character in Eliot's works. Grandcourt is presented in a way which connects his domestic tyranny (over Lydia, Gwendolen, Lush, and his dogs) to emergent British imperialism. In a discussion of the Governor Eyre affair Grandcourt takes Eyre's side, claiming that the Jamaican negro is "a beastly sort of baptist Caliban" (*DD* 29;303). Later in the novel the narrator comments that he would have made a good governor of a difficult colony, for he "would have understood that it was safer to exterminate than to cajole superseded proprietors, and would not have flinched from making things safe in that way" (*DD* 68;552). The ruling class is presented in the novel in Darwinian terms as a species whose fixed ideas and imperviousness to reason or culture have made it ill-equipped to survive in the future. As Gillian Beer notes, "The dwindling energy of England is directly related to the insistence on descent through the male line."[33] The estates of Mallinger and Grandcourt have been concentrated due to a paucity of male heirs, Lady Mallinger herself can only produce daughters, a fact which she regards as a judgment on herself, and Grandcourt leaves no legitimate male heir. Grandcourt is furthermore described in a series of scientific metaphors which suggest that he is a degenerate form of life, the product of an evolution which, instead of being governed by a teleological principle that can be described as an ascent, is a return to a previous, "lower" state of being. In the course of the novel Grandcourt is compared to or associated with a variety of "lower" forms of life: an alligator (*DD* 15;142), an insect (25;261), a fish (25;262), a sleepy-eyed animal on the watch for prey (35;384), a crab and a boa-constrictor (35;394), a lizard (48;546), and a serpent (64;626). Deronda regards him as a "remnant of a human being" (35;376), and in one striking image Grandcourt seems to be decomposing into the primal matter from which life began. He is described as lacking the regulated channels of habit "without which our nature easily turns to mere ooze and mud, and at any pressure yields nothing but a spurt or a puddle" (*DD* 15;141).

In spite of this depiction of Grandcourt several reviewers did not see him as a particularly wicked character. The reviewer for the *Athenaeum* noted in his review of book 4 that Grandcourt's character was worked out well, but that because he was a "gentleman" he would never have asked for the diamonds back.[34] George Saintsbury remarks disingenuously in the *Academy* that "the author would like us to detest Grandcourt," but suggests that Grandcourt is in no way, apart from his language, violent to Gwendolen, and that furthermore he is in the position of "being hated by his wife and having that hatred confided to a bewitching rival" (*CH* 372). Such reviewers make the mistake of Mr. Gascoigne in the novel itself; they assume that Grandcourt's behaviour in marrying Gwendolen in spite of her poverty is such a magnanimous gesture that he gains virtually absolute rights over her. In fact, many of Gwendolen's problems are due to Gascoigne's advice, which is characterized by an inadequate amount of the worldly wisdom which he imagines he possesses in a large degree. He encourages his niece to marry Grandcourt in spite of what he knows about Grandcourt's past, thinking with a pathetic lack of judgment that the marriage "might even strengthen the Establishment" (*DD* 13;124). Gascoigne also omits to insist on a settlement, which shows his lack of competence as Gwendolen's guardian by the very standards of the Victorian bourgeoisie which he espouses.

One reason why many reviewers did not grasp Eliot's satirical tone and purpose in *Daniel Deronda* is that they lacked a sufficiently sophisticated concept of the nature of the unity of a novel to appreciate Eliot's use of metaphor and allusion. As we saw in the discussion of *Adam Bede*, Victorian critics tended to concentrate on character to the exclusion of most other aspects of fiction, as is shown most obviously in their fascination with Mrs. Poyser. Furthermore, Eliot's frequent use of scientific metaphors, which were then not nearly so much a part of common discourse as they are now, annoyed readers who did not go on to try to understand the function of the scientific allusions in the novel. In addition, Eliot was often attacked for her authorial commentary, which was not a universally accepted technique even by Victorian readers.[35] The reviewers of *Daniel Deronda* often object to the quality of the thought and the style of the narrative commentary and the epigraphs, treating both as separable items which could be judged on their own merits, without reference to their function as parts of a larger whole. A typical example, one from among many, is R. H. Hutton's comment: "In the new story . . . there has seemed to us a vast deal more of effort and a vast deal less of fruitful wisdom in the incidental remarks, which have been at once less easy to apprehend, and when apprehended, less worth the labour of apprehending."[36] Both the *Athenaeum* and the *Spectator* use the word "pedantry" with reference to Eliot's use of scientific language in book 1, and both object to the word "dynamic" in the first sentence of the novel.[37] The prominence of this word meant that it was the target of every unfavourable reviewer. Blackwood confessed that the word gave him pause, but he added "I know no other word however that would so powerfully and strictly convey your meaning" (*Letters* 6:183). Eliot obviously had doubts herself about the word, for she changed it to "stinging" in the proofs, but in the first edition it reads "dynamic" once more. The *Examiner* complained that Eliot aims many of her illustrations "at a small cultured circle, a considerable portion of whose culture is scientific," while the *Edinburgh Review* complained of "the stony wilderness of big words, like the dried-up watercourses in which the harsh boulders have taken the place of living waters."[38]

The most intelligent response to such comments came from Edward Dowden, who argued that the true pedantry would be an insensibility to science, "for literature with its far-reaching sensibilities should be touched, thrilled, and quickened by every vital influence of the period" (*CH* 443). He compares science in the nineteenth century to the neoclassical mythology of the Renaissance, and says that "it is essential to the highest characteristics" of Eliot's art "that she should not isolate herself from the chief intellectual movement of her time" (*CH* 444). Science in *Daniel Deronda* functions like scriptural allusion in earlier literature; it provides an authoritative discourse on which an author can draw in order to place characters and events in a scale of moral value, as we have seen with the example of Grandcourt. Science also provides a model for the sort of rationality and the combination of imaginative inquiry and reason which Eliot suggests is needed in social thought. As the epigraph to the first chapter suggests, science, like poetry, is an attempt to make sense of a chaos of experiential data whose existence precedes any explanation which human beings can formulate. Science makes use of fictions and imagination in its attempt to provide explanations, and thus it is analogous to, rather than opposed to, the mythical and metaphorical grounds of culture expressed in religion and literature.

Reaction to *Daniel Deronda* varied widely; it was seen as both George Eliot's greatest and worst work. The primary focus of the controversy was the "Jewish part" or "Jewish subject matter." Reviewing the sixth book the *Athenaeum* commented that "The first third of the new part of 'Daniel Deronda' consists of Jewish scenes that will be even more completely wanting in interest to the general reader than were those which have gone before them," and in its final notice of *Daniel Deronda* the *Athenaeum* summed up the work as "both the least good and least interesting of George Eliot's works."[39] One of the most unsympathetic responses came from George Saintsbury, who described Daniel Deronda as "a person so intolerably dreadful that we not only dislike, but refuse to admit him as possible" (*CH* 373), and borrowed from *Alton Locke* the phrase "Samothracian mysteries of bottled moonshine" to describe the discourses of Mordecai to Deronda (*CH* 375). To many Christian readers the Jewish material was simply too foreign and remote, and they had no desire to attempt to understand it. No one minded the presence of romantic or villainous Jews in literature; Rebecca and Fagin provided recent precedents. However, the *Saturday Review* proclaimed, "When a young man of English training and Eton and University education, and, up to manhood, of assumed English birth, so obliging also as to entertain Christian sympathies, finishes off with his wedding in a Jewish synagogue, on the discovery that his father was a Jew, the most confiding reader leaves off with a sense of bewilderment and affront" (*CH* 377).

Eliot had expected that "the spirit of arrogance and contemptuous dictatorialness" which she had described in her letter to Harriet Beecher Stowe would inhibit the reception of *Daniel Deronda*, even though she also hoped to attack such prejudice by writing the novel. She noted in her journal on 12 April 1876 that the work had had good sales so far, but "the Jewish element seems to me likely to satisfy nobody" (*Letters* 6: 238). However, *Daniel Deronda* did satisfy its Jewish readers, whose reception of the work was conditioned not only by their experience of social disadvantages in English society, but also by literary history. The conventional depiction of Jews in English literature proceeds in an unbroken line from Chaucer and the romances through Marlowe and Shakespeare to Dickens and Thackeray. Thus Jewish readers evaluated Eliot's novel in relation to a tradition which saw Jews as either totally depraved or, less frequently, as noble sufferers like Scott's Rebecca or Dickens's Riah. (Shylock is not straightforwardly either of these extremes, but his character was conceived from within the same set of conventions Marlowe draws on in *The Jew of Malta*). A notice in the *Jewish Chronicle* describes Deronda as another in a series of noble Jewish characters, following Shylock, Rebecca, and Lessing's Nathan.[40] The same issue reports a lecture at the Jewish Working Men's Club which contrasted the anti-Semitism of Trollope and the unreal idealization of Riah with Eliot's depiction of Deronda.[41] Joseph Jacobs praised Eliot for avoiding the extremes that Dickens went to in Fagin and Riah,[42] and James Picciotto commented on Thackeray's anti-Semitism, and complained that the Jewish episodes were ignored by reviewers (*CH* 407–9). Eliot was praised by all her Jewish readers for her accurate and unprejudiced depiction of ordinary Jewish life, her remarkable knowledge of Judaism, its history, liturgy, and customs, and for her portrayal of the most noble and exalted aspects of Judaism in Mordecai. It is clear from these comments that Jewish readers were pleased by the same feature of the novel which so disturbed Christian readers, the fact that instead of portraying Jews through a series of conventions which made them— whether noble or evil—totally other, it depicted Jewish life in a sympathetic and unsensational manner, through the conventions of Victorian realism. Picciotto refers to the "photographic likeness" of Eliot's depiction of the Cohen family (*CH* 413).

Furthermore, *Daniel Deronda* implied that the Jewish religion was a living one, with at least as much power to excite human sympathies as Christianity. David Kaufmann praised Eliot's genius for seizing upon the historical moment when nationality had reasserted itself to write a poetic story which treated seriously the desire of the Jewish people for a homeland. He even claimed that the work was "pre-eminently fitted for being understood and appreciated by Jews; indeed, they only are qualified to embrace and enjoy its full significance."[43] But even as sympathetic a reader of *Daniel Deronda* as Kaufmann wrote that "at a first superficial glance it falls apart into two entirely unconnected narratives."[44] For many readers this perception lasted well beyond the first superficial glance, and the issue of the unity of *Daniel Deronda* has been debated since the first reviews. The novel did not lend itself to appreciation by the canons of formalist criticism, and it is only recently that it has received a great deal of favourable critical attention.[45] Eliot herself was quite unambiguous in her response to those critics who "cut the book into scraps and talk of nothing in it but Gwendolen," saying that "I meant everything in the book to be related to everything else there" (*Letters* 6:290). Once again, however, the majority of the first readers of the novel showed that they lacked the kind of understanding of fictional form which would at least have enabled them to comprehend what George Eliot was doing in *Daniel Deronda*, even if they did not value the achievement. This is not to say that Eliot's readers had no sense of how to read her work. The *Edinburgh Review* critic makes a revealing statement when he says that "George Eliot has taught us to look for a closeness of texture in her work, an unrelaxed tension of meaning, which we do not demand from other writers."[46] Thackeray and Dickens are cited as examples of the kind of writer from whom one does not expect unity. "But George Eliot is of a different habit; and as we have been trained to believe that she says nothing without solemn meaning and intention, our faculties are proportionably quickened, and our expectations raised."[47] Unfortunately, the *Edinburgh Review* critic did not find these expectations satisfied, for the work is described as "a disappointment, even a failure."[48] As Suzanne Graver comments, George Eliot's readers had in one sense "learned their lessons too well. Their response to her later work suggests that the expectations she had created in them caused them to resist new developments in her fiction."[49] Graver analyzes the divided response to what she calls "the poetry of community" in *Daniel Deronda*, by which she means the projection of an ideal myth of community, as opposed to the more analytical account of the failure of community which dominates *Middlemarch*. One group of readers, which would include critics like George Saintsbury, preferred works which attempted to nurture fellow-feeling through the portrayal of ordinary experience (precisely the project which George Eliot undertook in *Scenes of Clerical Life*). However, as Graver suggests, this view would exclude themes or characters—such as Jews—who were perceived by the majority of the reading public as out of the mainstream, or extra-ordinary.[50] A second group of readers, on the other hand, approached *Daniel Deronda* as a romance. For them "romance . . . becomes a way of fighting against the dead level of ordinary experience, affirming the idea of community in 'a life of mankind over, above, and around the life of the individual man or woman.'"[51]

The split which Graver identifies is clearly evident in many reviews. At least one reviewer seems to have recognized the direction that literature was taking, for *The Examiner* comments that "there is one thing, perhaps, which we shall not be considered irreverent if we take exception to, namely 'George Eliot's' increasing tendency to aim her illustrations and some of her humorous turns of phrase at a small cultured circle, a considerable portion of whose culture is scientific."[52] It is also significant that one of the few favourable non-Jewish reviewers was Edward Dowden, who became the first professor of English at Trinity College, Dublin. This split in reader responses is an early manifestation of the bifurcation of the English novel-reading public. Eliot had risen to popularity by writing a novel which, as I have argued in the preceding chapter, was read as an embodiment of the desires and values of the bourgeois reading public. In *Daniel Deronda* she tried to move away from a "realism" which fulfilled the expectations of this public, and through such things as her scientific imagery, the Jewish material, and the "open" form of the work, she challenged many of their assumptions. By doing so she risked alienating a majority of her readers, whose taste is reflected more in the reviews in weekly journals like the *Athenaeum* than in Dowden's more extensive review. Dowden's review is premonitory; it anticipates the criticism of early Modernism, which welcomed difficult or esoteric works and regarded popular success with suspicion.

In *Fiction and the Reading Public* Q. D. Leavis provides a highly influential account of the loss of homogeneity in the fiction-reading public. There are many inadequacies in this work, but it has not been replaced by a better study of the topic, although aspects of Leavis's subject have been more fully treated.[53] Leavis discusses the emergence of what the *Examiner* reviewer calls a "small cultured circle," and she seeks to provide an explanation for the breaking up of what was once a relatively homogeneous reading public. She points to "economic causes," but says that these were reinforced by the appearance of the "highbrow novelist,"

> who, unlike the serious novelists of the past, aiming like George Eliot, for instance, at moral ends easily comprehended by the half-educated, set out to develop the possibilities of his medium for ends outside the understanding of the ordinary reader, and which far from being "moral" only too often appeared to him the very opposite. Dickens and George Eliot were near neighbours, but there is an unbridged and impassable gulf between Marie Corelli and Henry James.[54]

There are several serious weaknesses in Leavis's analysis. She has a somewhat idealized view of literary history, and often writes as though there was no "trash literature" before the late nineteenth century. Thus, although Elizabeth Gaskell and Maria Edgeworth were inferior in many respects to lesser writers of a later period, in Leavis's mythological account "they had the inestimable benefits of a culture such as no modern writer is born to but must struggle for as best he can."[55] Her economic analysis is also faulty; she uses the very atypical example of George Eliot to suggest that before the emergence of "highbrow" culture one could make a living writing serious fiction,[56] when the evidence abundantly suggests that through the whole nineteenth century it was mainly the unremembered drudges who made a living from writing fiction.

One cannot argue with Leavis's basic point that the major novelists after 1880 never achieved the hegemony over the reading public that the major Victorians did. However, it is simplistic to suggest that a phenomenon called the "highbrow novelist" suddenly appeared on the scene, writing over the heads of readers who had cheerfully sat down with *Middlemarch*. Leavis's sociological methodology is imperfect and inconsistent; repeatedly assertions based on her own personal preferences take on the status of categories in her argument.[57]

She is unwilling to consider the fact that English culture has gone through repeated structural transformations in its history, because she prefers the apocalyptic fiction of a sudden "disintegration" of a hitherto unified reading public, akin to T. S. Eliot's "dissociation of sensibility." During the latter part of the nineteenth century those writers and readers who opposed the values of the Victorian bourgeoisie in its imperialistic phase used a notion of "culture" to separate themselves from the rest of society. This politics of culture developed into Modernism, and could manifest itself in a leftist manner in the political sphere, although more often it expressed itself in the form of a radical conservatism. George Eliot certainly, as Leavis asserts, captured the general reading public as well as being a "highbrow" writer, but a study of the reception of her fiction shows that this duality was obvious to many of her contemporaries, and that they tended to cope with it by responding to particular parts of her novels, depending on their own predilections. Furthermore, an analysis of the increase in popular education during the latter part of the nineteenth century suggests another reason for the rise of the "highbrow" novelist. More people read novels in the period after Eliot's death because more people were able to read, and also because disposable income increased significantly among the working and lower-middle classes so that leisure spending was more common.[58] These developments created a less unified literary sphere than had been the case when reading was less common and literary culture was a more exclusively aristocratic and middle-class phenomenon. The myth of a "fall from grace" which Leavis's work employs gives it something of the character of a belated polemic against democracy, a form of cultural criticism that comes with a long pedigree of Victorian practitioners, and which—as the prominence given recently to Allan Bloom's *The Closing of the American Mind* suggests—was not extinct by the 1980s.[59]

Two particularly perceptive reviewers who saw *Daniel Deronda* as a romance, expressive of the "poetry of community," were Dowden in the *Contemporary Review* and R. E. Francillon in *Gentleman's Magazine*, who thereby establish themselves according to my analysis as precursors of literary Modernism, and according to Leavis's as encouragers of the emergence of the "highbrow" novelist. Dowden begins his review by suggesting that *Middlemarch* has affinities with satire, whereas *Daniel Deronda* is dominated by a "poetical or ideal element" (*CH* 439–40). Dowden defends the Jewish subject matter by placing it in the context of contemporary European nationalist movements (*CH* 446). He also defends the portrayal of Deronda and argues that those who say that it is improbable are bound by their own narrow horizons:

> That some should find him incredible proves no more than that clever critics in walking from their lodgings to their club, and from their club to their lodgings, have not exhausted the geography of the habitable globe. If "knowledge of the world" consist chiefly in a power of

estimating the average force of men's vulgar or selfish appetites, instincts, and interests, it must be admitted that in such knowledge the author of *Middlemarch* and of *Felix Holt* is not deficient; but there is another knowledge of the world which she also possesses, a knowledge which does not exclude from recognition the martyr, the hero, and the saint. (*CH 441*)

Dowden's reaction against the realism expected by Eliot's readers and practiced by a writer like Trollope is clear in this passage. Eliot especially appreciated Dowden's review, and Lewes wrote to him to express their gratitude for it (*Letters* 6:336–37).

R. E. Francillon deals explicitly with George Eliot's confounding of her reader's expectations. He says that she has exchanged the role of "a natural historian of real life" for "the larger and fuller truth of romance" (*CH 382–83*). Francillon praises her for daring to break with her previous work:

> The author herself can have looked for no immediate fortune but that of battle. The very merits of the book are precisely the reverse of those to which the wide part of her fame is due. Not a few critics have already said that *Daniel Deronda* is not likely to extend George Eliot's reputation. That is unquestionably true—the sympathies to which it appeals are not, as in the case of *Adam Bede*, the common sympathies of all the world. But whether *Daniel Deronda* is not likely to *heighten* her reputation is an entirely different question. (*CH 382*)

For Francillon the Jewish subject matter does not need to be of interest to the reader in the literal sense for the novel to have an effect. Mordecai functions for readers, he says, "by keeping well before our eyes the existence of an ideal world, where all things, though but in dreams and visions, may seem possible" (*CH 393*).

Richard Holt Hutton praised *Daniel Deronda* in a number of reviews in the *Spectator*, although he had more reservations than either Dowden or Francillon. Hutton was a Unitarian turned Anglican, and he was an apologist for Anglican orthodoxy who had serious objections to Eliot for what he considered an overly intellectual and abstract view of literature's task.[60] He was therefore pleased by what he perceived as a new tone in *Daniel Deronda*, which suggested to him that Eliot had real faith in a power which acts purposefully in human life:

> What has been mostly wanting in George Eliot's books is this faith in the larger purpose which moulds men into something higher than anything into which they could mould themselves. And now that it is powerfully presented in one of her stories, though a story in which some of the elements of her genius are less visible than before, it certainly lends to her writing a force and a unity and a grandeur of effect which make up for many faults of execution.[61]

In the last of his reviews of *Daniel Deronda* Hutton confesses that he cannot make up his mind about Mordecai, and he concludes, "We cannot dismiss Deronda on his journey to the East without feeling uncomfortably that he is gone on a wild-goose chase,—to preach ideas which have only been hinted, and which rest on a creed that has hardly been hinted at all" (*CH* 370). This raises the important question of the relevance of Deronda's mission to the analysis of English society which dominates the novel. There is certainly some truth to Hutton's feeling that the novel's resolution depends upon an ill-defined creed. I shall conclude by looking at the question Hutton raises, and by considering the critical worth of the novel from the horizon of the present day, since it seems to me that in some ways it speaks to more questions of the present than any of Eliot's other works. It has certainly received a great deal of critical attention in the last decade, as I noted earlier.

George Eliot was well aware of the problems involved in writing a novel in which a young gentleman who has been to Eton and Cambridge is presented as the Jewish Messiah. Such a plot is worthy of the pretentious romances which she had ridiculed in "Silly Novels by Lady Novelists." One of the ways she deals with this difficulty is to adopt an ironic tone, so that the satire on English society is extended to an ironic treatment of Deronda's earnestness. This is the technique of Goethe in *Wilhelm Meisters Lehrjahre*, and the irony is of several different kinds. There is considerable irony at the simple verbal level. For example, while on one hand Deronda is compared with Titian's Christ in *The Tribute Money*,[62] the narrator also prevents the reader from seeing his crucial meeting with Mordecai in the terms of a Romantic historical painting: "It has to be admitted that in this classical, romantic, world-historic position of his, bringing as it were from its hiding-place his hereditary armour, he wore—but so, one must suppose, did the most ancient heroes whether Semitic or Japhetic— the summer costume of his contemporaries" (*DD* 63;694). Both the reference to ancient heroes and the Hegelian term "world-historic" function ironically, as the oxymoronic adjectives "classical" and "romantic" indicate, but viewed as a whole the novel suggests that Deronda is, or at least has the potential to be, a world-historic individual. The passage therefore both means what it asserts and yet casts a protective veil of irony over Deronda.

Deronda is also ironized through his relationship with the Meyrick family. He clearly enjoys being admired by the sisters, and his appreciation of this rather naive admiration makes him seem somewhat ridiculous. Hans Meyrick serves to undermine Deronda's seriousness by playing the role of the fool. Meyrick also accuses Deronda, not without justice, of wanting Gwendolen to "burn herself in perpetual suttee while you are alive and merry" (*DD* 69;744). Sir Hugo tells Deronda that he is "Jesuitical" (*DD* 32;332), and he is described as receiving Gwendolen as though he is a priest, in a library which is "as warmly odorous as a private chapel in which the censers have been swinging" (*DD* 36;419). Once again, the imagery has a dual function: it is indicative of the religious nature of Deronda's influence on Gwendolen, yet it is also ironic, given the sexual ambiguities involved in this meeting and in their whole relationship.

Another source of irony is the series of parallels between Deronda and Grandcourt. The two treat each other with an awkwardness which just falls short of hostility. It is interesting that Grandcourt, who says so little in the book, seems to have insights into Deronda's character which Deronda does not have into his: Deronda's "imagination was as much astray about Grandcourt as it would have been about an unexplored continent where all the species were peculiar" (*DD* 35;384). While Grandcourt does not see all of Deronda, he certainly perceives the weaknesses in the latter's self-regarding earnestness. When he first speaks of Deronda to his wife, Grandcourt comments that "he thinks a little too much of himself" (*DD* 29;302). Even Grandcourt's cruellest hit is not without truth. He tells Gwendolen that Deronda should not publicly praise Mirah, because "men can see what is his relation to her" (*DD* 68;547). Deronda at first will not admit his feeling for Mirah, and later he does in fact conceal his relation to her—that of betrothed lover—from Gwendolen. Furthermore, Grandcourt functions as a kind of diabolical parody of Deronda in relation to Gwendolen. Deronda is the messianic figure in the novel, but it is Grandcourt who is introduced by the epithet "prefigured stranger" (*DD* 11;97). Just as Grandcourt is already morally committed to Lydia when he marries Gwendolen, so Deronda involves himself in Gwendolen's life only after he has already made a kind of moral commitment to Mirah by rescuing her.

In his relations with both Gwendolen and Mirah, Deronda shows a combination of tenderness, disingenuousness, and naivety. He is in love with two women without even admitting to himself that he loves one. This ironical comedy, however, functions to bring in the mythological level of the novel, for as Elinor Shaffer persuasively argues, it is Deronda's sexual response to Gwendolen, and vice versa, which gives him the influence necessary to awaken her conscience.[63] Shaffer analyzes parallels between Eliot's portrayal of Deronda and Renan's *Life of Jesus*, suggesting that Eliot "recapitulates and refines" Renan's enterprise of "the minute scrutiny of the 'psychological miracle' left unsolved by Strauss, the process whereby traditional messianic expectations came to be applied to a specific living man."[64] Her argument is too intricate to be summarized here, but in essence she shows how Renan, like Feuerbach, located the sources of religious feeling and action in sexuality.[65] Shaffer gives a brilliant interpretation of the character of Deronda, which makes Eliot's portrayal of him seem much more explicable than many readers have suggested that it is. However, she ignores the relationship of the mythic aspect of the novel to the historicity of its "realistic" element, which makes her task of interpretation much easier. I think that by doing this she misses both some of the novel's most interesting unresolved tensions and some of the causes of its ambiguous reception. Eliot did not resolve the problems of renewing a religious mythology in the setting of nineteenth-century England in quite the triumphant way that Shaffer suggests.

If Christianity is made to live—albeit in a secular form—for Gwendolen, that animation is the result of a Jewish messianic figure. Although he is raised in the conventional manner of an English gentleman "of Eton and University education," Deronda is an "accomplished Egyptian" (*DD* 53;612) with a mysterious past and an indefinite future in the East. In telling his story Eliot skilfully mingles the mysterious birth and the accomplishments appropriate to a messianic hero with the conventions of the romantic novel, particularly as they were authoritatively determined for the English novel by Fielding. I have already discussed the way in which Eliot uses the sexual attraction between Deronda and Gwendolen to portray his spiritual authority. This, however, takes place in the private sphere, and is a matter of one man's spiritual influence over one woman of his own class and social circle. The novel also suggests that Deronda is to have a much wider spiritual destiny, as a potential leader of his people. We have seen how different readers emphasized one or the other of these aspects of Deronda's function, if they valued the "Jewish matter" at all. For Jewish readers the public aspect of Deronda's character was at least as important as the private. For such readers it was not incredible that the Jewish people should have a leader who would restore their scattered nation. As David Kaufmann wrote, "This ardent desire for a national future on the part of the Israelites forms the intellectual centre and heart of her book."[66] On the other hand, R. E. Francillon and other Gentile readers saw the Jewish material as another "husk" containing the kernel of the religion of humanity, rather like the Methodism of *Adam Bede*. However, the use of Judaism creates even more questions than the use of Methodism. Methodists were, after all, a part of English society, even if a somewhat marginal one. Deronda's new-found faith, on the other hand, requires him to give up all his past associations and friends, and to leave his country. Furthermore, it is dependent on an accident of birth. Thus it cannot easily function for most of Eliot's readers as an example of how to deal with the questions of what to believe and how to live a good life. Graham Martin notes that there is no sign in the novel that Judaism is of cultural or historical relevance to Christian England, or that Deronda's political cause has any bearing on English life.[67] This is true in a narrow sense. Eliot certainly has no faith in the possibility of a revolutionary change in English society. Deronda disappears at the end of the novel, "drifting off into legend" as higher criticism held that the life of Jesus merged with Jewish legend at the beginning and the end.[68]

In a more general sense, however, the novel does show that Judaism is of relevance to Victorian England, and I think that to suggest otherwise is to fall into the same trap as the Victorian reviewers who claimed that the subject matter was too remote. Eliot's point is that it is not at all remote if one considers the true sources of English culture. None of the Christian characters in the novel initially is willing to trust Judaism very far: the Meyricks' reception of Mirah is not without suspicion, and Deronda has many prejudices to deal with, too.

But through the notions of "pathways" and "separateness with communion" Eliot suggests that the Judaic tradition is bound up with and might have a vivifying effect upon the Christian tradition. Like Spinoza, Mordecai has rationalistically modified and kept alive the faith of his ancestors. Unlike Mordecai, Gascoigne and Sir Hugo (who are kind and well-intentioned men when compared with Grandcourt and the Arrowpoints) have reduced their faith to a corpse by refusing to take it seriously. The fact that Deronda, who is a messianic Jewish figure, can be for Gwendolen—even if at times against his own will and better judgment—a priest suggests that communication between faiths is possible. If Gwendolen is a better person as a result of knowing Deronda, then Judaism is in some way relevant to Victorian England.

This reading still limits the relevance of Deronda's mission to the private sphere. There is no attempt to deal with the political question of imperialism which is adumbrated throughout the text: as the source of Mrs. Davilow's income, as the concern of the politician Mr. Bult, and as the public manifestation of Grandcourt's private behaviour. Having raised these issues, Eliot leaves them entirely unresolved. There is a slight hint in one of Mordecai's speeches that a restored Jewish nation might be a "covenant of reconciliation" (*DD* 42;499), but it remains unexplored. Like most Victorian novelists, Eliot remains committed to personalized solutions to public issues. This is illustrated in a more complex and interesting way in her treatment of the issue of sexual politics in the novel, and it is here, I think, that one can most seriously question the relevance of Deronda's vocation to English life. The novel considers the topical question of the role of woman in society, and through the portrayal of Gwendolen shows the disastrous effects of the combination of great potential, limited scope for ambition, and a trivial and worthless education. Also, *Daniel Deronda* may be specifically related to a series of articles about "The Girl of the Period," published in 1868 by the novelist Eliza Lynn Linton. These articles decried the loss of the feminine English woman, who, Linton said, had been replaced by "the girl of the period." The "girl of the period" was dissatisfied with her lot, selfish, worldly, and assertive. Bonnie Zimmerman has persuasively argued that Eliot's portrayal of Gwendolen draws on this stereotype.[69]

In attempting to show the redemption of Gwendolen, Eliot also attempts to suggest a resolution to the crisis caused by the growing self-consciousness of women. In doing so she reveals her own uncertainty about and ambiguity of response to the question of the role of women. Unlike some of her feminist friends she had doubts about the value of education and the vote for women, fearing that these feminist innovations might diminish women's contribution to the domestic sphere. She told her friend Emily Davies to consider

the spiritual wealth acquired for mankind by the difference of function founded on the other, primary difference; and the preparation that lies in woman's peculiar constitution for a special

moral influence. In the face of all wrongs, mistakes, and failures, history has demonstrated
that gain. And there lies just that kernel of truth in the vulgar alarm of men lest women should
be "unsexed." (*Letters* 4:468)

Eliot's fear of politicized feminism is reflected in the way that Gwendolen
is described by the narrator and also in Deronda's advice to her. Gwendolen has
a restlessness and assertiveness, combined with an awareness of the power
relations involved in sexual interaction, which could easily have developed into
feminism, given the right circumstances. She tells Rex that she would like to
go to the North Pole, or ride steeplechase, or be a queen in the Middle East (*DD*
7;62); she tells Grandcourt that women are restricted because they cannot find
the Northwest Passage, or the source of the Nile (*DD* 13;119). Although she is
being frivolous, these examples all suggest the limitations under which she
lives. Men could, and in the nineteenth century did, go from England to Africa
and to the Northwest Passage. But women, for the narrator, are "the Yea or Nay
of that good for which men are enduring and fighting. In these delicate vessels
is borne onward though the ages the treasure of human affections" (11;109).
Deronda, when he advises Gwendolen about her future, is extremely vague
about the context of the "religious life" she should lead. He tells her "You are
conscious of more beyond the round of your own inclinations . . . " (*DD*
36;422), but it is not clear exactly what that "more" is. This is an issue which
Elinor Shaffer does not face in her otherwise exemplary treatment of *Daniel
Deronda*. Shaffer suggests that Gwendolen's nervous "Gothic" sensibility develops into "the religious awe that for Kant is hebraic and sublime and underlies
the assumption of moral responsibility that is the essence of the categorical
imperative, and then, through the complex transaction in the climactic scene
between Gwendolen and Deronda, into the assumption of moral responsibility
understood in Christian terms as imaginative crucifixion."[70] However, a moral
responsibility that is understood as an "imaginative crucifixion" is not a very
positive solution to Gwendolen's problems. Deronda's own language is equally
cheerless. He tells her that she must look at her life as a debt, as a duty from
which other duties will spring (*DD* 65;715). The secular Christianity to which
Gwendolen is converted lacks any ground beyond the conventions of the patriarchal society against which she rebelled in book 1. Her rebellion may have been
that of a "spoiled child," but Deronda's solution is that she should learn to
accept and love the limitations that are placed on her. If he had been free, the
narrator informs us, he would have sheltered her, loved her, and completed the
rescue he had begun in Leubronn (*DD* 65;712); instead, however, he abandons
her. Eliot does not "console" the reader by describing the marriage of Gwendolen and Rex, although she hints vaguely at it as a possibility. She was unable
to envision a more hopeful conclusion to Gwendolen's career than that of being

an angel in her family's house, but this conservative solution is rendered ambiguous by Gwendolen's rather bleak state when we last see her.

The resolution of the novel is further qualified by the depiction of two very different women: Mirah and Deronda's mother. Mirah's submissiveness and almost allegorical purity in adverse surroundings make her an obvious reworking of the "angel in the house" figure. The fact that Deronda marries her rather than Gwendolen, the woman whose energy and suffering provide much of the drama in the novel, is probably the most important reason for the dissatisfaction with the Jewish part of *Daniel Deronda* that many readers expressed. Mirah is obviously to be contrasted with Gwendolen, but unfortunately the contrast does not work in Mirah's favour. The situation is not helped by Ezra Cohen's description of the position of women in Jewish life: "A man is bound to thank God, as we do every Sabbath, that he was not made a woman; but a woman has to thank God that He has made her according to His will. And we all know what He has made her—a child-bearing, tender-hearted thing is the woman of our people" (*DD* 46;535). A "child-bearing, tender-hearted thing" is very similar to a "delicate vessel" bearing "the treasure of human affections," which suggests that the narrator endorses Cohen's views as to the appropriate destiny of woman, and also suggests what the "other duties" are which Gwendolen will learn to accept (*DD* 65;715). However, this message is seriously questioned by Eliot's portrayal of the Princess Halm-Eberstein, who shares Klesmer's devotion to art. For her, Judaism is a "bondage" (*DD* 51;584), a patriarchal and conservative religion which attempted to hinder her in her desire to be an artist. She tells Deronda:

> "You are not a woman. You may try—but you can never imagine what it is to have a man's force of genius in you, and yet to suffer the slavery of being a girl. To have a pattern cut out—'this is the Jewish woman; this is what you must be; this is what you are wanted for; a woman's heart must be of such a size and no larger, else it must be pressed small, like Chinese feet; her happiness is to be made as cakes are, by a fixed receipt.'" (*DD* 51;588)

This passage casts an unfortunate shadow over the diminutive Mirah, whose tiny feet are the object of the Meyrick girls' admiration (*DD* 20;193). Mirah's role as Deronda's wife highlights the arbitrariness and the problematic nature of the means Eliot employs to create a secular religion with some basis in the "laws of nature." Mirah is chosen by destiny in the form of heredity, by the fact that she was born a Jew and Gwendolen was not.

The Princess Halm-Eberstein reveals another important tension in the novel's moral argument. In the overall design of the work she must be seen as a tragic figure, whereas Deronda's grandfather is to be seen as the transmitter of a vital spiritual message. This means that the Princess's life as the Alcharisi must be regarded as an inadequate reward for the sacrifice of her capacity to love. The artistic life is one of worldliness, as is also suggested by Mirah's story of her life with her father, and it is to be contrasted with the religious life. However, in the Princess's story the grandfather appears as a repressive tyrant who refuses his daughter the right to self-expression in a far more vehement manner than the domestic tyranny of the Arrowpoints. One is moved to take the Princess's side as she tells the story of her life. Furthermore, art appears elsewhere in the novel both as an image of the religious life and as a secular substitute for religion. For the Meyricks and for Klesmer and Catherine, art is the key to an authentic life; for the Jewish characters it is a dangerous temptation whose danger is illustrated by the unloving parents of Mirah and Deronda. This attempt to use art in radically different ways in the same novel illustrates the complications which result from Eliot's attempt to revitalize religion while remaining a Victorian rationalist. It is probably no accident that the faith she chose as a vehicle of her religious theme was one which allowed her to valorize a conservative solution to the "woman question." However, although this makes the novel's ending in some ways unconvincing and unsatisfactory, the openness of that ending (if compared, for example with *Adam Bede*), and also the presence of Deronda's mother in the novel, show that Eliot did not attempt an easy escape from the contradictions of being a woman in the late nineteenth century. If she proposed a conservative solution to the difficulties, she nevertheless did not ignore any of the problems women faced.

4

From James to Woolf

Henry James wrote ten pieces of criticism on George Eliot, ranging from brief notices to full-length essays. In the collected edition of James's criticism these pieces amount to more than one hundred pages, which is twice as much as James wrote on Trollope, the nearest English rival to Eliot for his critical attention.[1] It is therefore not surprising that George Eliot was an important influence on James's fiction, especially on *The Portrait of a Lady*.[2] However, the following discussion will confine itself to the criticism alone: the influence of Eliot on later novelists such as Hardy and James is certainly an important topic, and one which could be helpfully approached through the use of *Rezeptionsästhetik*,[3] but this would require a separate study of considerable scope. Here I am concerned to develop an account of James's critical canons and his theory of fiction, with particular reference to George Eliot, since Jamesian aesthetics dominated criticism of fiction in the early twentieth century, and became a useful weapon in a systematic campaign against the influence of George Eliot.

James's criticism resembles his fiction in its multiple ironies and ambiguities, and in its detached descriptions of the way that an author's consciousness shapes his or her work. James wrote in "The Art of Fiction" that "the deepest quality of a work of art will always be the quality of the mind of the producer" (*EL* 64), and in a number of essays he follows the practice of Sainte-Beuve, whom he describes as "in purpose the least doctrinal of critics," and whose method he describes as "fairly to dissolve his attention in the sea of circumstance surrounding the object of his study" (*FW* 844). This style of criticism has close links with the phenomenological criticism practised by the Geneva school,[4] but, especially in his early essays, James is also concerned to make moral and aesthetic judgments. Like his fiction, his critical studies at first seem to hold back from commitment to a particular view, but they nevertheless imply a judgment which the reader must concretize for himself or herself. One can detect in his earliest critical pieces a struggle between moral and aesthetic criteria of judgment, which in James's criticism are not always as happily fused as in his major novels. His criticism is further complicated by the fact that he saw moral norms, and indeed all concepts of truth, as increasingly problematic as he evolved during his literary career into a stricter phenomenologist, concerned with "how we make reality by interpreting it."[5]

George Eliot is an interesting case study in James's criticism, for he clearly admired her greatly, and yet found her works seriously flawed in a number of ways according to the canons of criticism he formulated to define his own practice of fiction. The split between James the Victorian novelist and man of letters and James the philosophical modernist provides a great deal of insight into the horizonal change which produced the sharp decline in Eliot's reputation from 1880, when she was the leading figure in contemporary literature, to the early decades of the twentieth century, when—as we shall see in more detail later in this chapter—she was regarded as a tiresomely didactic and inartistic moralist. James himself was too intelligent and too sympathetic a critic to allow his own practice and concerns to obscure the significance of Eliot's achievement, but the altered social climate of the Edwardian period and the resulting change in aesthetic outlook which we know as the Modernist movement erected James's views of fiction—especially as expressed in the prefaces to the New York edition—into a dogma which was fatal to the reputation of all the Victorian novelists, and especially that of George Eliot.

Apart from one essay on Eliot's novels published in 1866, and a review of Cross's *Life* published in 1885, James's criticism of Eliot consists entirely of reviews of individual works. They belong to the earlier part of James's career, when he was more concerned with moral questions in the general idealist manner of a Victorian reviewer. Nevertheless, we shall see that a number of his later concerns are already evident in these pieces. One would expect that the later James would have had less patience with Eliot's fiction than the young Victorian reviewer did, for the famous prefaces (written 1906–8) advance a theory of fiction radically at odds with her practice. In the preface to *The Tragic Muse* James makes his celebrated statement of the importance of composition and artistic form, and asks of novels like *The Newcomes* and *War and Peace*, "what do such large loose baggy monsters, with their queer elements of the accidental and the arbitrary, artistically *mean*?" (*FW* 1107). In the preface to *The Princess Casamassima* James suggests that characters in fiction "are interesting only in proportion as they feel their respective situations; since the consciousness, on their part, of the complication exhibited forms for us their link of connexion with it" (*FW* 1088). He adds that "We care, our curiosity and our sympathy care, comparatively little for what happens to the stupid, the coarse and the blind; care for it, and for the effects of it, at the most as helping to precipitate what happens to the more deeply wondering, to the really sentient" (*FW* 1088-89). Neither of these passages would suggest that James would continue to value Eliot highly. Her sense of aesthetic form is quite different from the one James implies, and by his standards her novels, too, are baggy monsters. Furthermore, the emphasis on the need for characters with highly reflective consciousnesses is at odds with the realistic aesthetic of Eliot's early days. Throughout her fiction she insists on the importance of sympathy with the "coarse" and the "stupid."

In spite of his own theory of fiction, however, James appreciated Eliot's work throughout his career with a warmth which belies his analytical comments on it. He was impressed with Eliot as a person, too; in 1869 he described to his father his impression of a visit to her, the "one marvel" of his stay in London: "in this vast ugliness resides a most powerful beauty which, in a very few minutes steals forth and charms the mind, so that you end as I ended, in falling in love with her. Yes behold me literally in love with this great horse-faced blue-stocking. I don't know in what the charm lies, but it is a thoroughly potent, an admirable physiognomy."[6] There are several references to Eliot in the prefaces to the New York edition, and all are sympathetic, even affectionate. In the preface to *The Portrait of a Lady* he quotes a passage from *Daniel Deronda* in the context of a discussion of the problem of portraying heroines (*FW* 1077). In the preface to *The Princess Casamassima* he lists Eliot along with Shakespeare, Cervantes, Balzac, and a number of others as among "the fine painters of life" (*FW* 1092) and confesses to "a weakness of sympathy" with Eliot's determination to show the adventures and history of her characters "as determined by their feelings and the nature of their minds" (*FW* 1095).

The first piece that James wrote on Eliot was a review of *Felix Holt* in the *Nation* (16 August 1866). He begins by sounding what would be the dominant theme of everything that he would write about her, by saying that *Felix Holt* exhibits George Eliot's "closely wedded talent and foibles" (*EL* 907). The review follows the usual practice of Victorian reviewers. James comments in general on Eliot's strengths and weaknesses, then considers the plot and characters of *Felix Holt*, and concludes with some general comments on Eliot's place in English literature. Her weaknesses are in her construction of plot and conduct of story, and in the diffuseness of her style; her strengths include her delineation of individual character, her humour, and her morality (*EL* 907–8). It is interesting to see James discussing these various aspects of the novel as though they were separable parts of a machine. This is an almost universal practice of Victorian reviewers, and one which James himself decried in "The Art of Fiction" (1884), where he wrote that "a novel is a living thing, all one and continuous, like any other organism, and in proportion as it lives will it be found, I think, that in each of the parts there is something of each of the other parts" (*EL* 54). James concludes by warning that there is a danger that George Eliot will receive "excessive homage." It is so rare for a writer to combine powers of intellect with powers of imagination that one who does so may be overvalued. George Eliot has the powers of observation and expression characteristic of the female mind, but lacks the power of "those great synthetic guesses with which a real master attacks the truth." None of her novels to date can be described as a "master-piece" (*EL* 911).

This assessment of Eliot is more or less repeated, at greater length and with more detailed analysis, in the article "The Novels of George Eliot" (*Atlantic Monthly*, 1866). This is a general essay on Eliot's fiction up to *Felix Holt*, written in the manner of a critical article by Sainte-Beuve or Arnold. Arnold's influence is evident in the stress on intellectual culture and in the moral tone of James's early reviews (he wrote an appreciative review of *Essays in Criticism* in 1865).[7] In "The Novels of George Eliot" James appears as a disinterested seeker after truth in literature. He evaluates Eliot's novels as though there were an objective norm of "reality" against which her representations could be measured. He also praises her for her possession of Arnoldian virtues: "She is a thinker,—not, perhaps, a passionate thinker, but at least a serious one; and the term can be applied with either adjective neither to Dickens nor Thackeray. The constant play of lively and vigorous thought about the concerns furnished by her observation animates these latter with a surprising richness of color and a truly human interest" (*EL* 926). Eliot, James implies, writes fiction that is a criticism of life because of its fusion of disinterested observation of humanity with free and reflective thought. However, she falls short of the Arnoldian ideal because she does not render a sufficiently broad range of experience. In the review of *Felix Holt* James had suggested that there is "little genuine *passion* in George Eliot's men and women" (*EL* 909), and complained that her characters are all essentially decent and good-humoured: "The word which sums up the common traits of our author's various groups is the word *respectable*" (*EL* 915). After making a number of perceptive observations on each of the novels, James concludes "The Novels of George Eliot" with the general comment that George Eliot is a conservative in matters both of morals and of aesthetics. In respect to the latter, James accuses her of an "inclination to compromise with the old tradition—and here I use the word 'old' *without* respect—which exacts that a serious story of manners shall close with the factitious happiness of a fairy-tale." There are, he adds, "few things more irritating in a literary way than each of her final chapters" (*EL* 933).

Although James's point in this attack on Eliot's conservative optimism (or "meliorism," as she might have described it herself: see *Letters* 6:333) is essentially a moral one, it is the product of a specifically literary experience, namely James's detailed knowledge of the French literary scene and his consequent impatience with the relative prudishness and narrow moralism of the English publishers, critics, and reading public. Although, as I have suggested in my studies of *Adam Bede* and *Daniel Deronda*, Eliot deviated significantly from existing literary norms, by the standards of contemporary French literature her deviations are slight.[8] This is apparent in the accusation that she was inclined to "compromise" with the old tradition. In commenting on the relationship between morality and fiction in English criticism of this period Kenneth Graham notes that

> The moral ideal, or a specifically Christian ideal, or, most frequently, a belief in the absolute nature of the social code, continues to dominate the relationship of fiction to values right to the end of the century. The national sense of outrage at French naturalism came from this belief in the novel's attachment to certain indisputable ethical truths. The new fiction was honestly feared as the harbinger of a chaos that was more than literary.[9]

James, on the other hand, was widely read in the works of Balzac, Gautier, Flaubert, George Sand, and many lesser French writers. It was probably this reading, as much as any other factor, which caused him to react against the sunny respectability of Eliot's fiction—although he does find the Dodson family, in *The Mill on the Floss*, "in their way not unworthy of Balzac" (*EL* 930). James's comments are part of his general "dismissive" reaction to the English literary and intellectual scene.[10] Since a prescriptive moralism based on a timid conformity to perceived reader expectations dominated this scene, questions of artistic form, which involved more fundamental moral and philosophical questions, were not often raised. As an American and as a student of French literature James was well placed to challenge this English conformism, and this explains his reactions to George Eliot's willingness to compromise.

James gradually abandoned his own Arnoldian tendencies after he settled in Paris (1875) and then London (1876). In "The Art of Fiction" (1884) he formulated his own phenomenological view of the novel, in which the earlier view of an objectively ascertainable realm of experience is replaced by an emphasis on "impressions" and "aspects."[11] Even as early as his review of *Middlemarch* (1873), James judges Eliot by more purely aesthetic criteria. It is interesting to note that—in contrast to his first review—he now thinks that *Romola* "is especially a rare masterpiece, but the least *entraînant* of masterpieces" (*EL* 958). Although he has many generous things to say about *Middlemarch*, James finds it a flawed work from the point of view of composition. It "is a treasure-house of details, but it is an indifferent whole" (*EL* 958). While he hoped for "an organized, moulded, balanced composition, gratifying the reader with a sense of design and construction" he regretfully concludes that, as was to be expected, *Middlemarch* is "a mere chain of episodes, broken into accidental lengths and unconscious of the influence of a plan" (*EL* 958). The prelude raises the promise of "a definite subject," but the novel which follows is a "panorama" (*EL* 959). This complaint reminds one of James's explanation of the way his imagination produced novels from "germs." In the preface to *The Spoils of Poynton* he explains that the "germ" is "the stray suggestion, the wandering word, the vague echo" which gives rise to a novel. He says that "one's subject is in the merest grain, the speck of truth, of beauty, of reality, scarce visible to the common eye" (*FW* 1138). James was, therefore, not inclined to appreciate the formal qualities of *Middlemarch*, which Eliot originally conceived as two different works, and which strives for an epic inclusiveness. James comments in his review that *Middlemarch* gives a sense of the vastness and of the variety of human life "which it belongs only to the greatest novels to produce" (*EL* 963), and yet he found the same novel lacking in any form of artistic plan. This suggests the gap between his instinctive reaction to Eliot's work and his formal analysis of its structure and artistry.

This gap is even more evident in James's reaction to *Daniel Deronda*. The novel provided James with the basis for his first truly significant work of fiction, *The Portrait of a Lady*, but at the same time he obviously found the Jewish part of the novel unbearable. He dealt with his divided response by writing his review in the form of a conversation between three characters. The review was made famous (and infamous) by F. R. Leavis, who reprinted it as an appendix to *The Great Tradition* and also made it the basis of his own interpretation of the novel. It is obvious that the judicious views of Constantius are meant to carry the most weight, but the criticisms of Pulcheria are expressed with a lively wit and energy which draws attention to them, while Theodora's praise of the novel seems forced and unconvincing. For example, it is hard not to detect James's impatience in Pulcheria's question, "What can be drearier than a novel in which the function of the hero—young, handsome and brilliant—is to give didactic advice, in a proverbial form, to the young, beautiful and brilliant heroine?" (*EL* 984). In Pulcheria's reference to "a horrid big Jewish nose" (*EL* 974) there is an overt example of anti-Semitism, which no doubt underlies some of James's "aesthetic" strictures against the Jewish part of the novel.

James's most severe discussion of Eliot is found in his review of Cross's *Life*. In this piece the appreciative comments are still present, but they are more muted, and are overwhelmed by a mixture of criticism and an inadequate understanding of Eliot's character. Throughout the piece James is concerned with the development of George Eliot the novelist: for him a true novelist is someone— like himself or Flaubert—who consciously lives his or her entire life as an enactment of the role of novelist, rather than someone who turns his or her hand to writing novels for a particular end during a varied career. James says that for Eliot the novel "was not primarily a picture of life, capable of deriving a high value from its form, but a moralised fable, the last word of a philosophy endeavouring to teach by example" (*EL* 1002). She lacks "free aesthetic life," because for her "the world was, first and foremost . . . the moral, the intellectual world; the personal spectacle came after" (*EL* 1003). James is obviously uncomfortable with Eliot's mode of writing, which is more intellectual and didactic than his own, but at the same time he cannot dismiss "such fruit as *Romola* and *Middlemarch*" (*EL* 1002). Throughout the review James makes much of the fact that Eliot had found *Le Père Goriot* "a hateful book"; in her inability to appreciate Balzac, one feels, James has found the key to all that he objects to about her work. James's ambivalence towards Eliot is seen by the fact that on the one hand he examines her life as a process of "becoming a novelist," while on the other hand his comments quoted above suggest that, by James's definition, she was not really a novelist at all.

Henry James is often regarded as either the precursor to or founder of something called "Modernism." It is certainly true that the views on the novel expressed in his prefaces, and the practice of his later novels, were extremely influential in the twentieth century. Among other consequences, these views provided subsequent critics with the basis for a devaluation of George Eliot. It is significant that when Leavis undertook a revaluation of Eliot he also felt compelled to exalt the James of *The Portrait of a Lady* and to condemn James's later works. James's illogical ambivalence towards Eliot is an interesting phenomenon, because he represents so well in his individual career the transition from the late Victorian veneration for George Eliot to the Modernist disdain for her work. However, James's ambivalence, which combines these two positions in the same essay, is hard to explain adequately. I do not accept Elizabeth Coleman's contention that James's failure to appreciate Eliot's formal qualities resulted from an inadequate critical terminology and methodology, or from his emphasis on the "central critical value" of "life."[12] Coleman's argument is based on an insufficiently nuanced reading of James's criticism and an eccentric reading of "The Art of Fiction." She ignores a number of places where James reveals a very flexible and subtle understanding of literary works very different from his own. She also implies that "The Art of Fiction" exalts a hypostatized concept of "life" in a simplistic manner, whereas, as I have already suggested, the essay is concerned with the problematic nature, and thus the phenomenology, of perception.[13]

In a review of a new edition of Carlyle's translation of *Wilhelm Meister* (1865), James writes an appreciation of a novel whose form differs radically from his own compositions. He implies that the novel develops, according to its own internal logic, its own immanent form, and he says that it is a work which must be approached seriously to be comprehended. *Wilhelm Meister* is informed throughout, James says, by the unique quality of Goethe's mind, which is both extraordinarily calm and extraordinarily active, and which fills the novel with a "luminous atmosphere of justice" (*FW* 948). The work interests the reader without employing any of the devices of "clever" fiction: "It has no factitious qualities, as we may call them; none of those innumerable little arts and graces by which the modern novel continually and tacitly deprecates criticism. It stands on its own bottom, and freely takes for granted that the reader cannot but be interested" (*FW* 945). Some of these qualities are also found in Eliot's works, but James perhaps did not perceive her affinities with Goethe because he was, in his consciously analytical comments on her novels, too aware of her existence as part of an English literary horizon which he found very parochial in some ways, and in which he also wanted to compete and succeed. He certainly is no more generous to any other nineteenth-century English writer.

For James, Eliot seems to have been at once a literary parent and a rival whose connections with the old tradition of ill-composed baggy monsters meant that she had to be exposed, delivered from the burden of "excessive homage" in order to make way for a newcomer on the literary field. One can speculate further that Eliot may have hurt James by not making him a more intimate member of her circle, and that this accounts for the mixture of affection and cynicism in his criticism of her. The often-repeated story of James's visit to Eliot and Lewes in 1878 lends some credence to this interpretation:

> I see again our bland, benign, commiserating hostess beside the fire in a chill desert of a room where the master of the house guarded the opposite hearthstone, and I catch once more the impression of no occurrence of anything at all appreciable but their liking us to have come, with our terribly trivial contribution, mainly from a prevision of how they should more devoutly like it when we departed.[14]

James's mortification was completed when Lewes, as James was leaving with his companion Mrs. Greville, returned to her the two volumes of *The Europeans* which James had presented to her and she had insisted on loaning to Lewes and Eliot:

> Our hosts hadn't so much as connected book with author, or author with visitor, or visitor with anything but the convenience of his ridding them of an unconsidered trifle; grudging as they so justifiedly did the impingement of such matters on their consciousness. The vivid demonstration of one's failure to penetrate there had been in the sweep of Lewes's gesture, which could scarce have been bettered by his actually wielding a broom.[15]

Gordon Haight writes of the incident: "[James's] assumption that the Leweses did not connect it with him and had not read it was wrong. They had. But they failed to recognize James's projected vision of the occasion, in which George Eliot should recognize that he too was doing 'her sort of work.'"[16]

In the next section of this chapter I will examine the consequences of the general acceptance of Jamesian aesthetics for Eliot's reputation. Unlike James, the younger critics of the turn of the century had not lived through the heyday of the Victorian novel as young men and women. They therefore would continue, in a sharper manner, the attacks on Eliot for her didacticism and lack of artistry; they would not temper their attacks with admiration, which James retained to the last. At the end of his account of the disastrous visit to Eliot and Lewes, he wrote:

> It was the fashion among the profane in short either to misdoubt, before George Eliot's canvas, the latter's backing of rich thought, or else to hold that this matter of philosophy, and even if

but of the philosophic vocabulary, thrust itself through to the confounding of the picture. But with that thin criticism I wasn't, as I have already intimated, to have a moment's patience; I was to become, I was to remain—I take pleasure in repeating—even a very Derondist of Derondists, for my own wanton joy: which amounts to saying that I found the figured, coloured tapestry *always* vivid enough to brave no matter what complication of the stitch.[17]

It is well known among George Eliot scholars that Eliot's reputation in both literary and academic circles plummeted immediately after her death, and that her standing remained low until it was revivified by the place accorded to her in F. R. Leavis's *The Great Tradition*, by Gordon S. Haight's scholarly labours, which made available the raw material for subsequent critics and historians of ideas like Bernard J. Paris and U. C. Knoepflmacher, and by the critical studies of Joan Bennett, W. J. Harvey, and Barbara Hardy.[18] W. J. Harvey summarizes the reception-history of Eliot's fiction as follows:

> The body of published work on George Eliot may fairly be represented by the figure of a globe closely populated at its poles, yet at its equator but sparsely inhabited. On this analogy one pole represents the period beginning with the first reviews of *Scenes of Clerical Life*, reaching its point of greatest density in 1885 with Cross's official *Life and Letters* and ending roughly with Leslie Stephen's *George Eliot* (1902). The other pole represents essentially a post-1945 phenomenon. Between lies a long desert of neglect.[19]

The rest of this chapter will investigate the reasons for this extraordinary decline in Eliot's reputation, and for the period of relative critical neglect which followed. I will concentrate on a group of pieces of criticism and passages in literary histories of this period, which is also coincidentally the period during which the discipline of English studies was being formed.[20] These scattered pieces of criticism will serve to illustrate the effective horizons of critical opinion which conditioned the decline in Eliot's critical standing, and against which Leavis launched the onslaught of *Scrutiny*, which forms the subject of the next chapter.

To begin with I want to question the validity of another piece of received wisdom in George Eliot scholarship, namely the view that J. W. Cross's biography, *George Eliot's Life as Related in Her Letters and Journals* (1885), was somehow responsible—possibly through its deletions from her letters and journals and its policy of selection—for the decline in Eliot's standing. It is certainly true that Cross deleted passages that he thought might be too outspoken, or which might in some way detract from the image of his wife which he wished to leave to posterity.[21] However, such deletions do not significantly alter the overall tone of Eliot's letters in Cross's presentation. Reading through the volumes of Haight's edition is not an exciting experience, and I do not think that they present a radically different view of George Eliot. The picture is certainly more complete, but it is of a woman whose primary concern was to be precisely what Cross is falsely accused of representing her as: an earnest, sometimes ponderous Victorian intellectual who strove to make herself an embodiment of moral good. Even in Cross's *Life* the frequent references to Eliot's poor health and depressions reveal the extent of the effort which went into that striving, and thus, by implication, the extent to which George Eliot constructed her own image for the world. Cross's *Life* takes an inordinate amount of blame for what was in actuality a reaction against the persona that Eliot had evolved, and furthermore a reaction against the intellectual systems and the set of social expectations which produced that persona. The *Life* of George Eliot was thus only a symbol of the reaction against the life of George Eliot, which itself was a symbol of the pieties of Victorian bourgeois Radicalism and agnosticism. These pieties, as will be seen, were readily identified by turn-of-the-century critics in the fiction of George Eliot as well as in the life.

The effect of Cross's *Life* has often been remarked upon. In his introduction to *A Century of George Eliot Criticism*, Gordon Haight writes that

> Cross's life . . . seemed to confirm the image of the portentous Victorian moralist. Cross had known her only in her most sibylline years, and sought out the sententious passages in her letters for publication, omitting the natural, humorous touches that would have relieved his somber portrait. Most of his readers were disappointed at the absence of personal "revelations" about her private life, and repelled by the marmoreal image of the learned writer presented in Cross's volumes.[22]

Ruby Redinger says in *George Eliot: The Emergent Self*:

> Perhaps the most harmful, although indirect, influence of Cross's *Life* was upon the English-writing novelists who came of age, literarily speaking, within the first two decades of the twentieth century. Already natural rebels against the Victorian age, their symbolic parent, almost all of them accepted the legend as it had been hermetically sealed by the *Life* and assumed without further investigation that George Eliot had nothing to say to them.[23]

David Carroll expresses a similar view in the context of commenting on the shift from Eliot's works to her life (as Harvey notes in his survey of criticism and scholarship of this period, "biographies of George Eliot were frequent when good criticism was scarce").[24] Carroll's view is that

> the retreat from the hard clarity of the individual novel to the general assessments of the author's work, now culminates in Cross's lifeless silhouette. This was to intervene stubbornly between the novels and the reading-public for many years. George Eliot's contemporaries had been surprised to find that the novels they knew had been written by this woman; later generations assumed that this woman could not have written anything for them. (*CH* 40)

All three writers use similarly strong physical imagery to describe what they perceive as the effect of Cross's *Life*. For Haight it presents a "marmoreal image," to Redinger the work is a hermetic seal prohibiting access to the real George Eliot, and for Carroll it is a "lifeless silhouette."

It is interesting to note that Henry James—who unlike his younger contemporaries, did find that George Eliot had written something for him—found the work satisfactory. His review concentrates on Eliot the novelist in relation to the woman depicted in the *Life*, and even he concludes in surprise:

> What *is* remarkable, extraordinary—and the process remains inscrutable and mysterious—is that this quiet, anxious, sedentary, serious, invalidical English lady, without animal spirits, without adventures or sensations, should have made us believe that nothing in the world was alien to her; should have produced such rich, deep, masterly pictures of the multiform life of man. (*EL* 1010)

Similarly, Virginia Woolf, although a member of a circle which did not admire the pieties of the Victorian age, found much of interest in Cross's *Life*. She also stands out from among her contemporaries for the prophetic intelligence of her assessment of Eliot's fiction. Woolf wrote to her friend Lady Robert Cecil in 1919:

> I am reading through the whole of George Eliot in order to sum her up, once and for all, upon her anniversary, which happily is still months ahead. So far, I have only made way with her life, which is a book of the greatest fascination, and I can see already that no one else has ever known her as I know her. However, I always think this whatever I read—don't you? I think she is a highly feminine and attractive character—most impulsive and ill-balanced . . . and I only wish she had lived nowadays, and so been saved all that nonsense. I mean, being so serious, and digging up fossils, and all the rest of it.[25]

It seems likely that Cross's *Life* had little to do with the reaction against Eliot apart from providing a convenient focal point for the shift in aesthetic expectations which rejected the English fiction of the nineteenth century, with its accommodations to the popular taste of the age, for the more provocative and avant-garde fiction of the French tradition. Two strands can be identified, although they are often fused, in the latter reaction. One was a reaction to the notion of aesthetic teaching in fiction, especially in association with what were assumed to be Eliot's Positivist sympathies.[26] The other was a formalist objection to Eliot's fiction, based largely on a more severe application of Jamesian aesthetics than had been applied to George Eliot by James himself. In the pages which follow I will trace these strands through the criticism from the time of Eliot's death until the 1950s, and will then return to Virginia Woolf in an effort to come to some conclusions with regard to the critical horizon of this period.

In the years following Eliot's death a number of writers felt the need to attack the legend of the sage of the Priory by belittling Eliot's achievements. These attacks often used personal references to Eliot's appearance or moral earnestness as a means of attacking the fiction, which was assumed to embody the same objectionable qualities objected to in the writer. The nature of these attacks suggests the power of Eliot's public persona during the 1880s. It seems that younger critics were frustrated into such attacks because they felt the need to destroy that persona, and to make space for their own work by removing the prestige attaching to Eliot's. In addition there was undoubtedly resentment at the success of a woman writer who goes beyond both the bounds of the "lady-novelist" and the limits of socially acceptable behaviour, and I shall return to this aspect of the criticism when I consider Virginia Woolf at the end of the chapter. It is also worth noting that the strong physical imagery of these attacks recurs in the three passages I quoted from Haight, Redinger, and Carroll, none of whom could be accused of lacking sympathy for George Eliot. This provides a good example of the lingering effects of critical discourses.

One of the best-known attacks on Eliot comes in the *Views and Reviews* (1890) of the poet and critic William Ernest Henley (1849–1903), who writes ironically that "it was thought that with George Eliot the Novel-with-a-Purpose had really come to be an adequate instrument for the regeneration of human-ity."[27] He objects to the didactic aims of the novels, saying that "it is doubtful whether they are novels disguised as treatises, or treatises disguised as novels," and he concludes his diatribe against Eliot with a series of epigrams, characteriz-ing her among other things as "George Sand *plus* Science and *minus* Sex" and "Pallas with prejudices and a corset."[28] A similar tone is found in a later essay by Edmund Gosse (first published in the *London Mercury*, 1919) which re-calls—although with Gosse one wonders how trustworthy the recollection is—the author's memory of George Eliot towards the end of her life. He describes her as

> a large, thickset sybil [*sic*], dreamy and immobile, whose massive features, somewhat grim when seen in profile, were incongruously bordered by a hat, always in the height of the Paris fashion, which in those days commonly included an immense ostrich feather; this was George Eliot. The contrast between the solemnity of the face and the frivolity of the headgear had something pathetic and provincial about it.[29]

Gosse goes on to suggest that Eliot's present neglect was a just revenge for the excessive praise of her works in her lifetime. Unlike some other critics of his time, who confidently wrote Eliot out of the timeless canon of the great, Gosse is aware of the historical reasons for the decline in her reputation, and he concludes: "Another matter which mitigates against her faith today is her strenu-ous solemnity. . . . We are sheep that look up to George Eliot and are not fed by her ponderous moral aphorisms and didactic ethical influence. Perhaps an-other generation will follow us which will be more patient, and students yet unborn will read her gladly."[30] Like many other critics who devalued George Eliot, Gosse values the humour of the early works and has a low regard for the later novels. He describes his delight in the early works in the nauseating metaphors which are often characteristic of the belletristic critics of the early twentieth century:

> The solemn lady, whom might seem such a terror to ill-doers, had yet a packet of the most delicious fondants in the pocket of her bombazine gown. The names of these sweet-meats, which were of a flavour and a texture delicious to the tongue, might be Mrs. Poyser or Lizzie Jerome or the sisters Dodson, but they all came from the Warwickshire factory at Griff, and they were all manufactured with the sugar and spice of memory.[31]

Gosse's essay was collected in a work entitled *Aspects and Impressions*, and the two words which make up this title are important to an understanding of the criticism of the period. Critics were wary of any attempt to subsume an author's work in a critical system, or to make judgments of value which related the work to anything external to the realm of literature. In this respect critics like Gosse and Saintsbury (who published a work called *Corrected Impressions*) were following Pater's critical method, which was to attempt to describe not the Arnoldian "object as it really is," but one's *impression* of the object as it really is. These critics therefore abandoned the social goals which were part of Arnold's criticism. As Chris Baldick points out, Arnold's actual poetic preferences were too far out of the reach of the Philistines for them to have any practical effect, so that "a superficially English rendering of Arnold's cultural programme was left, then, to pioneers well outside the 'central' cultural position of Oxford classical studies—in large part to the Philistines themselves, and to their educators."[32] The "Philistine" tradition eventually would produce the criticism of F. R. Leavis. However, the early professors of English literature and the influential critics of the first part of the century took a more patrician approach. Their criticism tests the "flavour" and "colour" of literary works in the manner of a gentleman sampling old wines, and by its self-limitation to "aspects" (a word, as we shall see, important to E. M. Forster and Percy Lubbock) and "impressions" it avoided the need to make claims to any truth beyond the purview of the isolated perceiving consciousness of the individual critic. I should qualify this generalization by noting that my account here is mainly concerned with British criticism and universities. As Gerald Graff has shown, the kind of belletristic criticism I am describing was not nearly so important in the U.S.A. It was practised by isolated individuals such as James Russell Lowell, but in general the American universities were dominated by Daniel Coit Gilman's model, at Johns Hopkins, of "specialized departments and courses of study after the German pattern."[33]

Saintsbury wrote several works which include a discussion of George Eliot, and his judgments remain similar over a period of twenty years. He finds the value of her work to reside in "very carefully observed and skilfully rendered studies of country life and character, tinged, especially in *Adam Bede* and *The*

Mill on the Floss, with very intense and ambitious colours of passion."[34] For
Saintsbury, Eliot will never recover the "factitious height" of her contemporary
fame, but she will probably be "safely established" in "a high position among
the second class of English novelists."[35] *Middlemarch* is, like *Felix Holt*, a
study "of immense effort and erudition not unenlightened by humour, but on the
whole dead," and *Daniel Deronda* "is a kind of nightmare," the result of "a
parochial and grotesque idea having thoroughly mastered the writer."[36]

It would be tedious to cite all the examples of similar judgments from each
of the major literary histories contemporary with or following Saintsbury's *Short
History of English Literature* (1898) and *The English Novel* (1913), but it is
worth mentioning some representative examples. The account of Eliot in the
Cambridge History of English Literature (1916), although favourable, relegates
her to a chapter entitled "The Political and Social Novel," along with Disraeli,
Kingsley, and Gaskell.[37] Oliver Elton suggests that "the Positivist cult attracted
her strongly," and compares her with Meredith and Hardy to argue that, unlike
them, "she is apt to miss the spirit of life itself."[38] G. H. Mair's short history
of English literature, which was reprinted many times in the Home University
Library series, contains a chapter on the novel which devotes most of its space
to Richardson, Fielding, and Scott. Mair writes that he does not have the space
to deal with the Brontës, Gaskell, or George Eliot, "except to say that the last
is indisputably, because of her inability to fuse completely art and ethics, inferior to Mrs. Gaskell or to either of the Brontë sisters."[39] As late as 1948 Albert
C. Baugh's *Literary History of England* devotes chapters to "Charles Dickens,
Wilkie Collins, and Charles Reade" and "Thackeray and Trollope," but buries
George Eliot among "Other Novelists of the Mid-Century." After a discussion
of *Wuthering Heights* Samuel C. Chew, the author of this chapter of Baugh's
history, writes:

> Not without effort is the mind adjusted to a new point of view as one turns from a novel which
> has proved to be of enduring vitality to the writings of George Eliot. No other Victorian
> novelist of major rank is so little read today. The effort to lift fiction to a higher plane than
> that upon which her predecessors and contemporaries were satisfied to work, though it brought
> her immense temporary prestige, has ultimately been responsible for this decline.[40]

It is clear that for Chew fiction is to be judged according to the standards of a
narrowly defined English realistic tradition: the Continental tradition of philosophical fiction is either something of which he disapproves or something of
which he is unaware.

The literary histories praise Eliot, if they praise her at all, for her realism,
which is sometimes contrasted with French naturalism, and for her humour.[41]
The emphasis on the provincial humour and on Eliot's rustics suggests another
quality of early English literary scholarship which Chris Baldick and Terry

Eagleton have commented on—its nationalism.[42] Eliot is praised for continuing the tradition of Shakespeare and Scott, which is regarded as a tradition of English humour whose main virtue lies in the depiction, in realistic and individualized detail, of a world of rustics speaking home truths in an amusing way and in regional dialect. For the writers of literary histories, English literature provided a tradition of Englishness which could be drawn on to counter the equally nationalistic literary scholarship of Germany. This tendency was obviously most noticeable in the period surrounding the First World War.[43] For such critics Eliot's early works held obvious charms; however, the harsher tone of the later works, which also are far more overtly indebted to Eliot's study of French and German systems of thought, made them less palatable. Indeed, the early practitioners of "English" as a discipline conveniently forgot Arnold's injunctions that criticism ought to correct the English hostility to systematic abstract thought and to logical propositions.

By far the most intelligent critic of Eliot in the first forty years following her death was Sir Leslie Stephen. While he shares many of the assumptions of the critics I have referred to above, his criticism reveals much more familiarity with the texts of Eliot's fiction and far more understanding of the way that her novels are constructed. Stephen had the advantage of being a late Victorian himself, and he was therefore more in sympathy with Eliot's ways of thinking and feeling than were some of his younger contemporaries. (One remembers Virginia Woolf's portrait of Mr. Ramsay reading Scott in *To the Lighthouse*. It says much about her father's taste and affinities with an earlier age; Scott, of course, is the novelist most ridiculed by E. M. Forster in *Aspects of the Novel*.) Terry Eagleton argues that Stephen is the last of the Victorian men of letters, trying to hold together a literary sphere which was splitting into the opposing worlds of academic specialization and popular fiction.[44]

Stephen wrote several pieces on George Eliot: an obituary article in the *Cornhill* (1881), the article on her in the *Dictionary of National Biography* (*DNB*) (1888), and a book in the English Men of Letters series (1902).[45] His judgments are fairly consistent, although the praise in the obituary article is less qualified, for, as Stephen himself notes, "We are not at a sufficient distance from the object of our admiration to measure its true elevation" (*CH* 465). Like most of the early critics of George Eliot, Stephen values the early works more than the later, but unlike them he appreciates the nature of the later fiction. In the obituary notice (later reprinted in *Hours in a Library*, another title typical of the approach to criticism of the period) he says that no one could read *Romola* or *Middlemarch* "without the sense of having been in contact with a comprehensive and vigorous intellect, with high feeling and keen powers of observation. Only one cannot help regretting the loss of that early charm" (*CH* 481). The *DNB* article emphasizes Eliot's sympathies with Positivism, suggesting that the writings show this as well as the life.[46] The article also brings out a theme which will recur repeatedly in Stephen's book about Eliot: the notion that being a woman determined (and the implication is strongly that it *limited*) Eliot's literary and intellectual achievement. He writes that "in philosophy she did not affect to be an original thinker, and though she had an extraordinary capacity for the assimilation of ideas, she had the feminine tendency (no one was more thoroughly feminine) to accept philosophers at their own valuation."[47] One is reminded of Henry James's observation that Eliot is "a feminine—a delightfully feminine—writer" (*EL* 911).

Stephen's book contains an insightful account of the life of George Eliot as well as discussions of all her works. There may well be truth in Stephen's suggestion, which he leaves only as a possibility, that Eliot "listened with too much complacency to adoring and 'genial' critics who collected her 'wise, witty, and tender sayings' and took her for a great poet and philosopher as well as for a first-rate novelist" (p. 148). On her poetry Stephen is devastatingly accurate: "Passages often sound exactly like poetry; and yet, even her admirers admit that they seldom, if ever, have the genuine ring" (p. 168). Throughout the book Stephen comments frequently on Eliot's depiction of male characters, which is something that he finds inadequate throughout her work. In his discussion of *The Mill on the Floss* he makes the notorious comment that "George Eliot did not herself understand what a mere hair-dresser's block she was describing in Mr. Stephen Guest. He is another instance of her incapacity for pourtraying the opposite sex" (p. 104). In *Romola*, on the other hand, there is Tito Melema, who "is frequently mentioned as one of George Eliot's greatest triumphs. The cause of her success is, as I take it, that Tito is thoroughly and to his fingers' end a woman" (p. 139). It is interesting that male critics have rarely felt moved to make similar comments about the portrayals of women by male writers; there is little doubt that the confidence with which Stephen assigns Eliot's defects to inherent qualities of gender lies behind some of the anger and energy of his daughter Virginia Woolf's criticism.

Earlier I discussed Henry James's ambivalence towards the fiction of George Eliot. James's views of the novel were very influential in the early twentieth century, and they were reinforced by the efforts of other novelists, for example George Moore and Joseph Conrad, to write fiction that was in the French tradition. This shift in critical expectations was another reason, along with the reaction against the actual tone and content of Eliot's aesthetic teaching, for the attacks on her novels as treatises in the form of fiction. The application of Jamesian aesthetics can be seen in its purest form in the widely read work *The Craft of Fiction* (1921), by Percy Lubbock.[48] Although it modestly claimed to consider only a few novels, and those only from one "aspect," Lubbock's work was very influential as a treatise on the aesthetics of the novel, and provided a basis for refusing to consider nineteenth-century English fiction as worthy of serious critical scrutiny until Wayne Booth provided a very different and equally influential account in *The Rhetoric of Fiction*.[49]

Lubbock's book is still impressive. It is elegantly written, yet has an intellectual rigor beyond the range of more belletristic commentators. Essentially *The Craft of Fiction* is a codification of James's critical dicta on the novel in his famous prefaces, and beneath the modest claims and the graceful prose a powerfully systematizing purpose is apparent. This becomes overt on occasion, as when Lubbock wishes that, for the sake of precise critical terms, the novel could have fallen into the hands of seventeenth-century critical schoolmen (p. 22). He mocks the theoretical poverty of previous criticism of the novel, with its emphasis on a naively understood concept of mimesis. He implies that the pictorial analogy so beloved of Victorian reviewers is inadequate, and he ironically summarizes the prevailing mode of writing about fiction: "A novel is a picture of life, and life is well known to us; let us first of all 'realize' it, and then, using our taste, let us judge whether it is true, vivid, convincing—like life, in fact" (p. 9).

For Lubbock the essential requirement of a novel is unity of purpose. He suggests that one should be able to put the author's intention in a phrase (pp. 41–42). This brings to mind James's notion of the "germ" from which, he says, his novels and stories spring: "a single small seed, a seed as minute and wind-blown as that casual hint for 'The Spoils of Poynton' dropped unwittingly by my neighbour, a mere floating particle in the stream of talk"; a "virus of suggestion" (preface to *The Spoils of Poynton*, *FW* 1138). Thus, although it was written by "the supreme genius among novelists" (p. 58), Lubbock finds *War and Peace* an artistically unsatisfactory work. It is hard to tell what its true subject is; it is two books unsuccessfully united. On the other hand, *Madame Bovary* is an exemplary case of a work which is firmly fixed on its subject from beginning to end.

For Lubbock the essence of the craft of fiction is the narrative technique employed by a writer. He sums up this view towards the end of the book: "The whole intricate question of method, in the craft of fiction, I take to be governed by the question of the point of view—the question of the relation in which the narrator stands to the story" (p. 251). Although Lubbock began by discussing technical matters as merely an aspect of the criticism of novels, he concludes by a totalizing claim which excludes any concern at all with the referential, socially conditioned aspect of the meaning of fiction. One of the central examples which Lubbock relies on is *The Ambassadors*, which he considers from the point of view of the technical problem involved in dramatically rendering one person's point of view (p. 170). Lubbock implies that such an exaltation of the individual perceiving consciousness is a technical advance on preceding fiction. At the end of the book he explicitly rejects the notion of mimesis, saying that he is not interested in Jane Austen as an observer or in George Eliot's knowledge of the provincial character:

> It is their books, as well as their talents and attainments, that we aspire to see—their books, which we must recreate for ourselves if we are ever to behold them. And in order to recreate them durably there is the one obvious way—to study the craft, to follow the process, to read constructively. The practice of this method appears to me at this time of day, I confess, the only interest of the criticism of fiction. (p. 273)

It is clear from his preceding analyses of individual texts that by "following the craft" Lubbock does not mean the kind of examination of the way the text functions in relation to the reader that would be undertaken by Wolfgang Iser a generation later. Lubbock's hypostatized notion of the form of the novels he discusses exalts his own particular historically contingent perceptions of them, which are evidently those of a well-educated middle-class male, as absolute truths. His celebration of the isolated perceiving consciousnesses of James's fictions implies a rejection of the attempt of a novelist like George Eliot to construct a social vision that transcends such isolation. It seems, to a reader situated late in the twentieth century, curious to profess a notion of the "books" of Jane Austen which excludes any concern with the society which is observed in those books; in this respect Lubbock is a good example of the formalism which came to dominate the academic study of literature in the middle part of the twentieth century.

E. M. Forster is a far less dogmatic critic than Lubbock, at least in the range of his fictional taste, and in *Aspects of the Novel* (1927) he discusses a wide variety of types and experiences of fiction. He accords the Russian novel a greater status than Lubbock, for he is able to see it more fully on its own terms. Nevertheless, in one crucial way Forster reinforced the emphasis of Lubbock's book. Both neglect the cultural context which gives meaning to literary texts. Forster addresses us in his typically whimsical tone: "We are to visualize the English novelists not as floating down that stream which bears all its sons away unless they are careful, but as seated together in a room, a circular room, a sort of British museum reading-room—all writing their novels simultaneously."[50] The limitations of such an approach are so obvious as hardly to need mentioning. Forster is interested in such qualities as character, plot, fantasy, and pattern, which can readily be abstracted from novels from a number of centuries and written in a number of languages. But he is oblivious to those aspects of a novel's meaning which depend on a historically and socially determined context of shared ideas and language in order to be perceived and understood. His treatment of George Eliot compares a scene in *Adam Bede* with a scene in *The Brothers Karamazov* in order to show that George Eliot is a "preacher" and Dostoyevsky a "prophet."[51] By ignoring George Eliot's sociological and historical analysis of Methodism in *Adam Bede*, her use of the left-wing Hegelian critique of religion, and her complex interweaving of literary topoi and genres, Forster denigrates the achievement of *Adam Bede*, even though in itself one cannot object to the point he makes about the two passages. His intention seems clear; it is to show that George Eliot is inferior by virtue of being that most unpleasant and priggish of things: a "preacher."

In contrast to the ahistorical approaches I have just been considering, an attempt to evaluate George Eliot's importance by taking her ideas seriously was made by S. L. Bethell, in an article in *The Criterion* (1938). This article assesses Eliot in terms of the literary criticism of I. A. Richards and T. S. Eliot, and also seeks to appropriate her for the dogmatic neo-orthodoxy which T. S. Eliot sought to champion through his editorship of *The Criterion*. The article is interesting because it breaks with the tendency to value the early novels over the later ones, but, like the journal in which it was published, it seems unlikely that Bethell's article had much influence. Bethell unconvincingly tries to make Eliot—the Protestant turned agnostic, the bourgeois Radical with Positivist sympathies and conservative political tendencies—fit into a tradition of High Church Royalist orthodoxy:

> The fault lies, not in George Eliot, but in her period. Her catholic sympathies, profound intellect, and wide learning, are sufficient proof that had a fuller religious position been possible to her, she would have attained it. Analysis shows her to have derived her standards, not from the poverty-stricken utilitarianism or bleak positivism of her own times, but from the best thought and highest endeavour of the past: she has the *anima naturaliter Christiana*, with a keen awareness of the shortcomings of sects.[52]

Lord David Cecil's *Early Victorian Novelists* was one of the major critical works of the 1930s, and F. R. Leavis consciously wrote *The Great Tradition* against the "revaluations" of Cecil. The latter is best viewed as a late and unusually perceptive example of the belletristic critics, concerned primarily with the description of the impression made by a classic work on a sensitive literary critic of the appropriate educational background. Cecil describes his intention in the prefatory note as "to illuminate those aesthetic aspects of [the] novels which can still make them a living delight to readers."[53]

Cecil begins his chapter on George Eliot with a somewhat bizarre passage which, in its use of irrelevant and offputting detail, recalls the earlier denigrators of George Eliot:

> Only eight novels still remain upright on the shelves—the novels of George Eliot. And there is no doubt that one shrinks from tackling them as one has not shrunk from the others. Their very names—*Silas Marner, Felix Holt, Adam Bede*—are forbidding; there is at once something solemn and prosaic about them, heavy and humdrum, they are more like the names in a graveyard than the titles of enthralling works of fancy. Nor, if one turns from them to their

author's portrait, does one feel more encouraged. That osseous lengthy countenance, those dank, lank bands of hair, that anxious serious conscientious gaze, seem to sum up and concentrate in a single figure all the dowdiness, ponderousness and earnestness which we find most alien in the Victorian age. (p. 283)

This passage clearly reveals Cecil to be a critic who feels that he is writing in the repressive shadow of the Victorian age, and his blatant sexism and class prejudice also identify the source of his anxiety. He is struggling to maintain an aristocratic and trivial view of literature, and to defend it against the challenge of those who do not enjoy the style and grace which are the product of a leisure class. His use of the phrase "enthralling works of fancy" is revealing: it is evident that he has fairly low expectations of fiction, and does not want it to make serious demands upon him.

However, in fairness it must be noted that Cecil is not simply dismissive of George Eliot. He sees her as the first modern novelist, the first novelist to construct novels around an idea (pp. 283–87). He also sees her as a European novelist, comparing her—although not to her advantage—with the great Russian novelists. But, he says, she is hardly read any more, and when she is read she is not enjoyed (p. 318). Cecil's ambivalence seems to be motivated by his dislike of "intellectual" fiction and more profoundly by his dislike of Puritanism. The latter leads him constantly from a reasoned appreciation of Eliot into a sarcastically denigrating tone, which reads almost as though Cecil were personally threatened by Eliot's morality. "An exclusively moral point of view is, at any time, a bleak and unsatisfying affair," Cecil writes, and this is worse because Eliot's virtues are "drab, negative sort of virtues, they are school teacher's virtues" (p. 319). Thus, "the enlightened person of to-day must forget his dislike of Puritanism while he reads George Eliot" (p. 321). Cecil is so troubled by Eliot's moral framework that he ignores the other structures in her novels: the romance plots, the scientific analogies, the social analysis. He proceeds from the suggestion that readers must suspend their dislike of Puritanism to the suggestion that Eliot's loss of reputation is after all not undeserved. The problem is not only Puritanism; there is something "second-rate" in Eliot's inspiration, but she was not content to do second-rate things as Trollope was (p. 326). There was a congenital disproportion in the composition of her talent, and her intellect was too powerful for the machinery of her imagination (p. 327). Cecil returns to a more judicious mode in his final summation: "When all is said and done she is a great writer; no unworthy heir of Thackeray and Dickens, no unworthy forerunner of Hardy and Henry James. She stands at the gateway between the old novel and the new, a massive caryatid, heavy of countenance, uneasy of attitude; but noble, monumental, profoundly impressive" (p. 328). Even here, however, physical and sculptural imagery is prominent, and the negative subtext is therefore apparent.

A similar view of Eliot persists in the criticism of Walter Allen twenty years later. Like Forster, and like Cecil, Allen cannot avoid seeing Eliot as a preacher, although he values her achievement greatly. He comments in his history of the English novel that "it is not altogether pleasant to be lectured to by George Eliot"[54] and suggests that she "has to pay the price of her earnestness."[55] Allen repeats these reservations in a book-length study of Eliot, although he is enthusiastic in his discussion of *Middlemarch*, of which he claims, "Never was enthusiasm more justified," because "*Middlemarch* is unique in George Eliot's work in being a beautiful composition."[56] Allen's book usefully discusses Eliot in relation to both English and European fiction. It is a pity that when Leavis and his followers defended Eliot's morality and the aesthetic realization of her moral vision in her fiction, they neglected the European dimension of her work, while Cecil and Allen, for all their other limitations, had been fully aware of it. Although chronologically he comes after Leavis, Allen belongs with Cecil, for his approach is that of an engaging amateur, with none of the strident urgency which gives Leavis's criticism its unique flavour. Before turning to Leavis, however, I shall go back in time, and return to the criticism of Virginia Woolf, whose feminist perspective provides a radically different voice from the male chorus which I have been cataloguing throughout this chapter.

Of all the critics surveyed to this point, Virginia Woolf is undoubtedly the most important in terms of the interest she has for readers in the 1980s. Her view of George Eliot differs significantly not only from the writers of her father's generation, but also from her own contemporaries; Woolf's angry intelligence anticipates the George Eliot who interests contemporary feminist critics. One of these, Elaine Showalter, sums up Woolf's significance as follows: "Where the Victorians saw dullness or defiance, Woolf saw the awkward exigencies of a woman too brilliant for her age. Where they saw artificiality and stagnation, she saw the imprisoning role created by society for the exceptional woman. As an exceptional woman herself, Woolf was well situated to comprehend George Eliot."[57] In a series of essays and in *A Room of One's Own* Virginia Woolf analyzes the way in which women writers have been limited by their material circumstances, and the way in which their reception has been determined by a male literary world which sought to repress or delimit women's expression.[58] As she wrote in *A Room of One's Own*:

> And since a novel has this correspondence to real life, its values are to some extent those of real life. But it is obvious that the values of women differ very often from the values which have been made by the other sex; naturally, this is so. Yet it is the masculine values that prevail. Speaking crudely, football and sport are "important"; the worship of fashion, the buying of clothes "trivial." And these values are inevitably transferred from life to fiction. This is an important book, the critic assumes, because it deals with war. This is an insignificant book because it deals with the feelings of women in a drawing room.[59]

She expands this analysis in an article called "Women and Fiction" (first published in *The Forum*, March 1929) by saying:

> When a woman comes to write a novel, she will find that she is perpetually wishing to alter the established values—to make serious what appears trivial to a man, and trivial what is to him important. And for that, of course, she will be criticized; for the critic of the opposite sex will be genuinely puzzled and surprised by an attempt to alter the current scale of values, and will see in it not merely a difference of view, but a view that is weak, or trivial, or sentimental, because it differs from his own. (p. 50)

In her reading for the essay on George Eliot, Woolf found a case study of the male attitudes she analyzes in the above passages. Earlier in the chapter I quoted from her letter to Lady Cecil, which expresses far more interest in Cross's *George Eliot's Life* than was found by the male critics, who were often disappointed by the absence of "revelations." It seems that Woolf found revelations of a different kind. In a witty and brief article entitled "Indiscretions" (first published in *Vogue*, November 1924) she makes a serious point which would later be the basis of much reader-oriented criticism: apart from "the critics," this distinguished critic asserts, there is for everyone, in every book, "something— sex, character, temperament—which, as in life, rouses affection or repulsion; and, as in life, sways and prejudices; and again, as in life, is hardly to be analyzed by the reason" (p. 73). Woolf uses George Eliot to illustrate her contention:

> Her reputation, they say, is on the wane, and, indeed, how could it be otherwise? Her big nose, her little eyes, her heavy, horsey head loom from behind the printed page and make a critic of the other sex uneasy. Praise he must, but love he cannot; and however absolute and austere his devotion to the principle that art has no truck with personality, still there has crept into his voice, into textbooks and articles, as he analyzes her gifts and unmasks her pretentions, that it is not George Eliot he would like to pour out tea. (pp. 73–74)

In spite of the light tone of this passage, it is clearly a very serious indictment of the kind of criticism I have been quoting from and describing through much of this chapter: criticism which begins with the life rather than the works of George Eliot and which, by references to Positivism, or millinery, or gender, or dank, lank hair, passes almost unnoticeably from the life to a denigration of the fiction, before or after making the necessary genuflexion to Eliot's great gifts as a novelist.

Woolf's essay "George Eliot" is, when read in the context of its time, a truly remarkable piece of criticism. It was written to mark the centenary of Eliot's birth and published in the *TLS* on 20 November 1919. Woolf had spent the year in preparation for writing the piece, reading through Eliot's *Life* and all her works.[60] She begins by referring to the insidious effect of the tradition of writing about George Eliot which grew up at the end of the nineteenth century:

"To read George Eliot attentively is to become aware how little one knows about her. It is also to become aware of the credulity, not very creditable to one's insight, with which, half consciously and partly maliciously, one had accepted the late Victorian version of a deluded woman who held phantom sway over subjects even more deluded than herself" (p. 146). Indeed, Woolf suggests, her countenance must have "stamped itself depressingly upon the minds of people who remember George Eliot, so that it looks out upon them from her pages" (p. 147). She quotes the passage from Gosse which I quoted above to illustrate her point ("a large, thickset sybil," etc.), and she makes the vitally important suggestion that: "In fiction, where so much of personality is revealed, the absence of charm is a great lack; and her critics, who have been, of course, mostly of the opposite sex, have resented, half consciously perhaps, her deficiency in a quality which is held to be supremely desirable in women" (p. 148). Woolf provides her own account of Eliot's life, of the way that she made herself into the "elderly celebrated woman" (p. 148) of the hostile portraits, and she emphasizes the determination, the intellectual energy, and the suffering which brought Eliot to that point. Woolf counters the suggestion made by her father that Eliot's achievement was mitigated by the effects of the isolation resulting from her unconventional union with Lewes: "basking in the light and sunshine of *Scenes of Clerical Life*, feeling the large mature mind spreading itself with a luxurious sense of freedom in the world of her 'remotest past,' to speak of loss seems inappropriate. Everything to such a mind was gain" (p. 150).

Woolf also breaks radically with the critical tradition in her account of Eliot's fictional development and her assessment of the novels. While she recognizes the beauty of the nostalgic display of memory and humour in the early works she also finds in them, as later critics were to find in greater detail, "traces of that troubled spirit, that exacting and questioning and baffled presence who was George Eliot herself" (p. 152). Thus Woolf finds a continuity from the early novels, with their troubled heroines like Janet Dempster and Maggie Tulliver, to the later works, which were so frequently dismissed in Woolf's time. The most famous statement in the essay is Woolf's revaluation of *Middlemarch*, made with so much confidence that it is hard to remember that she was not repeating a received opinion, but rather challenging an orthodoxy: "to the reader who holds a large stretch of her early work in view it will become obvious that the mist of recollection gradually withdraws. It is not that her power diminishes, for, to our thinking, it is at its highest in the mature *Middlemarch*, the magnificent book which with all its imperfection is one of the few English novels written for grown-up people" (p. 152).

A final point which should be made about Woolf's essay is that it foreshadows such later feminist work as that of Gilbert and Gubar by retaining an interest in Eliot's life, but manifesting that interest by focussing on the form and content of the novels as an enactment or sublimation of the tensions and experiences of being a woman. Woolf suggests that Eliot's heroines intrude on her material: "the disconcerting and stimulating fact remained that she was compelled by the very power of her genius to step forth in person upon the quiet bucolic scene. The noble and beautiful girl who insisted upon being born into the Mill on the Floss is the most obvious example of the ruin which a heroine can strew about her" (p. 153). To the school of criticism represented by James and Lubbock such a discord between background and foreground would inevitably be an artistic flaw, since such critics judge exclusively by what they term aesthetic criteria. Woolf will have none of this; for her the heroines, for all their distorting effect, are the essence of George Eliot: "Yet, dismiss the heroines without sympathy, confine George Eliot to the agricultural world of her 'remotest past,' and you not only diminish her greatness but lose her true flavour. That greatness is here we can have no doubt" (p. 154). Woolf concludes the essay by emphasizing the significance of Eliot's heroines, which shows that for her literature both exists in its own world of the literary and at the same time impinges directly on social reality by exemplifying, distorting, representing, or arguing against social conditions and sexual-political structures and embodying the emotional lacerations caused by social and sexual oppression. Woolf writes of Eliot's heroines:

> They do not find what they seek, and we cannot wonder. The ancient consciousness of woman, charged with suffering and sensibility, and for so many ages dumb, seems in them to have rimmed and overflowed and uttered a demand for something—they scarcely know what—for something that is perhaps incompatible with the facts of human existence. George Eliot had far too strong an intelligence to tamper with those facts, and too broad a humour to mitigate the truth because it was a stern one. Save for the supreme courage of their endeavour, the struggle ends, for her heroines, in tragedy, or in a compromise that is even more melancholy. (p. 155)

The story of these heroines is, to Woolf, the story of George Eliot herself:

> Thus we behold her, a memorable figure, inordinately praised and shrinking from her fame, despondent, reserved, shuddering back into the arms of love as if there alone were satisfaction and, it might be, justification, at the same time reaching out with "a fastidious yet hungry ambition" for all that life could offer the free and inquiring mind and confronting her feminine aspirations with the real world of men. Triumphant was the issue for her, whatever it may have been for her creations. (p. 155)

George Eliot Scutinized and Particularized

As was seen in the previous chapter, George Eliot's fiction was not readily accommodated by the prevailing critical paradigms of the early twentieth century. While she was still admired for the "charm" of her early works she was perceived to be insufficiently an artist, and too much an intellectual, moralist, or philosopher. Furthermore, many critics believed that her gender prevented her from realizing certain artistic aims. Thus Eliot was given a relatively minor part in the formative critical texts of the discipline of "English." Virginia Woolf's criticism, which was not written from within the academy, was the major exception to prevailing views of George Eliot. However, by the mid-1960s Eliot's reputation had been dramatically rehabilitated and *Middlemarch* was canonized by many critics as the greatest of English novels. Many factors obviously conditioned this dramatic change; here I shall be primarily concerned with the criticism of F. R. Leavis, which embodies many of the critical—and also the social—tensions and conflicts of the 1930s and 1940s. I will discuss Leavis in some detail, not only because of this representative quality, but because he is undoubtedly—if significance is measured by influence—the most significant critic in the study of English fiction in this century, and any attempt to alter the course of English studies must take account of the influence of Leavis. After considering Leavis, I will turn to some other important examples of the formalist criticism which flourished at roughly the same time, in order to highlight similarities, but also to show where Leavis differs, and where he remains, for present-day criticism, exemplary. These other critics are probably more important in the context of the United States than was Leavis himself, since Leavis's involvement with peculiarly English cultural problems has doubtless restricted his influence outside England and those countries in which British traditions play a significant role.

To read the criticism of Leavis after that of most of the critics discussed in the previous chapter is to exchange whimsical, digressive, and diffuse prose for a highly charged critical discourse in which almost every word bears the pressure of passionate response to the text and passionate thought about the text and its bearing on social life. It is hard to believe that Leavis was virtually a contemporary of some of the writers discussed in the previous chapter. He rejects all their assumptions about the purpose and nature of literary studies, and substitutes for their generalities a rigorous discussion of individual passages of literary works. Where he differs most widely from them is in his radical humanism, his conviction that literature, far from being an elegant pastime for English gentlemen, is the central element of the cultural tradition and the basis of moral education and even social transformation.[1] Obviously Leavis's version of humanism no longer speaks directly to social concerns, and his practice of literary criticism no longer provides an authoritative model; nevertheless, part of my aim in this chapter is to suggest that if literary studies is to be defended as a valuable discipline Leavis must be considered an exemplary critic. This means that his work needs to be read in the vigorously combative manner with which he read the work of others, whether poets or critics. By seeing his work as a stage in the reception-history of Eliot's fiction I hope to avoid two different approaches to Leavis, both of which seem to me to be limited and unhelpful. The first looks on his criticism as something which is now safely in the past, and which can be ignored or condescended to, as though it no longer has any effect and as though it is no longer of contemporary relevance. This is probably the more common view of Leavis at present. But there are still some who see him as a fixed reference point to be emulated, a saving presence in the declining modern civilization. A great deal of what has been written on the Leavises falls into the latter category.[2] Works such as those of Ronald Hayman, P. J. M. Robertson, and—although to a lesser extent—R. P. Bilan present a homogenized *précis* of the criticism of the Leavises, seeking to explain away their rough edges and often unreasonable behaviour, and accepting at face value the rather questionable social analysis which underlies the critical project of *Scrutiny*.[3] It seems to me that the accounts of F. R. Leavis by Raymond Williams and Terry Eagleton, while often harshly critical, are nevertheless more faithful to the spirit in which the Leavises wrote their own criticism, for they never wanted to be sanitized into conventional figures of the academic establishment.[4]

For F. R. Leavis, literary criticism was in itself an activity that was profoundly moral and social in its implications. He insisted that criticism could be a discipline in its own right: in his well-known exchanges with F. W. Bateson and René Wellek he claimed that there could be no literary history independent of criticism, and that criticism was also sharply to be distinguished from philosophy.[5] Leavis was concerned to establish the critical study of literature, as distinguished from positivist scholarship or belletristic essays, as a serious intellectual discipline, and in so doing he instituted a system of analysis of literature which bears many resemblances to the formalist criticism of the American New Critics.[6] It now seems to the majority of commentators that Leavis sacrificed too much in his attempt to make criticism independent, and I shall return to these sacrifices later. However, he never abandoned his fundamental commitment to a view of literature which emphasized its moral aspect, its role within culture, and thereby its social function. One of the clearest statements of this commitment comes in *The Common Pursuit*:

> I don't think that for any critic who understands his job there are any "unique literary values" or any "realm of the exclusively aesthetic." But there *is*, for a critic, a problem of relevance: it is, in fact, his ability to be relevant in his judgements and commentaries that makes him a critic, if he deserves the name. And the ability to be relevant, where works of literary art are concerned, is not a mere matter of good sense; it implies an understanding of the resources of language, the nature of conventions and the possibilities of organization such as can come only from much intensive literary experience accompanied by the habit of analysis.[7]

Leavis rejected the crude literary judgments of the Marxist criticism of the 1930s, and he implied that a close reading of texts was in itself a political act, for it was an act of reasoned consideration of an artistic text which enacted and thematized moral and political questions. Thus, for Leavis, "discrimination" or "evaluation" were primary concerns. One had to assess which works of literature, which literary types, most rewarded close study, just as one had to evaluate which human actions were right or wrong in the social sphere if any social change was to be effected—and the whole project of *Scrutiny* and the related sociological studies associated with the journal were passionately committed to social change. This is the background to the rhetorical question Leavis asks in *The Great Tradition*: "Is there any great novelist whose preoccupation with 'form' is not a matter of his responsibility towards a rich human interest, or complexity of interests, profoundly realized?—a responsibility involving, of its very nature, imaginative sympathy, moral discrimination and judgement of relative human value?"[8] Leavis is here insisting on the need for the novelist, like the critic, to make judgments, or moral choices. Catherine Belsey's equation of the final phrase of the above quotation with the mentality that led to the concentration camps is a wholly inappropriate attack.[9] Belsey herself veers uncertainly between Marxism and feminism and an emphasis (derived from *Tel Quel*) on the ludic pleasures of an open text; she does not seem to realize that the former approach, at least, necessitates judgments of "relative human value" in the sense of determining which of two or more possibilities is more valuable to humanity in a given situation.

Leavis's social views are based on a regrettably simplistic and "literary" analysis of English society. Curiously, for a Cambridge intellectual (although not so curiously when he is seen in the context of a whole romanticizing trend of the early twentieth century), Leavis locates his ideal values in a mythologized pastoral idyll which he seems to have believed to be a historical reality. In

Culture and Environment, which Leavis wrote with the assistance of Denys Thompson, we read on the first page that literary education is to be offered as a substitute, in a modern world of sinister media influences, for a lost mode of being:

> What we have lost is the organic community with the living culture it embodied. Folk-songs, folk-dances, Cotswold cottages and handicraft products are signs and expressions of something more: an art of life, a way of living, ordered and patterned, involving social arts, codes of intercourse and a responsive adjustment, growing out of immemorial experience, to the natural environment and the rhythm of the year.[10]

The Leavises saw their task as twofold: to show, in books like *Culture and Environment* and *Fiction and the Reading Public*, what was lost when the traditional culture disappeared and to analyze the process of its dissolution, and, secondly, to create a literary tradition and promote a way of reading that would provide a substitute for the lost continuity of "organic community." *Culture and Environment* makes clear the virtually religious convictions of the *Scrutiny* group: "we are committed to more consciousness; that way, if any, lies *salvation*. We cannot, as we might in a healthy state of culture, leave the citizen to be formed unconsciously by his environment; if anything like *a worthy idea of satisfactory living is to be saved*, he must be trained to discriminate and to resist."[11]

The first of the above quotations (although it is repeated by numerous subsequent critics as though it were a statement of fact) reveals the essentially pastoral mode of Leavis's thought, with its use of such unexamined clichés as "immemorial experience" and "rhythm of the year." For anyone who has studied the history of English rural communities, with their periods of famine, unhygienic living conditions, and insecure tenure due to enclosure movements, such a statement obviously involves more fiction than fact, as Raymond Williams suggests in *The Country and the City*. Williams analyzes a series of historical occurrences of the topos of "the disappearance of Old England" at different points in English history, and he compares the progress of his retrospective investigation to an escalator journey that stops at Eden.[12] Later in the same book, Williams examines the specific historical moment which gave birth to *Scrutiny* and to many other romantic movements glorifying the English countryside and its vanished "community" (some of which were quite harmless, others of which were fascist in tendency). He sums up a discussion of the Georgian poets by saying "the underlying pattern is then clear. A critique of a whole dimension of modern life, and with it many necessary general questions, was expressed but also reduced to a convention, which took the form of a detailed version of a part-imagined, part-observed rural England."[13]

Q. D. Leavis's *Fiction and the Reading Public* was a pioneering work in its attempt to create a sociological method for studying literature, but it too contains its share of illusion. Chris Baldick has shown how Leavis tends to argue in this work from purely literary evidence, and to construct statements about the attitudes of consumers of popular culture based on her own distaste for such culture and the assumption that it was passively consumed.[14]

A further criticism which is often made, I think fairly, of the Leavises' social thinking, is that it ignores other possibilities for cultural expression than either the vanished "organic community" or the substitute literary tradition. It ignores the possibility of culture, as well as civilization, existing in urban social life, and it makes "salvation" dependent upon a narrowly defined tradition of literary works instead of a broad tradition of cultural products, such as is implicit in, for example, the writings of the Frankfurt School.

The social and critical assumptions which I have just outlined are implicit in Leavis's criticism of the novel, to which I now turn. George Steiner provides a fair assessment of the importance of that criticism when he writes:

> Undoubtedly, Leavis's principal achievement is his critique of the English novel. *The Great Tradition* is one of those very rare books of literary comment (one thinks of Johnson's *Lives of the Poets* or Arnold's *Essays in Criticism*) that have re-shaped the inner language of taste. Anyone dealing seriously with the development of English fiction must start, even if in disagreement, from Leavis's proposals.[15]

The contribution which Leavis made was to treat the novel as seriously as poetry, and to subject the language of the novel to the same kind of critical scrutiny which one applied to Donne or Keats. For Leavis the novel became, more and more, the place where an affirmative critique of modern civilization could be made (later in his career Leavis would narrow the focus down somewhat obsessively to the novels of D. H. Lawrence). When he approached the field of English prose fiction Leavis found a vast, insufficiently differentiated tract of large books, and recognized the need to make "some challenging discriminations" (p. 9). He defined the great novelists not in terms of their ability to create characters, people a world, or tell a story, nor of their ability to create formal beauty in the aesthetic sphere. For him, as he wrote in the introductory chapter of *The Great Tradition* (written after the completion of the sections on Eliot, James, and Conrad), the major novelists "count in the same way as the major poets, in the sense that they not only change the possibilities of the art for practitioners and readers, but that they are significant in terms of that human awareness they promote; awareness of the possibilities of life" (p. 10), and "they are all distinguished by a vital capacity for experience, a kind of reverent openness before life, and a marked moral intensity" (p. 17). The strong emphasis on affirmation almost certainly owes something to the fact that *The Great Tradition* was written in the period immediately following the end of the Second World War.[16]

Leavis organized the novels of the writers he considered to be the great English novelists into what he called "the great tradition." There are serious inconsistencies in his account, and there is much confusion in particular in his attempt to define exactly what he means by this tradition, but these need not detain us here.[17] Even if it is seen only as a convenient device to bring together those writers who satisfied Leavis's criteria for greatness, and to attempt to fuse them into some sort of totality, the "great tradition" served its purpose. It focused critical attention on the novel and stimulated a controversy over the evaluation of English fiction which continues to this day. From the moment that Leavis took issue with Lord David Cecil's gentlemanly amateurism, the novel could be seen as something worthy of serious intellectual scrutiny. (This, of course, had been recognized by Victorian journalists like Richard Simpson, but it was not so widely recognized in English universities.) For Leavis, Cecil and other critics had created a false dichotomy between Eliot the novelist and Eliot the moralist, as a result of their trivial view of the nature of fiction. Because they saw the novel as essentially a superior form of amusement, they valued her early works too much, to the detriment of the mature work of the later novels. Leavis argues that, contrary to popular belief, her novels contain no passages of "tough or dryly abstract thinking undigested by her art" (p. 43). In his analysis of the "good part" of *Daniel Deronda* Leavis is particularly persuasive in showing how Eliot's intelligence is manifested in her rendering of Gwendolen's experience: "It is precisely because she cares for the 'reason' of things that she can render the aspect so vividly; her intelligence informs her perception and her visual imagination" (p. 130). In arguing against Cecil's view of Eliot as a deeply flawed novelist who was both a Philistine and an intellectual, Leavis makes a convincing case, clearly showing the emptiness of the term "art" in Cecil's discourse. Reading what Cecil says about Eliot, Leavis observes, makes one wonder "why he should suppose he puts a high value on literature" (p. 134n.).

However, I do not want to suggest that Leavis's "revaluation" of Eliot is entirely satisfactory from the present perspective. His mode of reading and his view of the nature of literary art are curiously narrow in some ways, as his chapter on Eliot amply illustrates. Leavis seems to be striving for a type of criticism in which the critic becomes invisible, merely the unperceived catalyst to an unmediated communion of novelist and reader. That is, he wants to make his view of Eliot seem self-evident, and his characteristic mode of procedure is to attack a critic briefly, as he does with Cecil, and then to go on to quote long passages which "enact" or "embody" the qualities he himself finds in Eliot. In his stress on "concrete experience" and "close reading" Leavis at times comes close to making things out of words, like Swift's academicians in *Gulliver's Travels*. Leavis's notion of "art" is that it is something which absorbs all cognitive and normative perspectives on experience and "renders" them in "concrete" terms which strike the reader with so much "reality" that he or she is at once convinced of their truth and feels that truth as an immediate experience. A characteristic sentence occurs in the discussion of *Daniel Deronda*: Leavis refers to the portrayal of Gwendolen's response to Grandcourt's request for an interview and comments: "Here we have the most subtle and convincing analysis rendered, with extraordinary vividness and economy, in the concrete" (p. 114). For Leavis there can be no higher terms of praise, for he is describing a work which he considers to be "among the great things in fiction" (p. 94).

Leavis's approach is effective, when it is, because he is both a rigorous and subtle reader of texts, and he employs his key terms, like "concrete" and "realized"—when he uses them successfully—in a way which does render his response to the text quite graphically. The problem is that he is so persuasive that he can easily give the impression to an unresisting reader that there is no other possible response to the text, and he ignores the possibility that ideological, or purely cognitive, aspects of the work are involved in one's response. By calling attention to a few examples where an alternative critical perspective can be taken I will show some of the limitations of his methodology and expose some of the unexamined assumptions which are implicit in that methodology.

While he argues against the traditional dualist (i.e., artist vs. philosopher) view of George Eliot, Leavis introduces a new dualism of his own. He finds in all her works "a tendency towards that kind of direct presence of the author which has to be stigmatized as weakness" (p. 44). This, Leavis suggests, results in a tendency to idealize her heroines, to refuse to "place" them in relation to more mature experience. Such a tendency is responsible for weaknesses in the presentation of Maggie in *The Mill on the Floss* and Dorothea in *Middlemarch*, and for the whole of the "bad part" of *Daniel Deronda*. The dualism is thus one of Eliot the immature fantasist and Eliot the mature artist. In a passage which summarizes his discussion of Dorothea, Leavis conveniently illustrates the kind of emotional quality he is seeking to describe by a series of contrasts with the positive terms in his critical vocabulary:

> The emotional "fulness" represented by Dorothea depends for its exalting potency on an abeyance of intelligence and self-knowledge, and the situations offered by way of "objective correlative" have the day-dream relation to experience; they are generated by a need to soar above the indocile facts and conditions of the real world. They don't, indeed, strike us as real in any sense; they have no objectivity, no vigour of illusion. In this kind of indulgence, complaisantly as she abandons herself to the current that is loosed, George Eliot's creative vitality has no part. (p. 93)

One can contrast with Leavis's view of Dorothea the account—quoted in the previous chapter—which Virginia Woolf gives of George Eliot's heroines. For Woolf, too, George Eliot's heroines strike a discordant note, but this is because Eliot's novels represent an unresolved crisis in the lives of all women.

Eliot does not resolve the crisis in harmonious "mature art," not because she is immature, but because no such resolution was available, or even imaginable, to a woman living in a patriarchal society who wanted to represent her society realistically in works of art. For Woolf it is precisely the dissonant qualities of Eliot's depiction of her heroines, whose consciousness overflowed with an unformulated demand, which provides their artistic interest. In this disagreement it is Leavis, with his desire for an "objective correlative," who seems the narrow formalist, and who is unable to see, as he so often does see, the ideological promptings of a novelist's art. The question of what is meant by "mature art" is not always as straightforward as Leavis implies, and it is sometimes a highly contentious matter. Here it would be easy to see Leavis's "maturity" as a synonym for patriarchy.

Leavis did not think much of Woolf's essay on Eliot, describing it as "a characteristic and not very satisfactory essay" (p. 46). But subsequent criticism has endorsed Woolf's view of the matter more frequently and persuasively than Leavis's. It was another female critic, Barbara Hardy, who authoritatively challenged Leavis's contention that Dorothea is excessively idealized, in an argument which convinces through its careful reading of the "particularities" of *Middlemarch*.[18] Leavis is not sensitive to the function of the language he condemns as immature in the description of Dorothea. This language is part of one of the less "realistic" discourses in the novel, since it depends for much of its effect on conventional literary associations and scriptural symbolism. Leavis restricts his effectiveness as a commentator on Eliot by concentrating on the "realistic" discourse to the exclusion of other important elements, as we shall see in the remainder of the discussion of his chapter in *The Great Tradition*.

First, however, a final point should be made about Eliot's treatment of Dorothea. Leavis several times starts writing about her as though she were a character with an existence independent of the text in which she is a name and a function, which is an error that he and the whole *Scrutiny* group were quick to censure in others, most famously in the case of A. C. Bradley. In his discussion of *Middlemarch* Leavis writes that "George Eliot's valuation of Will Ladislaw, in short, is Dorothea's, just as Will's of Dorothea is George Eliot's" (p. 89). This ignores the fact that these two characters are "placed"—to adopt Leavis's own terminology for a moment—in a network of social roles involving a great number of characters, each with a point of view which has some claim to our attention, and that they are described in what is a highly complex text with many levels of discourse and different uses of language. To take just one example from the novel I shall briefly look at a passage from the end of *Middlemarch* to which Leavis objects. It offers a summary of the past relationship of Will Ladislaw and Dorothea: "Until that wretched yesterday—except the moment of vexation long ago in the very same room and in the very same presence—all their vision, all their thought of each other, had been as in a world apart, where sunshine fell on tall white lilies, where no evil lurked, and no other soul entered" (*M* 82;793). Leavis regards this as a typical example of the tone of "those impossibly high-falutin' *tête-à-tête*—or soul to soul—exchanges between Dorothea and Will, which is utterly without irony or criticism" (p. 89). However, in the passage he refers to, the image of the lilies has a dual function. It serves to represent—through the association of lilies with the Virgin and with Eliot's favourite archetype, the Annunciation—Dorothea's yearning for "something," she scarcely knows what. Because lilies more generally indicate virginity they can also suggest the barrenness of Dorothea's marriage and ironically—even critically—point to Dorothea's short-sighted refusal to acknowledge the sexual dimension of her feeling for Will Ladislaw. This lack of vision earlier in the novel prevented her from realizing that her friendship with Will made her husband jealous. The passage thus functions as a successful example of Eliot's use of a very conventional image or symbol to give added complexity to the texture of *Middlemarch*, a novel which, from its overall structure to its textual details, refuses to give anyone a privileged place which is secure from "irony" and "criticism."

In relation to *Daniel Deronda* Leavis's terms of reference led him to the absurd conclusion that a novel called *Gwendolen Harleth* could and should be quarried from within *Daniel Deronda*. It is only his strong preference for concrete rendering of moral drama, in the context of a carefully analyzed picture of English society, over all other kinds of fictional excellence, which could have led to this suggestion.[19] Leavis rapidly dismisses the "bad part," confident that "an interested reader will very easily choose representative specimens for himself" (p. 98) to illustrate the worst dialogue and prose in the book. Leavis ignores or is unaware of the fact that a serious cultural critique is being made in the "bad part" of the book, utilizing a radically different literary mode from the more "realistic" "good part." Eliot, as Elinor Shaffer has shown, is drawing on a Romantic tradition, and is representing experience in a heightened manner, using ideal characters. One may still want to question her success, but I would suggest that terms such as "concrete" and "realized" are not appropriate for the kind of literature that this part of *Daniel Deronda* is an example of, any more than they should appropriately be applied to certain works of the German literary tradition that Eliot was so familiar with, or—to cite another of Leavis's notorious dislikes—to the poetry of Shelley.[20]

This brings up a related point in relation to Leavis's treatment of Eliot and of "the great tradition" in general. Leavis's neglect of foreign literature is often alleged as a failing in his criticism. Sometimes this is done in a snobbish manner, in order to denigrate his achievement in one area by charging that he ignored another. However, sometimes Leavis's concentration on his English tradition does lead him astray. For example, he writes of Eliot that "except for Jane Austen there was no novelist to learn from—none whose work had any bearing on her own essential problems as a novelist" (p. 19). This ignores the influence of Goethe, who was of great importance to Eliot. I have already discussed this question in relation to the Victorian reviewers, who were well aware of Goethe's relationship to Eliot. In discussing the fiction of Goethe (and of Mann, a later writer in the same tradition) one is moved to discussion of the cognitive aspect of fiction much more quickly than in discussing, for example, Jane Austen. This is not necessarily to say that Goethe is any less of an artist, but he is certainly a very different kind of writer. Some consideration of Goethe might have shown Leavis new aspects of Eliot, or would at least have made his negative valuation of aspects of her work more convincing.

Perhaps Leavis did not seriously consider Goethe's influence for the same reason that he later developed an irrational identification with D. H. Lawrence: his almost mystical sense of his own Englishness. In a description of the enterprise of *Scrutiny* written in 1963, Leavis wrote: "We believed there *was* an English literature—that one had, if intelligently interested in it, to consider English literature as something more than an aggregate of individual works."[21] Something of the meaning of Leavis's concept of "Englishness" emerges in his early nostalgic description of the "organic community" in *Culture and Environment*, while in *The Great Tradition* it is associated primarily with a moral tradition that includes Bunyan and George Eliot. The evaluation of novelists in *The Great Tradition* stresses the degree to which the major novelists approximate, or fail to approximate, this moral tradition, and this perhaps accounts for the oddly critical tone and the very selective emphases in the chapters on James and Conrad, both of whom are not unequivocally within the English tradition, although they each have a place in "the great tradition."

The question of "Englishness" seems to have become more important to Leavis as he grew older. This is evident in an introduction to *Adam Bede* which Leavis published in 1961 (reprinted in *"Anna Karenina" and Other Essays*, 1967). In *The Great Tradition* Leavis had asked whether perhaps "the implicit valuation it [*Adam Bede*] enjoys in general acceptance doesn't represent something more than justice" and he had suggested that "the book is too much the sum of its specifiable attractions to be among the great novels . . . it is too resolvable into the separate interests that we can see the author to have started with" (p. 48). In the 1961 introduction he concentrates on the success of the novel, and implies a higher valuation of it. After comparing Eliot with Flaubert, to the disadvantage of the latter, he says that "she is at the centre of the creative achievements of the English language in the phase of its history to which we still belong, and incites to pregnant reflections on vital continuity in art: we see that there is indeed an English literature—something more than an assemblage of individual masterpieces or separate authors."[22] He emphasizes the value of Eliot's portrayal of a "rooted community." The historical value of *Adam Bede* "lies in her novelist's creation of a past England—of a culture that has vanished with the triumph of industrialism."[23] Eliot depicts a rural society with its traditional arts of living, such as the art of speech.

A similar tone is found in Q. D. Leavis's edition of *Silas Marner* (1967). Whereas her husband had seen it as a moral fable, like *Hard Times* (p. 60), Q. D. Leavis seems determined to show that *Silas Marner* is a realistic depiction of the lost "organic community." Describing the setting of the novel in her introduction she says that "in Raveloe the Industrial Revolution had not yet been felt and it is the countryside of the timeless past of pack-horses and spinning-wheel, of the organic community and the unified society" (*SM* p. 14). Leavis ignores two important aspects of the novel: she does not mention the way in which the novel provides an enactment in concrete terms of contemporary debates about biblical hermeneutics, and how it shows a positivist form of religion replacing a doctrinal one. She also ignores the way in which highly conventionalized literary topoi are utilized effectively to give a symbolic dimension to the work. It is indeed rooted in historical particulars, but the symbolic or allegorical aspects of the work emphasize that these particulars are vehicles for the novel's "unavowed" utopian vision. Thus the details which so interest Leavis are only one pole in a dialectical structure. An important example of the symbolism of *Silas Marner* is the garden which Eppie desires for the cottage (*SM* 16;197). Leavis, in one of her long and tendentious footnotes, maintains that "there should be no question of importing an undesigned symbolism here" (*SM* p. 263n.), and she provides a number of details about traditional flower symbolism to reinforce her own interpretation of the passage. However, if the novel is viewed as a representation of the process of secularization and as an illustration of a religion of humanity, then the more conventional literary topos of the garden is obviously relevant. The cottage garden is to be a restored Eden, and Eppie and Aaron are to fill the roles of Adam and Eve. The garden symbolizes the fact that Silas Marner has "recovered a consciousness of unity between his past and present" (*SM* 16;202) and has realized that "there's a good i'this world" (*SM* 16;205). While this fable obviously contains the local and precisely observed detail which Leavis stresses, and which is the product of Eliot's memory of her childhood, it also embodies the results of her study of higher criticism, Feuerbach, and Comte, and her attempt to find a way of maintaining a religious consciousness without denying her knowledge of and assent to the conclusions of these thinkers. If Eliot's fiction is to be read and understood in this dialectical mode then it is necessary to juxtapose a close textual and historical reading with an understanding of a variety of important intellectual contexts: Biblical hermeneutics, positivist sociology, Philosophical Radicalism, and nineteenth-century science. A number of modern commentators have treated these topics, notably Elinor Shaffer, Gillian Beer, Sally Shuttleworth, and Suzanne Graver. The danger of their approach, however, is that the reading of Eliot might become an *academic* pursuit in all senses of the word. In contrast, the criticism of the

Leavises, when juxtaposed with most of the more sophisticated recent academic criticism, has a passionate response to the text and a conviction of the relevance of the text to the concerns of contemporary society which makes it still relevant and stimulating even though it ignores important dimensions of Eliot's art.

At the same time that Leavis was drawing his own map of English literature, the movement known as "New Criticism" was conducting a parallel, although not entirely similar, campaign in the U.S.A. This movement concentrated more on poetry than on fiction, but it produced one very significant essay on George Eliot: Mark Schorer's study of *Middlemarch* in "Fiction and the 'Matrix of Analogy.'"[24] Schorer, like Leavis, maintains that "fiction is a literary art" and that a proper reading of fiction "must overcome corrupted reading habits of long standing."[25] Schorer's method is much more formalist than Leavis's; he focuses on "the dominant metaphorical quality" in the novels he examines, and reads with the kind of scrupulous attention to the logic of metaphor which one now associates with deconstruction. In one of his observations about the novel, that it "is a novel of religious yearning without religious object,"[26] Schorer also anticipates the type of conclusion that deconstructionists come to when reading George Eliot, or, one is tempted to add, any work of literature.

In England significant formalist studies of George Eliot's fiction were produced by W. J. Harvey and Barbara Hardy. Harvey's main contribution was to argue against the earlier formalism of Lubbock, and to maintain that Eliot's fiction has its own form of artistry. Harvey suggests that "whether she is dealing with the moral consequences of one individual act or with the interaction of character and society, George Eliot submerges her philosophy in the very texture of her novels."[27] He defends the omniscient author convention as a mode of narration as artistic as any other; for Lubbock, as was observed in the previous chapter, omniscient narration ranks distinctly lower in the hierarchy of modes, and third-person limited is the ideal mode.

The work of Barbara Hardy on George Eliot spreads over twenty-five years, and forms an important and distinguished corpus of criticism.[28] Hardy's main contribution has been her extremely subtle and clever attention to all the implications of particular passages in George Eliot; she is less interesting on wider issues and tends to make theoretically naive statements about the nature of fiction and reality. But in her commentary on the "particularities" of the text she is unsurpassed, and her readings have made a whole generation of readers more perceptive to the symbolic rhetoric of Eliot's prose. Hardy's method is clearly exemplified in an essay on chapter 30 of *Middlemarch*, where she writes:

> The whole has undoubtedly had a better press than the part, "unity," as William James observed in *Pragmatism*, "being more illustrious than variety." There is no need to labour our recent concern with unity in theoretical and analytical criticism, but what is perhaps slightly

surprising is the neglect of parts and details even in Victorian criticism. . . . I start with the assumption, more easily accepted than acted upon in practice, that some details are more local and superficial than others. The objects, events, and images in this treasure-house of detail are not all equally profound, microcosmic, or symbolic. Some details lie casually on the surface, taking their place in a rendering of people, feelings, places and ideas.[29]

Hardy's careful noting of such details as the imagery, the style of speech attributed to different characters, and the evocation of affective states does much to counter the once-common notion that after one had observed that Eliot's style was "ponderous" or "heavy" there was little else that could be said about it. Hardy has done as much as any critic to justify treating the language of fiction with the same scrupulousness as the language of poetry. However, as we observed to be the case with Leavis, her criticism is narrow in its assumptions as to the nature of literary art, and she lacks Leavis's compensatory passionate involvement with the text, and his sense of social mission.

Hardy, like Leavis, underplays the cognitive dimension of literature, and the increasing stress in her criticism on "affectivity" has culminated, in *Forms of Feeling in Victorian Fiction*, in a type of affective reader-response criticism. Her most theoretical work, *The Appropriate Form: An Essay on the Novel*, makes evident the empiricist assumptions which underlie her criticism. She writes, "The novelist, whoever he is and whenever he is writing, is giving form to a story, giving form to his moral and metaphysical views, and giving form to his particular experience of sensations, people, places, and society."[30] Hardy downplays the significance of the middle term, for she is not sympathetic to art with a didactic structure. Her interest lies clearly with the third term, in which her favourite word "particular" appears coupled with the key empiricist notion of "experience." For Hardy, ideology in the novel is simply a matter of the overt moral and metaphysical views and design of the novelist; there is no suggestion that either "experience" or literary form may be shaped by ideology. She attempts, as she does in her earlier work on Eliot, to develop a broad concept of form which gets away from the Jamesian notion of design, and stresses the need to consider the novelist's use of an "appropriate form" to express his or her "criticism of life."[31] This appropriate form is the "form of truth" or "the form of particularity," to be distinguished from both narrative structure and thematic organization.[32] Hardy's criticism is here strikingly like Leavis's, and her "form of truth" resembles his "enactment in concrete terms." Catherine Belsey has termed this position "expressive realism," and has shown how it demands that the artist both represent the objects portrayed faithfully and express the thoughts and feelings they evoke.[33] Obviously there is a contradiction between the empiricism of the first part of this formulation and the idealist notion implied by the second. In her practice Hardy moves steadily away from the first term, but without entering into a consideration of the ideological aspects of the second.

There is no discussion of the epistemological problems involved in saying that something is "true to life." Thus she is limited in her criticism by the fact that she remains caught within the ideological premises embodied in the texts she is reading. The assumption is that we, the middle-class humanist readers, agree with both Hardy and Eliot (middle-class humanist critic and novelist) on what is right and wrong and what is the emotional response appropriate to a particular scene or event. This is quite clearly illustrated in the conclusion to *The Novels of George Eliot*. Hardy writes that Eliot

> succeeds, as all good novelists must, in making that intense particularization for the moment, which engages our imagination. Many of the superficial attitudes and appearances of characters and society—and some of the narrative conventions, though not many—have become a part of history, but beneath their remoteness lies the questioning and the sympathy of a humanism which speaks warmly and directly to this century and even to this decade.[34]

Eliot's humanism can be seen to speak directly to contemporary readers only because fiction for Hardy is primarily concerned with moral truth, and because she conceives of morality in radically individual terms. Such naive and individualistic humanism dramatically limits the pedagogical value of much of Hardy's criticism. It is hard to conceive how Eliot's humanism could speak directly to a working-class student in Liverpool in the 1980s or to a student reading *Middlemarch* in a school in the Third World. Since Hardy's criticism is still regarded very highly in the institutions of literary study, it is important to separate her insightful readings from the repetitions of an outmoded ideology which are inscribed in her criticism. If this is not done the result can only be to make George Eliot, and literary study in general, seem progressively more irrelevant to those (increasingly numerous) students who do not share Hardy's ideological presuppositions.

If Hardy had allowed greater place to the cognitive function of literature, and had broadened the range of literary types or modes she refers to (her constant terms of reference are Eliot, Lawrence, and Tolstoy), the negative effect which I have described above would have been mitigated. The structures of ideas in Eliot's novels provoke intellectual responses which prevent the reader from having to respond (or fail to respond) solely on an affective level. In conclusion, I will look at two examples where Hardy's narrow approach leads her to make an impoverished interpretation of Eliot's fiction.

In an essay entitled "Objects and Environments," Hardy undertakes a discussion of Eliot's handling of the inanimate world.[35] This is done entirely by close textual analysis, with almost no reference to the wider philosophical implications of such a topic. Although the essay contains a number of interesting observations, Hardy also makes statements that are banal and trivial. She notes that objects are "instrumental" in the *Scenes of Clerical Life* because the plot of the first Scene is advanced by the spilling of a boat of gravy, and the plot of the last by the discovery of a bottle of brandy.[36] Equally obvious is Hardy's observation that "the Bartons' poverty and Milly's hard work and anxiety are shown through domestic items of mending, clothes, food, furniture, and bills," while "the Cheverels' wealth and connoisseurship are shown through architectural details, objects of luxury, cultural accessories, and collector's items."[37] An analysis of Eliot's use of objects in phenomenological terms, or a more developed use of her brief reference to Marx, might have given point to the essay. Remarkably, there is also no reference to Balzac, a novelist whose rendering of the inanimate is so striking that a comparison would seem almost inevitable. Finally, Hardy could also have made use of the writings of the thinkers whom Eliot read, for example Feuerbach or the scientific writers, to bring out the intellectual assumptions about the material world and about human attitudes to inanimate objects which may have influenced or determined Eliot's perceptions. Instead, however, Hardy has produced a mediocre anthology of citation and commentary.

A similar problem is apparent in the essay "Rituals and Feeling."[38] This piece is concerned with the different uses of ritual in Eliot's novels, but there is no reference to the intellectual consequences of higher criticism, which radically modified perceptions about ritual, nor any reference to the Positivists' attempt to provide a secular ritual. Both of these historical phenomena are of the utmost relevance to Eliot's view of ritual and the sacred, and they were important concerns for her from her earliest work as the translator of Strauss to her last novel. This omission seriously impoverishes Hardy's essay, and it leads her into at least one serious error when she maintains that the shared meal of Bartle Massey and Adam Bede is not a symbolic reenactment of the Last Supper, "since the meal shows the way life often needs to become personally and individually ritualistic, in private ceremonies of loving or unloving."[39] However, Hardy's words here are a virtual restatement of Feuerbach's humanistic interpretation of the meaning of the Last Supper, and the passage in question is, as I noted in chapter 2, an important strand in Eliot's presentation, in *Adam Bede*, of a secularized Christianity or "religion of humanity." The resonances of the Last Supper are therefore not irrelevant, but essential, since the meal that the two men share is the eucharist of the religion of humanity, in which the spiritual meaning of the original meal is preserved while the outer form is annulled or transformed.

The similarities in the work of Leavis and Hardy should by now be apparent. But the differences between them are more important. Hardy's commentary has permanently enriched our response to the text of Eliot's novels, but taken as a whole her criticism seems dated, the product of an outmoded critical discourse, in a way in which Leavis's does not. Leavis, unlike Hardy, was aware of the nature of ideology. He was also willing to enter into disputes about the particular beliefs expressed in works of literature or in the writings of other critics. This makes him unusual in a period that was dominated, especially in the U.S.A., by a school of criticism that denied that literature even expressed beliefs.[40] While a comparison with critics like Benjamin or Adorno reveals the limitations of Leavis's work, as does a comparison with Raymond Williams, who was in many ways his successor, I think that Leavis, like Virginia Woolf, still challenges our critical horizons, and for this reason they are both exemplary critics, of continuing relevance to present critical concerns.

6

Marxists Reading George Eliot: The Case of *Felix Holt, the Radical*

For a generation of critics the dominant picture of George Eliot's work was that created by F. R. Leavis and Barbara Hardy. A selective reading of Eliot's fiction, which concentrated on *Middlemarch*, celebrated her as an emblem of liberal individualism; her strengths were seen as her social and psychological realism, and in particular her skill in creating character. In Barbara Hardy's words: "Within the great event and the large group, she is always interested in individual man, sometimes energetic and powerful, often dwarfed, frustrated, and alone. He is placed in history and in society, given his local colour—in the most precise sense of the word—but emerges primarily as a moral being."[1]

A number of critical developments have combined to break up the view of George Eliot which I have just outlined. Among these are Marxist criticism, feminism, deconstruction, and a revived interest in the scientific, sociological, and other intellectual sources of Eliot's thought. My concern in this chapter is with Marxist criticism, and in particular with Marxist readings of *Felix Holt, the Radical*.

As late as 1975 Terry Eagleton was able to lament that there was no English tradition of Marxist aesthetics.[2] That this is no longer the case is the result of, among other things, Eagleton's own work and the responses it has produced, and of Raymond Williams's progressive move towards Marxism. Before discussing Williams and Eagleton I will first consider two critics who represent English Marxist criticism of the pre-1975 phase. Lacking a genuine theory of aesthetics, Marxist critics of this period tend to share with Leavisites a naively empiricist theory of reading. Their Marxism is largely a matter of a political engagement, which leads them to judge literature on the basis of its approximation to the progressive political movements of the time in which it was produced. This, as Williams has suggested, is the most simplistic kind of Marxist criticism, although in some form an evaluative concern with the degree of resistance to established norms embodied in a work is common to all Marxist critics.[3] However, the early English Marxist critics never move beyond this simple evaluation of "content" to a concern with literary form, or with "literariness." There is no attempt in them, as there was in the work of Georg Lukács, to rethink aesthetic categories in the light of Marxism as a philosophical system, let alone to see literature as anything other than a "reflection" or "transcription" (translating the German *Widerspiegelung*) of reality.

David Craig and Arnold Kettle have both written influential essays on George Eliot, focussing on *Felix Holt*. The novel attracts them because of its treatment of English politics at the time of the 1832 Reform, but repels them by its manner of treating this subject. Each of these critics has a definite notion of what *Felix Holt ought* to be about, and each of them has an explanation for what he sees as its artistic failure. They see it as a flawed political novel in which the author lacks the courage to develop the logic of her most radical insights about the nature of society, so that the work ends in a compromise whose failure as a solution to pressing social problems reproduces or reflects the inadequacies and contradictions of Eliot's own political position and that of English bourgeois radicalism in general. This analysis is undoubtedly true as far as it goes, but I will argue that it is an inadequate account of the novel, and that it paradoxically excludes the most radical questions produced by *Felix Holt*.

For David Craig, *Felix Holt* is an example of the problems that "literature"—his case might have been more effective if he had said "the middle-class realist novel"—has had in facing up to "problems of a mass kind."[4] Craig has a reductively mimetic theory of the novel. His discussion concentrates on chapter 30 of *Felix Holt*, which describes contrasting speeches by a Chartist leader and by Felix. Craig praises Eliot's sympathetic description of the Chartist, then says, "What is not acceptable is the implication that there was some finer alternative attitude which could replace or seriously compete with that kind of militancy. The state of social struggle at that time was such that only antagonism (allied to acuteness) could conceivably have made any headway in quickening people to a sense of all they lacked."[5] Literature is thus for Craig a document of social movements, to be evaluated according to its conformity to a supposedly objective, Labour-Marxist account of social history. He provides an outline of such a history of the working-class movement in the nineteenth century. *Felix Holt* is valuable because it incorporates aspects of this history, but ultimately fails because it falsifies it.

Kettle's account is somewhat more subtle. He translates Craig's analysis into formal terms, arguing that he does not find the novel a failure because of his disagreement with Felix Holt's political creed, but because Felix does not play the kind of hero's role that the structure of the novel demands.[6] This is basically a Leavisite argument: Kettle is suggesting that George Eliot does not sufficiently enact her theme in the concrete form of the novel. He says that George Eliot's introduction to *Felix Holt* leads one to believe that it "is to be a novel about the personal fortunes of people whose lot is organically bound up with the condition of England, with class-conflicts and the moral problems involved in social advance, with the two faces of Radicalism and what political responsibility implies."[7] However, Kettle suggests, because of the complicated legal plot and because of the author's emotional involvement with the separate theme of Mrs. Transome's nemesis, the political issues are not adequately faced and the novel draws back "from certain of the realities of the social situation" with which it has concerned itself.[8]

Craig and Kettle both limit themselves to a discussion of the novel's treatment of Radical politics. Neither takes the Transome plot or the story of Esther Lyon very seriously, and as a result they both condemn the novel, Craig because it does not meet his documentary requirements; Kettle because it does not satisfy his own definition of its purpose. Both are limited by their inadequate theoretical categories; my own account will attempt to suggest how a more complete reading of *Felix Holt* might be developed without denying the political engagement which Craig and Kettle bring to the novel. I will argue that the novel operates outside the received categories of "realism" and "political novel" and that it is interesting in spite of the conservative political doctrines which can be abstracted from it.

In the case of *Felix Holt* there is a stronger temptation than with most literary works to abstract the overt ideological content and regard it as equivalent to "the work," because of the existence of George Eliot's political essay "Address to Working Men, by Felix Holt" (*Essays* 415–30). This article was produced at the instigation of John Blackwood, who wrote to her on 7 November 1867—more than a year after the novel first appeared—and asked, "Do you never think of writing any miscellaneous papers for the Magazine? It strikes me that you could do a first rate address to the Working Men on their new responsibilities. It might be signed *Felix Holt*" (*Letters* 4:395). In spite of the doubts of George Henry Lewes (*Letters* 4:397), the article was written and published in *Blackwood's* in January 1868. It is one of the many documents recording the Victorian bourgeoisie's fear of the consequences of the Second Reform Bill. The essay is written in the form of a speech by Felix Holt, and advises the newly enfranchised workers to use their political power wisely. Felix employs the traditional metaphor of the body politic, and he uses the figure of inherited wealth to describe the nation's culture. He argues that revolutionary action by one member of the body endangers the wealth safeguarded by more privileged members. There is a recurrent slippage from the metaphorical sense of wealth, as the nation's culture, to a more literal sense of wealth as private property. The "Address to Working Men" crystallizes the attitudes expressed by Felix Holt in his most activist phase in the novel, and puts them into a far more dogmatic form than we find in the novel, where—as I shall argue shortly—the presence of Esther Lyon problematizes any attempt to see Felix as George

Eliot's mouthpiece. To conflate the "Address" and the novel is to ignore differences of literary genre, and to overlook the significance of the formal aspects of fiction.

Raymond Williams has struggled throughout his critical career to clarify his ambiguous response to George Eliot, a novelist with whom he feels deep personal affinities. In *Culture and Society* (1958) Williams does not allow the personal note to obtrude as much as he would later, and his conclusion is similar to that of Craig and Kettle, although the case is argued with greater intellectual subtlety. He writes:

> When she touches, as she chooses to touch, the lives and the problems of working people, her personal observation and conclusion surrender, virtually without a fight, to the general structure of feeling about these matters which was the common property of her generation, and which she was at once too hesitant to transcend, and too intelligent to raise into any lively embodiment. She fails in the extension which she knows to be necessary, because indeed there seems "no right thread to pull."[9]

Williams emphasizes both questions of literary form and his personal response to George Eliot in his discussion of her in *The English Novel from Dickens to Lawrence*. This discussion is repeated with significant modifications in *The Country and the City*.[10] He contrasts Eliot's attempt to restore "the real inhabitants of rural England to their places in what had been a socially selective landscape" with Jane Austen's view of the country, "which becomes real only as it relates to the houses which are the real nodes" and otherwise exists only as "weather or a place for a walk."[11] Williams is interested in the problem Eliot has in representing a class of people who do not, unlike the more prominent middle-class characters, share her own idiom and assumptions. He values the formal disturbance caused by this almost insuperable difficulty over abstract criteria such as "unity":

> What we have to emphasize, on the contrary, is the creative disturbance which is exactly George Eliot's importance: the disturbance we shall see also in Hardy. That is where the life is, in that disturbed and unprecedented time. And those who responded most deeply, who saw most, had no unified form, no unity of tone and language, no controlling conventions, that really answered their purposes.[12]

In this analysis Williams is able, as Lukács was in works such as *The Historical Novel*, to evaluate the way in which ideological and social structures reproduce themselves in literary *form*. However, like Lukács again, Williams remains locked in a mimetic view of literature, which accounts for the fact that, as Eagleton points out, he remains as committed to "the moment of nineteenth-century realism—a moment supposedly paradigmatic of 'fiction' as such" as are Lukács and Leavis.[13] Williams uses his concept of the "structure of feeling"—

which Eagleton suggests means roughly the equivalent of "ideology"[14]—in such a way that he regards novels as embodiments of ideology, reproducing the structures which ideological formations produce in human consciousness. There is not in Williams's work on the novel an acknowledgment that literary form is itself the location of ideological division and conflict; such an analysis is only to be found in Marxist critics who have incorporated the thinking of Russian Formalism, the Frankfurt School, and structuralism.[15]

In *The Country and the City* Williams adds a passage to the earlier analysis of Eliot, and it suggests the degree to which he feels a personal involvement in Eliot's work: "I can feel enough connection with the problems George Eliot was facing to believe I could make these points in her presence; that I am, in a sense, making them in her presence, since her particular intelligence, in a particular structure of feeling, persists and connects."[16] However, the discussion of George Eliot in *The Country and the City* concludes with another new passage, which reflects a disillusionment with the realist tradition and with Eliot's habit of looking to the past. One can speculate that this reaction is a product of Williams's growing political frustration. He concludes that, for Eliot, "value is in the past, as a general retrospective condition, and is in the present only as a particular and private sensibility, the individual moral action."[17] This assessment accurately sums up the political programme embodied in the character of Felix Holt, but for the radical aspects of Eliot's novel one must look not here, but rather to the depiction of women and to the concern with questions of hermeneutics and epistemology, to the examination of the problem of grounding ethical imperatives in a secularized world. Williams gives little indication that Eliot was preoccupied by these questions, or that she examines them in the formal innovations and disjunctions of her novels. Thus in many ways Williams repeats F. R. Leavis's view of George Eliot, since although he consciously attempts to rewrite *The Great Tradition* he remains limited by some of that work's theoretical assumptions.

Terry Eagleton begins his book *Criticism and Ideology* with a long critique of the work of Raymond Williams, and Eagleton implies that since he, unlike Williams, is equipped with a tradition of Marxist aesthetics—one derived from Althusser and Macherey—he will therefore be able to transcend the limitations of English Marxist criticism and deal at last with literary form from a truly Marxist, rather than a left-Leavisite, standpoint.[18] Later in the same work he includes a brief essay on George Eliot in a series of accounts of nineteenth-century and early twentieth-century writers. He suggests that Eliot's writing is an attempt to resolve a structural conflict between two forms of mid-Victorian ideology:

> a progressively muted Romantic individualism, concerned with the untrammelled evolution of the "free spirit," and certain "higher," corporate ideological modes. These higher modes

(essentially, Feuerbachian humanism and scientific rationalism) seek to identify the immutable laws to which Romantic individualism, if it is to avoid both ethical anarchy and social disruption, must conform.[19]

Eagleton describes this ideological conflict as "the productive matrix" of Eliot's fiction, but cautions that "the ideology of her texts is not, of course, reducible to it. For Eliot's literary production must be situated, not only at the level of 'general' ideology, but also at the relatively autonomous level of the mutation of literary forms."[20] In spite of this caution, Eagleton's account does not move beyond the level of a simplified and abstract description of Eliot's *oeuvre* as an allegory of conflicting and hypostatized ideological formations. Because he does not discuss any of the novels in detail, Eagleton does not fulfil his intention of considering the "relatively autonomous level of the mutation of literary forms." Instead, he remains almost completely on the level of what he calls "'general' ideology," describing a battle between various ideological forms, some of which (e.g., "Romantic individualism") are so general as to be almost meaningless. He throws out a number of suggestive insights, but these are mixed with a characteristically extravagant rhetoric, which often seems to presuppose the sort of vulgar transcriptional Marxist aesthetic theory which Eagleton's valuable theoretical work is concerned to transcend.

Daniel Cottom has recently published the most extensive Marxist study of George Eliot to date, *Social Figures: George Eliot, Social History, and Literary Representation*.[21] In spite of Cottom's ambitious claims and his use of Foucault and other theorists, his book does not add much to the briefer discussions which I have already mentioned. He does not consider literary history to any significant extent, and his study is further flawed in two respects. He treats Eliot as an example of a category he describes as "the liberal intellectual: the social figure who takes the ideal of intellectual discourse to be the reality of society."[22] Cottom treats virtually every nineteenth-century English writer as a member of this category, which suggests that Cottom's use of the term "liberal" is broad virtually to the point of meaninglessness, something that is surprising in a critic who insists so much on the historical specificity of discourse. Even more serious is Cottom's refusal to consider issues of gender. He states in his preface that "in treating Eliot as a liberal intellectual, I am treating her as a figure of patriarchy."[23] This limitation, astonishing in a work of socially committed criticism published in 1987, means that Cottom ignores the most powerful source of contradictions and tensions in Eliot's writing, as Terry Eagleton points out rather gently in his foreword to the work. [24]

The fundamental problem with all the Marxist readings that I have surveyed is that they either concentrate almost exclusively on the overt ideological content of *Felix Holt*, which they find inadequate as a transcription of a reality which can be objectively described, or they regard the form of the artistic work as a reflection or reproduction of ideology and the contradictions in ideology. There is no suggestion that the text's own processes of ordering and structuring, or its particular combination of contradictory positions, can play a constitutive role, suggesting a way beyond the horizons of particular discourses or ideological systems. Even Eagleton's account, in spite of his theoretical claims, conflates the novel and the "Address to Working Men." For Eagleton, the Radicalism of Felix in the novel "consists in a reformist trust in moral education and a positivist suspicion of political change—a combination heroically opposed by the text to an unsavoury alliance of opportunist Radical politics with the insensate irrationality of the masses."[25]

In my view Eagleton and the other Marxist critics ignore the extent to which *Felix Holt, the Radical* is a questioning of the Positivist view of social and political change, because they ignore the productive nature of the tensions and discontinuities in the novel. Traditional Marxist critics are also reluctant to recognize that literature has a potentially constitutive, rather than simply a transcriptional, function. But a great Marxist critic, Theodor W. Adorno, cautions in "Lyric Poetry and Society":

> We must be especially wary of the present insufferable tendency to drag out at every slightest opportunity the concept of ideology. For ideology is untruth—false consciousness, a lie. It manifests itself in the failure of art works, in their own intrinsic falsehood, and can be uncovered by criticism. . . . The greatness of works of art lies solely in their power to let those things be heard which ideology conceals.[26]

Adorno thus emphasizes the fact that artistic works can transcend the horizons of ideology. A similar view is asserted by Jauss in "Literary History as a Challenge to Literary Theory":

> The gap between literature and history, between aesthetic and historical knowledge, can be bridged if literary history does not simply describe once again the process of general history as reflected in its works, but rather discovers in the course of "literary evolution" that properly *socially formative [gesellschaftsbildende]* function that belongs to literature as it competes with other arts and social forces in the emancipation of mankind from its natural, religious, and social bonds.[27]

In *Felix Holt* George Eliot presents her first really overt challenge to Christianity as the ground of morality and social action. She presents it as an outmoded form of expression, according to the Positivist analysis of human development, and she examines the resulting hermeneutic confusion and the Positivist claim that both religion and metaphysics can be superseded by Positive knowledge. Through her portrayal of women in the novel, Eliot exposes the shortcomings of Positivism, but female action and female speech—in the society Eliot describes—are not able to produce a fully articulated alternative moral position.

The novel uses the conventions of the inheritance plot in order to question the *telos* of that plot as manifested in its typically socially conservative form in novels of the tradition of Fielding and Scott (or, closer to her own time, in a novel like Disraeli's *Sybil*). But *Felix Holt* also qualifies Eliot's own realist project, by questioning the ease with which realism assumes that it can read the world, and in this way the novel anticipates *Middlemarch*. It dramatizes the epistemological problems of Radicalism and Positivism, but does not retreat into a sentimentalizing of the past. There is no suggestion that the social changes which are so graphically depicted can be undone, nor that the landowning class is possessed of a special wisdom or culture. The novel does not produce the kind of ideological closure which produces, in Marxist terms, false consciousness; the value of *Felix Holt* lies precisely in its resistance to the temptations of such a consciousness.

In the character of Rufus Lyon, George Eliot sympathetically depicts a Christian minister whose ministry is nevertheless, in the context of nineteenth-century English society, seen as marginal if not anachronistic. In earlier works Eliot had used clergymen or religious figures like Dinah Morris as privileged speakers of humanistic truths, but there is little suggestion in *Felix Holt* that Lyon possesses any real insight into the political or personal crises of the novel. He is valued by the narrator and by Felix for his integrity of purpose, but Felix refuses to submit to Lyon's dogmatic creed. When Esther asks Felix why he doesn't always attend chapel and why he doesn't join the Church he replies: "There's just the difference between us—I know why I don't do those things. I distinctly see that I can do something better. I have other principles, and should sink myself by doing what I don't recognise as the best" (*FH* 10;108). There are suggestions, in the depiction of Lyon's relationship with his wife, Annette, that he himself has had difficulties with his dogmatic creed, and throughout the novel we see that his faith involves him in problems of interpretation which will be perceived as unnecessary by the more liberal reader assumed by the narrator. As Robin Sheets suggests, Lyon believes that he can use language effectively, but he is an inadequate interpreter and communicator.[28] We first see him meditating upon an apparently straightforward biblical text: "And all the people said, Amen." Due to Lyon's interpretive labours, however, the text begins to spread out "into a many-branched discourse" (*FH* 4;48). The ramifications of biblical discourse are seen to extend even further in Lyon's subsequent conversation with Felix Holt's mother, who distresses Lyon by justifying her prejudices by—in Lyon's words—"giving a too private interpretation to the Scripture" (*FH* 4;51). The minister believes that "the word of God has to satisfy the larger need of His people" (*FH* 4;51), but the examples I have just cited show that the novel begins by problematizing the interpretation of scripture, and it also—this is one of its most striking features—asks what the larger need of "God's people" is, and dramatizes the interpretive problems involved in determining that need.

At the end of the novel, Lyon is seen surrounded by a wall of books, "absorbed in mastering all those painstaking interpretations of the Book of Daniel, which are by this time well gone to the limbo of mistaken criticism" (*FH* 41;326). In order for him to reach Esther, the minister has to upset a pile of books, "thus unintentionally making a convenient breach in his wall" (*FH* 41;327). This is a telling image, revealing Eliot's faith in the power of human affections to provide the basis for a new "religion" which will depose Evangelical dogmatism. However, even this Feuerbachian faith is not the last word in *Felix Holt*. The novel shows that material and ideological constraints prevent the affections from functioning in an untrammelled way. As the narrator comments, in a famous passage, "there is no private life which has not been determined by a wider public life" (*FH* 3;45). The most powerful example of this, of course, is the relentless analysis of Mrs. Transome's tragedy; her social position and the culture which is a part of it have prevented the free operation of her natural affections, so that her whole life has been poisoned.

Felix Holt foregrounds questions of interpretation and epistemology more than any of Eliot's works. It does not do this, as one might easily suppose, simply to problematize the notion of "Radicalism" in order to advocate a privatized bourgeois humanism; rather, the work examines the difficulties of grounding interpretation in a system which will guarantee some degree of communication, but which will not be oppressive of socially beneficial change. In other words, Eliot is squarely facing the issue of the consequences of secularized thinking on discursive theory and practice. The consideration of interpretation is effected in part through the example of Lyon's biblical exegesis, which is shown to be no less arbitrary and private—to the world outside the dissenting chapel—than the interpretations of Mrs. Holt.

Another major motif is a concern with the nature, effect, and consequences of human speech. The narrator observes, "The one speech, sometimes uttered under great responsibility as to missiles and other consequences, has given a text to twenty speakers who are under no responsibility" (*FH* 19;175). As Robin Sheets points out, Felix believes, like Lyon, in the possibility of truthful speech, but he is in fact "a very clumsy rhetorician who consistently fails to carry his point in public."[29] Thus he is unable to save himself at his trial, where Esther Lyon shows that she—unlike Mrs. Holt and Mrs. Transome—has learned to speak honestly and effectively. At the beginning of the novel, Esther's attitude to speech only adds to Mr. Lyon's hermeneutic problem, as he tells Felix:

> "My daughter is a critic of words, Mr. Holt," said the minister, smiling complacently, "and often corrects mine on the grounds of niceties, which I confess are as dark to me as if they were the reports of a sixth sense which I possess not. I am an eager seeker for precision, and would fain find a language subtle enough to follow the utmost intricacies of the soul's pathways, but I see not why a round word that means some object, made and blessed by the Creator, should be branded and banished as a malefactor." (*FH* 5;62–63)

At the trial Esther speaks out plainly, and shows that she has progressed beyond the limited world of ladylike behaviour in which she was confined at the beginning of the novel, but Eliot does not idealize the power of this speech. Esther does not secure Felix's acquittal by her testimony; the local gentry only arrange for his pardon because they are moved by her beauty and because they regard Felix as "a good fellow at bottom" (*FH* 47;379), in other words, as a covert Tory. Esther's speech is responsible for Felix's freedom, but only in the unpredictable manner in which speech in general disseminates itself, according to the narrator's description quoted earlier.

Another aspect of the novel's concern with interpretation is its emphasis on the duplicitous nature of names and naming. Felix Holt the Radical is, as everyone observes, really a Tory. One of the villains in the novel is called Maurice Christian. Esther's claim to the estate rests on the fact that she is really a Bycliffe, not a Lyon, while the "Transomes" are really Durfeys. Harold is doubly not a Transome, since his real father is Jermyn the lawyer. The novel is also full of equivocations as to the meaning of the word "Radical," and puns on the word's etymology, as when Harold tells his uncle that he is "a Radical only in rooting out abuses" (*FH* 2;39). By this demonstration of the inadequacy of naming, Eliot—as Catherine Gallagher has pointed out—reveals an impatience with and skepticism about realism, and in particular with the metonymic connections which realism assumes.[30] Gallagher also maintains that Eliot "attempts the direct representation of pure political value in the characterization of her protagonist."[31] However, as critics like Craig and Kettle were eager to point out, the novel does not successfully achieve such a realization. And if one avoids committing the intentional fallacy, one can read the novel in a very different way, not as the quest for a transcendental realm of value through the depiction of Felix, but as a questioning of the values embodied in both Felix and Harold Transome. The work does not fully endorse the Positivism of Felix Holt,[32] and it questions the patriarchal *telos* of the inheritance plot, in which the will of the absent father determines the fate of subsequent generations. In its subdued conclusion, the novel enacts the ideological blockage produced by an impasse of Radicalism and feminism. The recurrent thematization of hermeneutic uncertainty enacts this blockage and produces the need for the reader to effect a synthesis in which the choices for the Esther Lyons of the world are no longer limited to either the emptiness of the life of a Mrs. Transome, or the chosen obscurity of the future that is sketched out for Esther as the wife of Felix Holt.

As Gillian Beer observes, one of the ironies of *Felix Holt* "is that if *law is male story* ('patriarchal and genealogical'), as its identification with Jermyn and its patriarchal organisation of inheritance imply, that story unexpectedly produces a female inheritor—Esther Lyon—and one at liberty to repudiate her inheritance."[33] Law in the novel functions as a metaphor for a more abstract law of determinism.[34] It is through his own legal machinations and his attempts to

conceal them that Jermyn ultimately exposes himself, before the Treby establishment, as no gentleman (*FH* 48;382-83); Harold's attempt to right the wrongs
done to his estate produces the discovery that he has no title to the estate; and,
most memorably, Mrs. Transome's punishment for her past indiscretions, which
is seen against the background of Greek tragedy, is worked out at the level of
plot through the tangled legal connections between Jermyn and Harold. There
is no mercy provided by the nemesis of patriarchal law, which repeats the stern
imperatives of the originating father throughout the novel. The complex legal
plot was dismissed by an earlier generation of critics as a defect in a flawed but
obviously important realist novel. It is now possible to see the plot in a different
and more positive light, as a symbolically successful repetition and repudiation
of the complex inheritance plots of the Fielding-Scott tradition.[35] Eliot repeats
this formal structure in order to show its punitive weight, but she repudiates it
by suggesting that the attempt to master the tortured web of interconnections,
and to trace them back so as to get power over them, represents an obsessive
search for patriarchal origins which it is possible to avoid. Esther does so by
concentrating on the figure of her deceased mother, by an identification with
her step-father rather than with her biological father's inheritance, and by her
eventual rejection of Harold Transome and the inheritance. Even Mr. Lyon
initially finds himself absorbed by the story of the inheritance, and he is only
rescued from a Casaubon-like search for an originative type by an affective
response to his daughter's situation, which aligns him with her against the
manipulators of narrative—Jermyn, Johnson, Christian, and Harold Transome.
Lyon

> was so accustomed to the impersonal study of narrative, that even in these exceptional mo-
> ments the habit of half a century asserted itself, and he seemed sometimes not to distinguish
> the case of Esther's inheritance from a story in ancient history, until some detail recalled him
> to the profound feeling that a great, great change might be coming over the life of this child
> who was so close to him. (*FH* 38;306)

Felix Holt suggests that a very different type of plot, different social values,
and different modes of consciousness are necessary for a truly radical transformation of society. The definition of these alternatives emerged only by implication, for Eliot's utopian vision is even more unavowed here than elsewhere.[36]
But it is clear that neither the patrician Radicalism of Harold Transome nor the
Positivist organicism of Felix Holt is valorized in the novel. As Gillian Beer
points out, it opens with the suppression of a woman's independence, which is
an event that had previously been put at the conclusion of Eliot's works (notably
in *Adam Bede*). Opening with this image allows it to be questioned, and much
of the questioning is done through the juxtaposition of the two plots, the private
and the public, the romantic and the political. Beer notes that none of Eliot's

contemporary critics connected the public story of class politics with the private story of sexual politics, and she suggests that "this is one of the instances where one can readily radicalize George Eliot way beyond her own control. By this I mean that this book potentiates radical questioning without itself being in command of it."[37] As Beer suggests, *Felix Holt* is unexpectedly open to radical interpretation, once one reads all of it with equal attention, instead of focussing on those parts which best illustrate the overt design of the work. Thus, although it tries to create a resolution to the tension between the private story and the public, Eliot's novel leaves the impression of a private world which, if seen in terms of a feminist politics, does not fit harmoniously into the larger political resolution she offers in the public world.

Harold Transome's Radicalism does not extend to the private sphere, as his treatment of his mother and his attitude towards Esther make abundantly clear. Felix tries to educate Esther above the narrow concerns of a conventional lady, but only so that she can become the Positivist ideal of an inspirational Madonna figure. He asks rhetorically whether anyone will ever measure "the force there would be in one beautiful woman whose mind was as noble as her face was beautiful—who made a man's passion for her rush in one current with all the great aims of his life" (*FH* 27;223). As David Carroll observes, Felix initially sees the reform of Esther and political reform as independent, and he assumes that he cannot continue with his implied commitment to her as well as be a political reformer.[38] But Carroll suggests that, by marrying Esther, Felix overcomes this separation of the private and the public worlds, and implies that the conclusion of the novel is therefore a harmonious and relatively optimistic one, offering a satisfactorily totalized version of true "radicalism." However, this seems to me a rather myopic and conservative reading of the novel. Felix's organicist theory of society claimed to be able to reconcile the radically divergent codes of interpretation and signification of the various classes of society, but the reader of *Felix Holt* is more aware of the separateness of these classes, which are divided by gulfs of power, wealth, and linguistic and cultural incomprehension. The novel is full of reminders of these barriers: obvious examples are the scene where Mrs. Holt's plea for help to free her son causes Mr. Lingon and Harold to burst out laughing (*FH* 43;348); the difference between the Christianity of the Rector of Treby Magna and that of Mr. Lyon; and the apparent absurdity of Mr. Lyon's desire that if Harold Transome were to marry Esther he should also join the Independent Chapel (*FH* 41;328–29). Felix attempts to demonstrate that the interests of the classes in society need not be opposed when he tries to save the Debarrys' estate from damage during the election riot, but the gulf between the classes is demonstrated when he is put in prison for his actions.

Felix may assume the unity of the social organism, but he assumes an incompatibility between the destinies of men and women which his Radicalism does not address. When Esther speaks for him in court, eventually influencing those who secure his pardon, she does what his own speeches are unable to do. However, Esther's action does not have any relation to Felix's failed political quest. He is only rescued because Esther's speech contributes to the picture, in the patronizing minds of the local gentry, that Felix is a harmless fellow, a Tory "at bottom." The novel is thus unable to figure a resolution which could incorporate political activity—based on the recognition of the determination of private life by public life—with the utopian image of a private life in which a woman had the right to speak truthfully and of her own volition. Mrs. Transome's life has been one of long enforced silence. Esther gains the right to speak, but the novel does not generalize this image of female assertiveness to a public life in which both Esther and Felix could play a significant role. The story of the biblical Esther, as Sheets points out, ends not only with the legal vindication of Mordecai, but with his elevation to a public role.[39] For Felix and Esther in George Eliot's novel, the future is only faintly indicated in the closing pages of the novel, but it is certainly one of obscurity. The repudiation of her inheritance opens up a space for Esther to stand free of patriarchal determination; she can reject the burden of male plotting, but there is no indication of the course of a truly female story. The true radicalism of *Felix Holt, the Radical* lies not in the title character, but in the momentary possibility that is opened up for the novel's all-too-often unrecognized heroine before she is enclosed once again by the imperatives of society.

7

George Eliot in the University: Some Recent Approaches

There has been a great deal of scholarly work on George Eliot in the last forty years. By editing the letters and producing a "definitive" biography, Gordon Haight made available the documentary materials that enabled a generation of scholars to investigate the intellectual background of the novels and to trace the intellectual development of the woman who became the novelist. Since that time, Eliot's relationship to higher criticism, Positivism, scientific thought, and social theory has been documented with varying degrees of thoroughness. While all this research has greatly enriched our understanding of both the historical individual Mary Ann Evans and the novelist George Eliot, it has not in itself radically altered the way that we read her novels. One must look elsewhere to find the factors which have produced genuinely new and different readings of George Eliot. Jauss's account of literary reception suggests that we read texts to seek new answers to new questions, or more specifically, to find the questions of the present which the art of the past can answer for us. Thus the text that we read is not only the product of literary evolution and of historical conditions, but also the product of the reader's own historical horizon, his or her own specific situation in history and society. It is therefore not surprising that the most challenging readings of the literature of the past—those readings which seem to alter the shape, structure, and significance of texts the perception of which has become automatized—are produced by readers whose mode of reading addresses the text forcefully with questions of present concern. It is this which makes F. R. Leavis and Virginia Woolf such important and influential critics of George Eliot: their criticism was produced under the pressure of questions of historical moment, which forced themselves on minds unusually sensitive both to these questions and to literary texts.

Leavis's mode of reading was developed by subsequent critics—among whom Barbara Hardy is prominent—into a critical methodology, with a system of governing assumptions. I have already considered one challenge to this methodology, that of Marxist criticism, and in this concluding chapter I will consider two other challenges, each of which has offered the possibility of new ways of reading. Feminist criticism has had a revolutionary impact on the way that nineteenth-century literature is perceived, and post-structuralism, in its most radical form, has challenged the humanist privileging of an overly aestheticized idea of literary discourse, and stimulated ways of reading which are attentive to the contradictory and dissonant nature of language and of the literary work.

Between the late 1960s (Kate Millet's *Sexual Politics* appeared in 1969) and the early 1980s, feminist criticism radically affected the study of literature in the Anglo-Saxon world. Although it drew on the work of earlier writers such as Virginia Woolf and Simone de Beauvoir, the women's movement of the 1970s was also characterized by a remarkable and sudden outpouring of sociological, psychological, historical, and literary studies. The effect of feminism in literary studies has been two-fold. It is now difficult to present the work of writers like D. H. Lawrence and Norman Mailer from an uncritically masculine perspective; their writings, like all literary texts, are now seen in the context of sexual politics. Secondly, a tradition of women's writing has been rediscovered, and it is now being used to construct a poetics of women's writing. This has major implications for aesthetic theory, but more immediately relevant to the present study is the fact that it has resulted in a major revaluation of nineteenth-century fiction. F. R. Leavis had suggested in *The Great Tradition* that although Charlotte Brontë could claim "no part in the great line of English fiction (it is significant that she couldn't see why any value should be attached to Jane Austen)," she nevertheless "has a permanent interest of a minor kind."[1] Since a tradition of women's fiction has been established by literary historians like Elaine Showalter, Leavis's judgment is no longer generally accepted; recent critical discussions suggest that Brontë is now regarded as an extremely important English novelist, while such comfortably Victorian gentlemen as Trollope and Thackeray have slipped from the prominent place they held in the literary histories of the first half of this century. (Leavis, of course, anticipated and contributed to the current estimation of Thackeray and Trollope.) In this section I will sketch a history of the various stages of feminist criticism, in order to show how it has struggled with George Eliot's work, and how it has significantly altered received perceptions of it. Feminist criticism provides an exemplary case of criticism which addresses past works with questions of urgent present concern—in this case questions about women's rights, the social construction of sexuality and sexual roles, and the nature of patriarchy—and which reconstitutes works of literature in their socially formative role, so that they can provide answers to these questions.

I have already, in chapter 4, contrasted the way that F. R. Leavis and

Virginia Woolf read George Eliot, but it is worth returning to this contrast for a moment. I shall focus here on *The Mill on the Floss*, since this is an important novel for many feminist critics. Leavis comments on the "emotional" tone of the novel. He suggests that "we feel an urgency, a resonance, a personal vibration, adverting us of the poignantly immediate presence of the author." This quality, Leavis suggests, entails "limitations" which "are inseparable from disastrous weaknesses in George Eliot's handling of her themes": "the emotional quality represents something, a need or hunger in George Eliot, that shows itself to be insidious company for her intelligence—apt to supplant it and take command."[2] By contrast, Virginia Woolf found in the expression of this emotional quality one of the features of George Eliot's novels which made them valuable. The exorbitant emotion depicted in her heroines is an expression of the unfulfilled aspiration of women in patriarchy: "The ancient consciousness of woman, charged with suffering and sensibility, and for so many ages dumb, seems in them to have rimmed and overflowed and uttered a demand for something—they scarcely know what—for something that is perhaps incompatible with the facts of human existence."[3] Similarly, Simone de Beauvoir found in *The Mill on the Floss* an expression of her own frustration as a young woman in an ossified society, experiencing the dilemma of wanting self-fulfilment but being expected to live for others:

> I saw my own isolation not as a proof of infamy but as a sign of my uniqueness. I couldn't see myself dying of solitude. Through the heroine I identified myself with the author: one day other adolescents would bathe with their tears a novel in which I would tell my own sad story. . . . Maggie Tulliver, like myself, was torn between others and herself: I recognized myself in her. She too was dark, loved nature, and books and life, was too headstrong to be able to observe the conventions of her respectable surroundings, and yet she was very sensitive to the criticism of a brother she adored.[4]

The Mill on the Floss, as a novel focussing on the education of a young woman, and as a novel repeating and rewriting the masculine genre of the *Bildungsroman*, has been a focal point for feminist criticism of English literature. It provides a perfect example of the way that formal deviations are motivated by extraliterary factors. The conventional *Bildungsroman* tells the story of a young man's assumption of his identity through rites of passage such as sexual initiation and discovery of a vocation, and perhaps renunciation of romantic desires and accommodation to the exigencies of the world. Goethe's *Wilhelm Meisters Lehrjahre* was read in this way by Victorian readers, including George Henry Lewes and George Eliot. But, as Susan Sniader Lanser and Evelyn Torton Beck ask in a study of critical theory: "If we posit a female hero, the same growth pattern is not only viewed as inappropriate, but yields disaster and decline. How then do we name the female *Bildungsroman*?"[5] It is possible that the celebratedly problematic nature of the ending of *The Mill on the Floss* results from precisely this problem of defining a female *Bildungsroman*. Eliot wants to follow the upward curve of the masculine model, and to end affirmatively, but at the same time she remains true to the narrative logic of woman's experience. It would be interesting to construct a full reading of *The Mill on the Floss* in relation to Goethe's novel, in order to examine more precisely, and in much greater detail than is possible here, the formal divergences, repetitions, and deviations which Eliot's text performs.[6]

There have been two major phases of Anglo-American feminist criticism[7] (although they have not followed one another in a perfect chronological sequence, and there is a great deal of overlapping), and a third seems to be in the formative process. I will describe each of these stages in turn, continuing to use Eliot's *Mill on the Floss* as a point of reference, in order to give some continuity to the narrative. In the first stage, typified by works such as *Sexual Politics*, feminist critics were primarily concerned with identifying images of women in the work of male writers, and also to some extent with evaluating the characters of female writers according to their value as role models (the latter emphasis persists in what I shall identify as the second stage). This type of feminist criticism is parallel to the Marxist criticism which concerns itself with evaluating the political tendency of literary works. A striking negative appraisal of George Eliot from such a viewpoint is found in Ellen Moers's *Literary Women*. Moers comments that "George Eliot, as her readers have always been surprised to find out, was no feminist." Thus it is not surprising that

> Dorothea Brooke in *Middlemarch* is the worst kind of product of the myth of Corinne (and the worst sort of influence on novelists like Doris Lessing) for she is good for nothing *but* to be admired. An arrogant, selfish, spoiled, rich beauty, she does little but harm in the novel. Ignorant in the extreme and mentally idle (without feeling any of the guilt of Jane Austen's heroines for their failure to read) Dorothea has little of interest to say, but a magnificent voice to say it in. . . . She also has what must be the most stunning wardrobe in Victorian fiction.[8]

I have quoted Moers because her book has been widely read; references to a number of earlier feminist dismissals of George Eliot are given in Zelda Austen's article "Why Feminist Critics Are Angry with George Eliot," which coincides with a general trend in feminist criticism towards the construction of a history and a poetics of women's writing, and a turn to the more positive and even utopian aspects of women writers who had previously not seemed to have much to say to feminists.[9] This phase has been named "gynocritics" by Elaine Showalter, and defined as "the study of women *as writers*, and its subjects are the history, styles, themes, genres and structures of writing by women; the psychodynamics of female creativity; the trajectory of the individual or collective female career; and the evolution and laws of a female literary tradition."[10] Showalter has admirably exemplified her definition in her study of the female literary tradition in English literature, *A Literature of Their Own* (first published in 1977). This work begins by attacking the "residual Great Traditionalism" which separated a few major women writers from their context in a vast activity of writing; in contrast to this approach Showalter offers a vision of "the lost continent of the female tradition [which] has risen like Atlantis from the sea of English literature."[11] Showalter's work is the product of a generous feminist humanism, and she values above all the realistic depiction of women's experience in literature. Her book tells the story of a progress towards an ever more complete realism, so that

> in the fiction of Iris Murdoch, Muriel Spark, and Doris Lessing, and the younger writers Margaret Drabble, A. S. Byatt, and Beryl Bainbridge, we are beginning to see a renaissance in women's writing that responds to the demands of Lewes and Mill for an authentically female literature, providing "woman's view of life, woman's experience." In drawing upon two centuries of the female tradition, these novelists have been able to incorporate many of the strengths of the past with a new range of language and experience.[12]

However, it would be equally possible to see writers such as Drabble and Murdoch as mere epigones of the bourgeois realist novel, which would make Showalter's triumphal progress suspect, particularly when, as Toril Moi observes, Showalter puts herself in the position, by her valorization of a Lukácsian theory of realism, of being unable to do justice to Virginia Woolf, who for Moi is the great woman writer in English of the twentieth century (and who certainly marks a divergence from the Victorian bourgeois novel in a way that Margaret Drabble does not).[13]

It is therefore not surprising that Showalter fails to respond wholly enthusiastically to George Eliot. Like Raymond Williams she fails to find the kind of answers she seeks in Eliot's texts because she addresses them in the language of the expressive realist tradition. Thus for Showalter *The Mill on the Floss* is less valuable as a study of woman's experience than *Jane Eyre*, because Eliot's book contains less rebellion and questioning of patriarchal conventions. Showalter concludes, rather like Elizabeth Ermarth and Carla Peterson, that Maggie Tulliver "is the progenitor of a heroine who identifies passivity and renunciation with womanhood, who finds it easier, more natural, and in a mystical way more satisfying, to destroy herself than to live in a world without opium or fantasy, where she must fight to survive."[14] In an interesting article which is in a sense a postscript to *A Literature of Their Own*, Showalter seems more sympathetic to George Eliot. She considers the ways in which, for twentieth-century writers, Eliot has become "an image as well as an influence in their narratives, and a model for fictional heroines."[15] This article in some ways modifies the impression of Eliot in *A Literature of Their Own* by recognizing the degree to which Eliot is a living influence on and preoccupation of the modern realist novelists

whom Showalter prizes: "If the images of Eliot in contemporary women's literature are disenchanted, her demystification as the superior woman, above pain,
conflict, and compromise, has led to a firmer acceptance of her sisterhood with
all other women."[16]

Another significant product of "gynocritics" is *The Madwoman in the Attic*,
by Sandra Gilbert and Susan Gubar. This very influential study is a reading of
nineteenth-century women's literature which emphasizes two determining aspects of a women's tradition in literature. It adapts Harold Bloom's model of
literary history by reading women's literature as a struggle against male precursors' readings of women, and it discusses in phenomenological terms the way
that women's writing is a representation of women's consciousness, which is
described as formed by experiences of confinement, disease, and neurosis. The
authors write:

> Even when we studied women's achievements in radically different genres, we found what
> began to seem a *distinctively female literary tradition*, a tradition that has been approached and
> appreciated by many women readers and writers but which no one had yet defined in its
> entirety. Images of enclosure and escape, fantasies in which maddened doubles functioned as
> asocial surrogates for docile selves, metaphors of physical discomfort manifested in frozen
> landscapes and fiery interiors—such patterns recurred throughout this tradition, along with
> obsessive depictions of diseases like anorexia, agoraphobia, and claustrophobia.[17]

Instead of treating Eliot's work chronologically, and locating her in some sort
of largely male intellectual and literary tradition, Gilbert and Gubar begin with
the minor short story "The Lifted Veil," which they see as an important key to
understanding George Eliot. Its science-fiction qualities make "The Lifted Veil"
a very different work from Eliot's novels, and it provides the authors with a way
of linking Eliot's work with the tradition of "female Gothic" and of evaluating
her "ambivalent response to Romanticism" (p. 462). Gilbert and Gubar largely
ignore the cognitive aspects and historical contexts of Eliot's work, in order to
concentrate on the way that her rewriting of male stories, myths, and genres
enables her to represent, by indirection, the inner experience of nineteenth-
century women. In one of a series of metaphors of duplicity and concealment
which they apply to women's writing, they suggest that her male pseudonym
and the male narrative voice of the early novels serve as a kind of "camouflage
. . . to conceal the dramatic focus of the plot" (p. 491).

The effect of Gilbert and Gubar's commentary is to view Eliot's fiction as
an example of a trans-historical female consciousness, which embodies feminine
resistance to patriarchy by its use of the equally trans-historical mythological
figures of the angel and the madwoman. This leads them, like Nina Auerbach,
to see *The Mill on the Floss* as a more angry and rebellious book than did
Showalter.[18] They comment on the doubleness of the archetypal images of
women, and show how when Maggie Tulliver tries to become an angel of

renunciation she instead makes herself an angel of destruction, enacting the author's "female (even feminist) vengeance" (p. 491). The following passage from their discussion of *The Mill on the Floss* is typical of Gilbert and Gubar's mode of argument:

> Like Lucy Snowe, Maggie is both Jael and Sisera, both a Satanic inflictor of pain who pushes her pretty cousin Lucy Deane into the mud and a repentant follower of Thomas à Kempis who associates love with self-inflicted martyrdom. In addition, besides being both Madonna and Medusa, Maggie is nature's child, for her rapt, dreamy feelings constantly carry her away in floods of feeling suggestive of the rhythms of the river that empowers the mill. But the brother to whom she is so passionately devoted inherits the mill itself and is thereby associated with the grinding, crushing process that transforms primordial matter into civilized stuff fit for consumption, much as Nelly Dean in *Wuthering Heights* is identified with the secondary, socializing arts of cooking. (p. 492)

This illustrates the highly allusive nature of Gilbert and Gubar's prose. Their analogies and mythological parallels often serve to dissociate Eliot's writing from one's received ideas about it, and their phenomenological method at times provides brilliant insights about the nature of women's experience, and suggests the basis of a possible poetics of women's writing. However, the passage quoted also reveals one of the weaknesses of their approach: in their development of the meaning of the image of the mill at the end of the passage the authors lose sight of Eliot's text altogether, and substitute for it their own mythological system. While they rightly observe the way that literary genres are largely male constructions, "devised by male authors to tell male stories about the world" (p. 67), they do not take much interest in the way that women writers have attempted to modify these genres in particular works. In other words, Gilbert and Gubar, like many phenomenological critics, do not pay much attention to the specificity of the individual work, and the complex overdetermination of its formal features.

Gilbert and Gubar in fact run the risk of subsuming all literature, or at least all women's literature, into "one single thing," to quote Paul de Man on a similar tendency in Northrop Frye's poetics.[19] The cumulative effect of their style, with its plethora of mythic parallels and references to archetypal situations—as illustrated above—is to sever the intertextual links between the works of the writers they study and other literary works and other discourses, and thereby to cut them away from their location in history. Instead, they tend to relate the works back to their author, both to the specific biographical facts which are known about her life and to a more generalized female experience or consciousness which speaks through all the works they study. Moi criticizes Gilbert and Gubar for implying that

> in a given patriarchal society all women (because they are biologically female) will adopt certain strategies to counter patriarchal oppression. These strategies will be "female" since they will be the same for all women submitted to such conditions. Such an argument relies

heavily on the assumption that patriarchal ideology is homogeneous and all-encompassing in its effects.[20]

The effect of this assumption is that Gilbert and Gubar curiously diminish George Eliot's achievement. The fact that a "fallen woman" could become a Victorian sage, the aesthetic teacher of a whole generation, suggests that there were major contradictions within Victorian patriarchy. In her writing, Eliot appropriates ideas from philosophy, science, anthropology, and sociology, and reconsiders them as both a woman and a Victorian intellectual. A feminist reading which ignores this fact has the paradoxical effect of relegating Eliot to a ghetto of neurotic disease and confinement from which she had managed to escape (although admittedly not without bearing the scars of the struggle, which are clearly visible in the kind of experience which Gilbert and Gubar record in their chapter on Eliot). A valuable corrective to the excessively personalized, subjective, and phenomenological reading of *The Madwoman in the Attic* is Gillian Beer's recent book on George Eliot, which restores the intellectual structures of Eliot's fiction to the centre of critical attention, but which insists throughout that Eliot was, contrary to Ellen Moers's assertion, a feminist.[21]

The most recent stage of feminist theory and criticism has been the attempt to construct a poetics of feminine writing which does not rely on New Critical notions of the ontology of a work of art, on phenomenological theories of the subject, or Lukácsian theories of realism and reflection. This third stage of critical thought is attempting to rethink aesthetic categories themselves from a politically engaged position, and it draws on the work of Derrida, Lacan, and such French feminists as Hélène Cixous, Luce Irigaray, and Julia Kristeva. In her introduction to feminist literary theory, Toril Moi seeks to make this type of feminist thought better known in the English-speaking world, and she undertakes an extended critique of Showalter's chapter on Virginia Woolf from a Kristevan standpoint.[22] Moi convincingly draws detailed parallels between the literary theories of Showalter and Lukács, since both seek to rid the world of contradiction and ambiguity, believing in the value of a totalizing realism which effects the reunification of public and private, and in the ability of an author to express such a vision in an organic form. For Kristeva, and for other post-structuralists, however, language and literature are characterized by their "already written" quality. All writing is intertextual, and therefore its meaning is largely shaped by such factors as gender, genre, class, literary institutions, and discursive formations. Kristeva has been greatly influenced by V. N. Vološinov, who, by emphasizing the contextual nature of meaning, endeavoured to dissolve the boundaries between linguistics, rhetoric, and poetics, in favour of semiotics.[23] The influence of such post-structuralist thinkers as Derrida, Kristeva, Lacan, and Foucault has become prominent in feminist literary theory and criticism, and it seems likely that the work of such critics as Moi and Nancy

K. Miller will result in an increasing tendency to historicize feminist literary theory and criticism, and to deconstruct its belief in the privileged author and her autonomous literary work.[24] Several recent essays on *The Mill on the Floss*, of which Nancy K. Miller's is the most noteworthy, exemplify the post-structuralist turn in feminist criticism.[25] In "Emphasis Added: Plots and Plausibilities in Women's Fiction," Miller attempts to separate the plots of women's fiction from the lives of women, and thus to steer feminist criticism away from its concern with biography. She begins with a discussion of Mme. de Lafayette's *La Princesse de Clèves*, noting that upon publication it met charges of *invraisemblance*, or "implausibility." The critics who made this charge believed that "art should not imitate life but *re*inscribe received ideas about the representation of life in art. To depart from the limits of common sense (tautologically, to be extravagant) is to risk exclusion from the canon" (p. 36). Miller suggests that to write a fiction which puzzles by its contravention of received ideas that can be expressed in maxims is "to fly in the face of a certain ideology (of the text and its context), to violate a grammar of motives that describes while prescribing, in this instance what wives, not to say women, should or should not do," and she asks whether such "ungrammaticalities" characterize women's fiction (p. 37). She suggests in her analysis of *La Princesse de Clèves* that the process of "demaximization" the novel effects is an example of the difference of female writing from male. Similarly, in *The Mill on the Floss* the "implausibility" of the ending is to be explained by turning away from maxims. In fact, Miller argues, attacks on the implausibility of women's writing result from the fact that

> the maxims that pass for the truth of human experience, and the encoding of that experience in literature, are organizations, when they are not fantasies, of the dominant culture. To read women's literature is to see and hear repeatedly a chafing against the "unsatisfactory reality" contained in the maxim. Everywhere in *The Mill on the Floss* one can read a protest against the division of labor that grants men the world and women love. (pp. 46–47)

For Miller:

> The plots of women's literature are not about "life" and solutions in any therapeutic sense, nor should they be. They are about the plots of literature itself, about the constraints the maxim places on rendering a female life in fiction. Mme. de Lafayette quietly, George Eliot less silently, both italicize by the demaximization of their heroines' texts the difficulty of curing plot of life, and life of certain plots. (p. 46)

Miller's article recognizes the socially formative (*gesellschaftsbildende*) nature of literature; rejecting notions that literature is either a reflection of reality or an exemplary model for imitation, she nevertheless links the literary text with the extraliterary sphere of lived praxis. And like so many other feminists, she finds *The Mill on the Floss* a particularly important text.

All people of broad, strong sense have an instinctive repugnance to the man of maxims; because such people early discern that the mysterious complexity of our life is not to be embraced by maxims, and that to lace ourselves up in formulas of that sort is to repress all the divine promptings and inspirations that spring from growing insight and sympathy. And the man of maxims is the popular representative of the minds that are guided in their moral judgment solely by general rules, thinking that these will lead them to justice by a ready-made patent method, without the trouble of exerting patience, discrimination, impartiality—without any care to assure themselves whether they have the insight that comes from a hardly-earned estimate of temptation, or from a life vivid and intense enough to have created a wide fellow-feeling with all that is human. (*MF* 7,3;438)

My discussion of feminist criticism ends with Nancy Miller's view of women's writing as a process of "demaximization," or of writing against the authority of a hegemonic discourse. The final critics whom I will consider in this study undertake an even more radical demaximization, which seeks to expose the fundamental doubleness or indeterminacy of all literary discourse. However, the radicalism is more in the area of epistemological claims than in the sphere of social praxis. By an examination of two essays by J. Hillis Miller and one by Cynthia Chase, I will argue that the Yale School's mode of criticism in fact represents a *maximizing* discourse in its own right, which works—in the three essays on Eliot in question—rigorously to exclude the kind of questions asked by Marxist and feminist critics, and which approaches literature with a narrow set of presuppositions ratified by reference to the originating masters, Derrida and Nietzsche. Miller's work, in spite of these limitations, is valuable as a mode of rhetorical analysis. He draws attention to metaphoric structures and contradictions in Eliot's novels, and to the philosophical assumptions that inform them, in a remarkably lucid and precise style; he reads Eliot with a subtlety hardly equalled among critics of English fiction, and he commands an enviable knowledge of literature and philosophy. Yet his analyses have a disturbingly hermetic quality, ignoring the contextual, intertextual, and interdiscursive nature of meaning in literary works, and the kind of determining factors of literary production and reception that I have been trying to emphasize throughout this study. By so ruthlessly repressing the historical, the ideological, and the relation of literary and extraliterary discourses, and by focussing exclusively on canonical works of "great literature" without reference to the literary horizons in which they were produced, Miller runs the risk of erasing the social function of literature (one might less charitably attribute this to him as a covert design). In a detailed reading of Miller's career, Donald Pease identifies this danger in Miller's criticism, suggesting that he "verges dangerously close to conscripting deconstructive strategies as forms of what Herbert Marcus[e] earlier referred to as 'repressive tolerance.' "[26]

My account of the Yale criticism is an attempt to define the ambivalent nature of my own response to it. The preceding pages certainly bear traces of the influence of the Yale critics, and especially of Paul de Man. But my primary commitment is to a mode of criticism which transcends the scholastic world of Miller's abysses and indeterminacies, and which sees literature as embedded in history and society in addition to having its own specificity and relative autonomy. By ignoring the historicity of literature, Miller propagates the insidiously North American form of pluralistic tolerance which allows any challenge to the system a place to stand and speak, while at the same time ensuring that no one will take what it has to say seriously. Deconstruction has potentially radical and far-reaching implications, but Miller, as a "wily conservative,"[27] neutralizes these. If literature is entirely outside society it can have no bearing on social practice, however radical are the ideas it thematizes. It is therefore necessary to put Miller's interpretations of Eliot in a wider frame by looking at the horizons of expectations in which both Eliot's work and Miller's criticism of it were produced. My reading of Miller thus returns me to my beginning, to the criticism of Jauss, which should now also be seen in the new context of the sharply engaged criticism of Marxists and feminists. The questions asked by Marxists and feminists are part of the current horizon of critical discourse, and they may be able to correct a lack of focus in Jauss's own social programme.

In "Narrative and History" Miller examines the relationship between fiction and history. He makes use both of Nietzsche's critique of Hegel and of the theories of Walter Benjamin. Miller begins by asserting that notions of fictional form "are displaced versions of ideas about history."[28] Assumptions of *arche* and *telos*, of unity, progress, and causality, characterize the Western idea of history, and

> all the elements of this system of ideas about history may be transferred without distortion to the customary notion of the form of fiction. The formal structure of a novel is usually conceived of as the gradual emergence of its meaning. This coincides with its end, the fulfillment of the teleology of the work. The end is the retrospective revelation of the unity of the whole, its "organic unity." (pp. 460–61)

The corollary of this is that if a novel "'deconstructs' the assumptions of 'realism' in fiction, it also turns out to 'deconstruct' naive notions about history or about the writing of history" (p. 462).

Middlemarch, commonly considered as the "English masterpiece" of realistic fiction (p. 462), is then taken as an example of this deconstructive process. It shows each main character operating under a mystified belief that the details he or she confronts all can be explained by a single master key which unlocks the secret of their coherence (pp. 464–66). George Eliot's narrative deconstructs its own historicist ground:

> The concepts of origin, end, and continuity are replaced by the categories of repetition, of difference, of discontinuity, of openness, and of the free and contradictory struggle of individual human energies, each seen as a center of interpretation, which means misinterpretation, of the whole. History, for George Eliot, is not chaos, but it is governed by no ordering principle or aim. (p. 467)

Thus, "the only origin is an act of interpretation, that is, an act of the will to power imposed on a prior 'text,' which may be the world itself seen as a text, a set of signs" (p. 468). This Nietzschean world, for Miller, allows acts of free moral choice to George Eliot's characters, so that although "Dorothea's life does not have a given aim any more than it has an other than accidental origin, nevertheless she may give it an aim, as she u'.imately does in her decision to marry Ladislaw" (p. 468).

There are several fundamental problems with Miller's logic in "Narrative and History." He begins by assuming a global coherence between the realist project of fiction and what he sees as both a Hegelian, and more generally the Western logocentric, idea of history. He does not consider the possibility that George Eliot herself examines and possibly questions radically this idea of history in *Middlemarch*, and that she might address the problem of history directly rather than deconstructing it, as it were, accidentally, through the unconscious operation of textuality. Her study of higher criticism and other aspects of nineteenth-century thought had made Eliot acutely aware of the problematic of history which Miller addresses. She situates *Middlemarch* neither at the extreme of the simplified Hegelian model which Miller sets up as a straw theory of history, nor at the radically decentred libertarian and Nietzschean extreme celebrated in Miller's deconstructive reading. She recognizes, with Miller, that "signs are small measurable things, but interpretations are illimitable" (*M* 3;24), but she also attempts to analyze the way that interpretations are produced by particular discourses, so that it is possible to gain some knowledge of the nature of these proliferating ways of seeing things. The characters in the novel discover very painfully the way that social circumstances limit and deform the projects they have formed for reading the text of the world and defining their relationship to it. The examples of Lydgate and Dorothea are the most obvious:

> What he really cared for was a medium for his work, a vehicle for his ideas; and after all, was he not bound to prefer the object of getting a good hospital, where he could demonstrate the specific distinctions of fever and test therapeutic results, before anything else connected with this chaplaincy? For the first time Lydgate was feeling the hampering threadlike pressure of small social conditions, and their frustrating complexity. (*M* 18;176)

> Marriage, which was to bring guidance into worthy and imperative occupation, had not yet freed her from the gentlewoman's oppressive liberty: it had not even filled her leisure with the ruminant joy of unchecked tenderness. Her blooming full-pulsed youth stood there in a moral imprisonment which made itself one with the chill, colourless, narrowed landscape, with the

shrunken furniture, the never-read books, and the ghostly stag in a pale fantastic world that seemed to be vanishing from the daylight. (*M* 28;268)

Eliot implies that the way to emancipation from these circumstances is above all by means of *knowledge*, but the novel is far from being a Positivist utopia. We see far more failures to attain knowledge in the novel than examples of it, as the narrator suggests in a particularly important passage:

That opposition to the New Fever Hospital which Lydgate had sketched to Dorothea was, like other oppositions, to be viewed in many different lights. He regarded it as a mixture of jealousy and dunder-headed prejudice. Mr. Bulstrode saw in it not only medical jealousy but a determination to thwart himself, prompted mainly by hatred of that vital religion of which he had striven to be an effectual lay representative—a hatred which certainly found pretexts apart from religion such as were only too easy to find in the entanglements of human action. These might be called the ministerial views. But oppositions have the illimitable range of objections at command, which need never stop short at the boundary of knowledge, but can draw for ever on the vasts of ignorance. (*M* 45;433)

This quotation clearly shows that objections, like interpretations, have a way of ramifying and proliferating when there is no transcendental ground of certainty. Eliot applies the same word "illimitable" to both "interpretations" and "objections." She refuses, in *Middlemarch* as elsewhere, to figure "knowledge" as a transcendental ground. The above passage indicates that "knowledge" has boundaries in a way that "objections" do not, and that the "ministerial views" of two institutionalized discourses are equally incapable of stopping the multiplication of lights in which the affair of the New Fever Hospital can be viewed. To this extent the passage states what I take to be J. Hillis Miller's basic point about *Middlemarch*. However, Eliot's narrator does not approve of this situation of infinite deferral, and the text suggests that, although it may be unavoidable, there are ways of dealing with the proliferation of objections and gaining a space in which to construct a purpose which is more than a voluntaristic declaration of intent.

Middlemarch opens up possibilities for its main characters which they do not realize, but which exist as moments in which it is possible for the future to be both different from and more purposeful than the past. Miller's celebration of the decentred conclusion of the novel does not allow for these possibilities, because for Miller all hierarchies can be subverted or deconstructed. But *Middlemarch* clearly valorizes certain terms above others, for example in the way that Dorothea's experience is judged. She cannot, as Miller implies, simply give her life an aim; this is surely the whole point of the novel, and especially the point of the Prelude and the Finale. Her life has no given aim at the beginning of the novel, not because she inhabits a Nietzschean groundless universe, but more immediately because she is a gentlewoman, for whom no vocation is prescribed, but whose lot is predetermined as "the gentlewoman's oppressive liberty" (*M* 28;268). Similarly, the Finale is far more tragic than celebratory. Eliot does not celebrate the diffusion of causality among an infinite number of connections; rather she laments the waste of a life which might have been lived otherwise: "Her full nature, like that river of which Cyrus broke the strength, spent itself in channels which had no great name on the earth" (*M* Finale;825). The word "spent" obviously includes a sense of waste, as does the diffusion of the novel's imagery of the stream of life into "channels which had no great name on the earth" (nothing in the novel suggests the existence of anywhere else where a compensatory "great name" might be located). Miller's reading ignores the involvement of *Middlemarch* in the "woman question" of its time, and ignores the questions which twentieth-century women have been asking the novel. This is not in itself necessarily reprehensible; what is regrettable is that his reading not only ignores these questions but considers the novel in a way which excludes them.

Miller considers another aspect of the language of *Middlemarch* in "Optic and Semiotic in *Middlemarch*" (1975). There he argues that the novel both implies an omniscient narrator and deconstructs the very nature of omniscience by demonstrating that all seeing is interpretation, so that there can be no objective stance.[29] The novel embodies this contradiction in two contradictory models of metaphor. Miller quotes a famous passage from *The Mill on the Floss* (*MF* 2,1;123) in order to show that already there she had formulated "her recognition of the deconstructive powers of figurative language, its undoing of any attempt to make a complete, and completely coherent, picture of human life" (p. 144). Once again Miller sets up two false extremes. If we cannot know everything, he seems to be saying, we should renounce all action and attempts at interpretation, since we will only *mis*interpret; instead we should celebrate the aporia which lies at the heart of being. The force of Miller's argument depends on the assumption that one can "double-read" *Middlemarch* as the combat of two extremes of omniscience and radical skepticism, which are embodied in two different types of figure. One reading assumes an omniscient narrator whose knowledge is as absolute as that of God, and thus assumes a mystified view of language and epistemology; the other reading recognizes that all knowledge depends on metaphor and that all interpretations are "false interpretations" because all naming is "falsification" (p. 143). However, by introducing the notion of "falsification" Miller implies a transcendental basis of objective knowledge, against which his deconstructive reading pronounces acts of naming to be falsification. But if naming *constitutes* its object, which is a possible reading of George Eliot, then the dichotomy between Miller's two readings would be broken.

George Eliot does not ever assume that we could or should know everything, so for her the failure of such an ambition is less catastrophic than it seems to be to Miller. She is more concerned with the instrumental uses of knowledge, and with protecting the forms of knowledge which produce beneficial results from the effects of stupidity and misinterpretations. Eliot's skepticism is therefore not complete, but rather sufficient to prevent her from claiming transcendental status for any claim she makes. In *Middlemarch* she clearly demonstrates the contingent and tentative status of the "truths" spoken by her narrator. The narrator is located in history, and distinguished from Fielding's very different omniscient narrator, who could assume far more agreement with his assumptions and judgments, and who has the leisure to digress:

> Fielding lived when the days were longer (for time, like money, is measured by our needs), when summer afternoons were spacious, and the clock ticked slowly in the winter evenings. We belated historians must not linger after his example; and if we did so, it is probable that our chat would be thin and eager, as if delivered from a camp-stool in a parrot-house. (*M* 15;138–39)

Unlike Fielding's narrator, George Eliot's does not presume to be able to expatiate "over that tempting range of relevancies called the universe" (*M* 15;139).

Another way in which Eliot avoids absolute claims for her narrator is by emphasizing the "literariness" of *Middlemarch*, which, like *The Mill on the Floss* in Nancy Miller's reading, is at least as much about the plots of literature as about the lives of women. In "Narrative and History" J. Hillis Miller based part of his argument on the fact that *Middlemarch* is not obviously an antinovel, but rather "solidly within the tradition of realistic fiction" (p. 462). However, the omniscient narrator is a device which lends itself to the shattering of the illusion of realism, and, as Gilbert and Gubar maintain in *The Madwoman in the Attic*, *Middlemarch* is "a self-conscious literary text."[30] They mention the chapter epigraphs, which are a significant way in which the narrator's authority is relativized through the provision of a built-in form of intertextuality. The epigraphs juxtapose the narrative discourse with a series of fragments, from famous texts or invented by George Eliot, which are not part of the narrator's own discourse, and which interact with it.[31] The epigraphs come from a diverse range of literary works, and they introduce parodic, satirical, even carnivalizing elements which play against the more judicious and scientific tone of the narrator. For example, chapter 2 begins with a passage from Cervantes, which emphasizes the quixotic nature of Dorothea's aspirations; chapter 5 begins with a quotation from the *Anatomy of Melancholy* that presents a satirical perspective on Casaubon, which the narrator does not so overtly allow herself. Miller is disingenuously relying on a naive theory of realism, when he must be fully aware of the way that, for example, Barthes's *S/Z* shows at length the way that literary realism is produced by a series of "codes," while even a critic like George Levine, who is concerned to defend realism against its structuralist

demythologizers, nevertheless shows the way it depends on literary conventions.[32]

Middlemarch does not offer any positive—in the Comtean or more general
sense—solution to the confusing situation in which it depicts its heroine. It does,
however, permit an opening up of possibilities for Dorothea before some of
them are closed once again by her marriage to Ladislaw. Significantly, this is
done through images drawn from religious allegory, but they are offered here
without their metaphysical freight, as emblems of a social task:

> She opened her curtains, and looked out towards the bit of road that lay in view, with fields
> beyond, outside the entrance-gates. On the road there was a man with a bundle on his back
> and a woman carrying her baby; in the field she could see figures moving—perhaps the
> shepherd with his dog. Far off in the bending sky was the pearly light; and she felt the largeness
> of the world and the manifold wakings of men to labour and endurance. She was a part of that
> involuntary, palpitating life, and could neither look out on it from her luxurious shelter as a
> mere spectator, nor hide her eyes in selfish complaining. (*M* 80;777)

Miller's essays, for all their attention to the texture of the novel, do not allow
for this opening towards the future and towards society which is what makes
an analysis of *Middlemarch* a worthwhile task in the first place. Perhaps the
best way to sum Miller up is to see him as a New Critic who has inverted all the
assumptions of the New Criticism without transforming the nature of its critical
practice. This is the conclusion of Paul A. Bové, in an excellent discussion of
the Yale critics:

> The similarities in technique between New Criticism and deconstruction produce a critical
> impasse not easily broken. Since neither New Criticism nor deconstruction bothers to account
> for its own function and position historically in society—precisely because they are both
> radically anti-historicist—even the most sophisticated employment of the latest reading tech-
> niques merely repeats and extends a power formation already in place.[33]

Cynthia Chase's article on *Daniel Deronda* is a far less interesting piece
of Yale-style criticism. Indeed, I am only mentioning it because it has gained a
great deal of attention, perhaps because it recycles the Yale way of reading as
an easily learned method which can be readily applied to any text. Chase uses
a frivolous letter by Hans Meyrick to Daniel Deronda (*DD* 52;597–602) as an
allegory of the novel as a whole. She maintains that when Meyrick's letter refers
to the "present causes of past effects" it draws attention to the double structure
of the novel, which requires the narrative of Deronda's origin to be read in two
ways: "On the one hand, the narrator's account emphatically affirms its causal
character. On the other hand, the plot and the overall strategy of the novel
conspicuously call attention to its status as the effect of tactical requirements."[34]
So far all Chase has done, as commentators on her interpretation have pointed
out, is to confuse plot and story, or at least to express astonishment at the fact

that plot is an ordering of story.[35] She is not able to put this insight to any significant interpretive use, however, although she seems to believe that her deconstruction of Deronda's identity in the novel has alarming implications for Western metaphysics: "Since Deronda is the character whose consciousness coincides most closely with that of the narrator, and who thus represents the exemplary subject, the deconstruction of his identity has radical implications for the concept of the subject in general."[36]

In order that this study of George Eliot does not end in the bathos of Cynthia Chase's facile deconstruction of the concept of the subject, it may be advisable to attempt a brief recapitulation of what has been said. My aim in this history has been to read both George Eliot's writings and writings about them through the dual consciousness of an awareness of present questions and a willingness to listen to the alterity of past texts. I have sought to avoid the implication that literary texts are somehow stable entities, which can be measured and weighed by judicious critical tools. Rather, they seem to me unstable, liable to change shape according to the presuppositions of the perceiver, but they also have an influence on the perceiver's way of seeing and may alter it. To change the metaphor, "George Eliot" is not a monological deity who appears before those who formulate the right question. She is rather a goddess capable of multiple incarnations, and who has appeared in different forms to differently situated believers, none of whom has access to an empyrean realm inhabited by an unchanging presence. George Eliot has something to say to all who have enough faith to seek her and invoke her, and so is able to answer very different questions; but there are some faiths to which she will have little to say, and some believers to whom she will not appear to partake of divinity.

My "pre-judgments" have led me to regard highly Virginia Woolf's criticism of George Eliot, and to find something of value, contrary to popular taste, in the criticism of F. R. Leavis. I also admire J. Hillis Miller's skill as a reader, but am puzzled by the narrow uses he makes of it. One of the aims of this book has been to transcend the limitations of formalist criticism, of which J. Hillis Miller seems to me the latest influential exemplar in the North American tradition. Gerald Graff observes that

> deconstructive textual transgressions have obliquely served to patronize literature and keep it on its cultural pedestal, just as much as New Critical organic-unity readings did—and not just because deconstructionists have tended to deal with canonized texts. . . . The New Critical fetish of unity is replaced by a fetish of disunity, aporias, and texts that "differ from themselves," but criticism continues to "valorize" that complexity in excess of rational reformulation that has been the honored criterion since the forties.[37]

As I have worked on this book I have realized that it is a small part of a growing movement within literary studies to situate literature within history once more, but a history understood not in the simplistic manner of the positivist paradigm, as "background," but instead as the "cultural text, which is the matrix or master code that the literary text both depends upon and modifies."[38] My particular contribution to this movement has been to develop the implications of Jauss's *Rezeptionsästhetik*, which I see as a valuable theory of literary history because of its mediation of specifically literary history and the processes of general history. In addition I have sought to accommodate reception theory to the issues posed by Marxist and feminist criticism. The latter especially has a great deal to teach us not only about issues of gender, but about methodology in the practice of literary history. As Judith Newton argues, "barely alluded to in most of the histories of 'new historicism' so far are what were in fact the mother roots—the women's movement and the feminist theory and feminist scholarship which grew from it."[39]

Marxist criticism has the great virtues of relating literature to nonliterary discourses and social structures, and of insisting on the political nature of even the most abstruse academic investigation, and therefore the political responsibility of the investigator. Post-structuralist theory has made us read literary texts with more scrupulous attention to their language and rhetoric. For these reasons I have found these approaches valuable in my thinking about literature, but I remain convinced that the work of Jauss offers the most comprehensive attempt at formulating a theoretical basis for a new critical practice. Jauss's own essays on literature have both illustrated and developed his theoretical contributions. In these concluding remarks I will reiterate what I see as the most important contributions of reception theory.

Marxist theory provides a more sharply defined political agenda than does Jauss, and for this reason I have pushed reception theory much closer to Marxism than Jauss himself would probably think was legitimate. However, those Marxist theories which resolutely exclude an idealist component are unable to account for the role of literature in society, and for the enduring effect of literature (the question which puzzles Marx in the *Einleitung zur Kritik der politischen Ökonomie*). Marxist critics who assert the primacy of the economic base of society over the cultural superstructure are forced to concentrate exclusively on literary *production*, or at least to view literary reception in a highly simplistic manner. Western Marxism has tended to concentrate on questions of culture more than has the Marxist-Leninist tradition, as can be seen in the writings of the Frankfurt School or the English New Left. But such thinkers frequently focus on the negative aspects of culture, seeing it at times as nothing more than a giant conspiracy to control minds. Against both schools of Marxists, Jauss asserts that literature is capable of a socially formative role, and that it is able to formulate alternative ways of thinking, perceiving, and feeling. In making this assertion Jauss is not falling into a naive humanist belief that literature exists in a realm of pure consciousness, as though above the wreckage of history. Rather, he locates literature at all times within history, but asserts its power to affect history.

Jauss's concept of the "reception" of literature is a very broad one. A study of the reception of a literary work can include an investigation into the way that actual historical readers concretized it, as in the case of the readings of *Madame Bovary* recorded in the transcript of the proceedings against the novel. But the horizon of expectations can also be projected from the text itself, and in some cases—as in the medieval texts with which Jauss began his career—it must be so projected, since documentary evidence of the historical reception of a work is not always available. This aspect of reception theory incorporates a phenomenological hermeneutics which utilizes the distance between work and interpreter as a basis of constructing an interpretation.

Jauss's work is an important contribution to the theory and practice of literary history. He has absorbed the work of the Russian Formalists and Prague structuralists, which constitutes the most significant advance over the positivist models for literary history, but Jauss takes them further in two ways. His insistence on the relationship of literary history to "general history" checks a tendency towards narrow formalism in the Russian, and to some extent in the Czech theorists, and allows for the writing of literary history from a politically engaged position. Secondly, Jauss makes literary history inseparable from literary interpretation by his awareness of the hermeneutic issues involved in literary studies. Just as there can be no literary-historical statement without literary interpretation, so all literary criticism depends upon acknowledged or unacknowledged historical assumptions. While literary history is the dialectical process of formal innovation, repetition, and deviation, one can only describe the formal properties of literature through interpretation. The texts which are canonized and made the objects of literary study are valued for reasons which are not purely formal, but which incorporate the extra-aesthetic sphere of general history. Jauss's theory recognizes these interrelationships in a subtle and profound manner, drawing on such diverse sources as literary sociology, Marxism, phenomenology, the aesthetics of Jan Mukařovský, and the hermeneutics of Hans-Georg Gadamer. It provides a promising basis for literary study, especially if modified by more empirical, and also more politically committed, approaches. There are a number of ways in which reception theory could make further contributions to the study of George Eliot. I think that valuable work could be done on the relationship between Eliot and Goethe, which has been inexplicably .neglected by almost all George Eliot scholars, on the place of Eliot's texts in nineteenth-century literary history and on the re-reading of the philosophical tradition in Eliot's fiction. Such investigation would in its ideal form unite formal analysis, historical scholarship, and an awareness of the various functions of literature in society. It would embody an awareness of both the extent to which discourse is socially produced and of the possibilities of being which are opened up through literature. Eliot is profoundly aware of both of these aspects of human existence. In *Middlemarch* she dramatizes in a profound manner the interaction of the public and the private in all the characters, and most memorably in the depiction of Dorothea:

> What she would resolve to do that day did not yet seem quite clear, but something that she could achieve stirred her as with an approaching murmur which would soon gather distinctness. . . . Dorothea wished to acknowledge that she had not the less an active life before her because she had buried a private joy. (*M* 80;777–78)

> Certainly those determining acts of her life were not ideally beautiful. They were the mixed result of young and noble impulse struggling amidst the conditions of an imperfect social state, in which great feelings will often take the aspect of error, and great faith the aspect of illusion. For there is no creature whose inward being is so strong that it is not greatly determined by what lies outside it. (*M* Finale; 824–25)

Notes

Chapter 1

1. Paul de Man, "Literary History and Literary Modernity," in *Blindness and Insight*, 2nd ed. (Minneapolis: University of Minnesota Press, 1983), p. 165.

2. These matters are briefly discussed in Wlad Godzich, introduction to Hans Robert Jauss, *Aesthetic Experience and Literary Hermeneutics*, trans. Michael Shaw (Minneapolis: University of Minnesota Press, 1982), pp. vii–xxiv, and at greater length in Peter Uwe Hohendahl, *The Institution of Criticism* (Ithaca: Cornell University Press, 1982).

3. See Edward Pechter, "The New Historicism and Its Discontents: Politicizing Renaissance Drama," *PMLA*, 102 (1987), 292–303.

4. For the word *idealist* see Hans Robert Jauss, "The Idealist Embarrassment: Observations on Marxist Aesthetics," trans. Peter Heath, *New Literary History*, 7 (1975), 191–208. For McGann see Marjorie Perloff, "Ca(n)non to the Right of Us, Ca(n)non to the Left of Us: A Plea for Difference," *New Literary History*, 18 (1987), 633–56. Among McGann's many significant contributions to literary history and criticism in the last few years, his *A Critique of Modern Textual Criticism* (Chicago and London: University of Chicago Press, 1983) is especially noteworthy, setting out the basis of a materialist theory of textual scholarship.

5. "Paradigmawechsel in der Literaturwissenschaft," *Linguistische Berichte*, no. 3 (1969), 44–56. Translations are my own. Subsequent references are given parenthetically in the text.

6. "Literary studies" seems to me the closest translation of "*Literaturwissenschaft*," and preferable to the rendering "literary theory" used by Timothy Bahti in his translation of Hans Robert Jauss, *Toward an Aesthetic of Reception* (Minneapolis: University of Minnesota Press, 1982).

7. Jean-Paul Sartre, *What Is Literature?*, trans. Bernard Frechtman (New York: Harper & Row, 1949). For discussions of the sociology of literature see Robert C. Holub, *Reception Theory* (London and New York: Methuen, 1984), pp. 45–52; Peter Uwe Hohendahl, "Introduction to Reception Aesthetics," trans. Marc Silberman, *New German Critique*, 10 (1977), 29–63 [this is a translation of Hohendahl's introduction to a collection of essays he edited on reception theory, *Sozialgeschichte und Wirkungsästhetik* (Frankfurt: Athenäum, 1974)]. Further perspectives on the sociology of literature can be found in a recent issue of *Critical Inquiry* devoted to the topic, vol. 14, no. 3 (Spring 1988).

8. Two influential collections of essays on this topic are Susan R. Suleiman and Inge Crosman, eds., *The Reader in the Text* (Princeton: Princeton University Press, 1980); and Jane P.

Tompkins, ed., *Reader-Response Criticism* (Baltimore and London: Johns Hopkins University Press, 1980).

9. *Phenomenological Hermeneutics and the Study of Literature* (Toronto: University of Toronto Press, 1987), pp. 22–23.

10. Hans-Georg Gadamer, *Truth and Method*, no trans. (1975; rpt. New York: Crossroad, 1984), p. xiii. Subsequent references are given parenthetically in the text.

11. Holub, p. 53.

12. See Friedrich Schiller, "Was heisst und zu welchem Ende studiert man Universalsgeschichte?—Eine akademische Antrittsrede," in *Historische Schriften*, vol. 4 of *Sämtliche Werke*, ed. Gerhard Fricke et al. (München: Carl Hanser, 1962), pp. 749–67.

13. *Literaturgeschichte als Provokation der Literaturwissenschaft* (Konstanz: Universitätsverlag, 1967). A revised version of the essay appears in *Literaturgeschichte als Provokation* (Frankfurt: Suhrkamp, 1970), pp. 144–208.

14. *Toward an Aesthetic of Reception*, pp. 9–10. Subsequent references are given parenthetically in the text.

15. "*La douceur du foyer*: Lyric Poetry of the Year 1857 as a Model for the Communication of Social Norms," in *Aesthetic Experience and Literary Hermeneutics*, pp. 263–93.

16. See Holub, pp. 134–46.

17. See "The Alterity and Modernity of Medieval Literature," *New Literary History*, 10 (1979), 181–229, a translation by Timothy Bahti of the introductory chapter of *Alterität und Modernität der mittelalterliche Literatur* (München: Fink, 1977).

18. Jauss, "Alterity and Modernity," p. 183.

19. Wellek, "The Fall of Literary History," in *The Attack on Literature* (Chapel Hill: University of North Carolina Press, 1982), p. 77.

20. Herbert Dieckmann et al., "Interview/Hans R. Jauss," trans. Marilyn Sibley Fries, *Diacritics*, 5, no. 1 (1975), 53.

21. Wellek, "Zur methodischen Aporie einer Rezeptionsgeschichte," in *Geschichte: Ereignis und Erzählung*, ed. Reinhart Kosellek and Wolf-Dieter Stempel (München: Fink, 1973), p. 516. Translation mine.

22. E. D. Hirsch, Jr., *Validity in Interpretation* (New Haven and London: Yale University Press, 1967), p. 27.

23. Robert Scholes, *Textual Power* (New Haven and London: Yale University Press, 1985), p. 40.

24. "The Identity of the Poetic Text in the Changing Horizons of Understanding," in *Identity of the Literary Text*, ed. Mario J. Valdés and Owen Miller (Toronto: University of Toronto Press, 1985), p. 165. In *Aesthetic Experience and Literary Hermeneutics*, Jauss seeks to rehabilitate the notion of aesthetic pleasure, and he undertakes a detailed critique of Adorno's *Aesthetics*, pp. 13–21. See also Pauline Johnson, "An Aesthetics of Negativity/An Aesthetics of Reception: Jauss's Dispute with Adorno," *New German Critique*, 42 (1987), 51–70.

25. *Aesthetic Experience*, p. 270.

26. This matter is discussed at greater length and from a historiographical viewpoint in "History of Art and Pragmatic History," in *Toward an Aesthetic of Reception*, pp. 46–75.

27. See Bernd Jürgen Warneken, "Zu Hans Robert Jauss' Programm einer Rezeptionsästhetik," in *Sozialgeschichte und Wirkungsästhetik*, ed. Peter Uwe Hohendahl (Frankfurt: Athenäum, 1974), p. 291.

28. See the diagram of these modalities, *Aesthetic Experience*, p. 159.

29. For a detailed account of the disputes of this period see Hohendahl, *The Institution of Criticism*.

30. See Godzich, Introduction to *Aesthetic Experience*, pp. ix, xiii.

31. Robert Weimann, "'Reception Aesthetics' and the Crisis in Literary History," trans. Charles Spencer, *Clio*, 5 (1975), 22.

32. Weimann, pp. 21–22.

33. Weimann, p. 25.

34. Weimann, p. 30.

35. Weimann, p. 24.

36. *Aesthetic Experience*, p. 4.

37. Warneken, p. 294.

38. Manfred Naumann, "Literary Production and Reception," trans. Peter Heath, *New Literary History*, 8 (1976), 119. This is a translation of portions of Naumann et al., *Gesellschaft, Literatur, Lesen* (Berlin and Weimar: Aufbau-Verlag, 1973).

39. Jauss, "Racine und Goethes *Iphigenie*—Mit einem Nachwort über die Partialität der rezeptionsästhetischen Methode," in *Rezeptionsästhetik*, ed. Rainer Warning (München: Fink, 1975), pp. 384, 389.

40. Quoted in "The Idealist Embarrassment," p. 203.

41. Quoted in "The Idealist Embarrassment," p. 191.

42. "The Idealist Embarrassment," p. 207.

43. Holub, p. 134.

44. *Toward an Aesthetic of Reception*, pp. 30–31. See also *Aesthetic Experience*, p. xxxvi.

45. *Marxism and Literary History* (Cambridge: Harvard University Press, 1986), p. 126.

46. I am thinking here primarily of Jameson's *The Political Unconscious* (Ithaca: Cornell University Press, 1981).

47. See Rien T. Segers, "An Interview with Hans Robert Jauss," trans. Timothy Bahti, *New Literary History*, 11 (1979), 88–89; and Hans Robert Jauss, "Theses on the Transition from the Aesthetics of Literary Works to a Theory of Aesthetic Experience," in *Interpretation of Narrative*, ed. Mario J. Valdés and Owen Miller (Toronto: University of Toronto Press, 1978), pp. 140–42.

48. Perloff, p. 646.

49. Pechter, p. 301.

50. Pechter, p. 295.

51. "Literary Criticism and the Return to 'History,'" *Critical Inquiry*, 14 (1988), 741.

52. Simpson, p. 743.

53. Simpson, p. 742. See Perloff on McGann, pp. 649–53.

54. "Publishing History: A Hole at the Centre of Literary Sociology," *Critical Inquiry*, 14 (1988), 574–89.

55. *The Origins of the English Novel 1600–1740* (Baltimore and London: Johns Hopkins University Press, 1987).

56. *Modes of Production of Victorian Novels* (Chicago and London: University of Chicago Press, 1986).

57. *Toward an Aesthetic*, p. 139.

58. See *Toward an Aesthetic*, p. 140, and Gadamer, *Truth and Method*, pp. 274–78.

59. *George Eliot's Early Fiction* (Berkeley and Los Angeles: University of California Press, 1968), p. 1.

Chapter 2

1. See John Holloway, *The Victorian Sage* (London: Macmillan, 1953). Basil Willey also includes Eliot in a book largely devoted to writers of nonfiction prose, *Nineteenth-Century Studies* (1949; rpt. Harmondsworth: Penguin, 1964).

2. Although, as Anthony McCobb points out, "there is no definite proof that George Eliot ever read a word of Hegel's," it is unlikely that she did not read at least part of the *Aesthetik*. See McCobb, *George Eliot's Knowledge of German Life and Letters* (Salzburg: Universität Salzburg, 1982), p. 114. G. H. Lewes had written a review article she may have known: "Hegel's Aesthetics: Philosophy of Art," *The British and Foreign Review*, 13 (1842), 1–49. Eliot also corresponded with John Sibree, the translator of the *Philosophy of History*. She seems to echo the theory of tragedy in the *Aesthetik* in a passage in the *Letters* (1:247), and Darrel Mansell, Jr., argues for the presence of Hegelian influence in her essay "The Antigone and Its Moral" (*Essays* 261–65) in "A Note on Hegel and George Eliot," *Victorian Newsletter*, 27 (1965), 12–15.

3. See George Levine, "George Eliot's Hypothesis of Reality," *Nineteenth-Century Fiction*, 35 (1980), 1–28, for an interesting account of the way in which Eliot's later work draws on scientific thought. This question is taken up at length, with somewhat different emphases, in Sally Shuttleworth, *George Eliot and Nineteenth-Century Science* (Cambridge: Cambridge University Press, 1984).

4. *The Mirror and the Lamp* (Oxford: Oxford University Press, 1953), p. 53.

5. Abrams, p. 53.

6. For example, compare Eliot's early and later view of Hannah More (*Letters* 1:7 and 1:245) and of another early favourite, Edward Young (*Letters* 1:7 and "Worldliness and Other-Worldliness: The Poet Young," *Essays* 335–85).

7. See Knoepflmacher, *George Eliot's Early Novels*, p. 95.

8. "Preface to *Lyrical Ballads*," in *English Critical Texts*, ed. D. J. Enright and Ernst de Chickera (London: Oxford University Press, 1962), p. 165.

9. Wordsworth, p. 166.

10. See Abrams, p. 229, and generally, chapter 9, "Literature as a Revelation of Personality," pp. 226–62.

11. Wordsworth, p. 164.

12. Abrams, pp. 104–5.

13. Useful accounts of the criticism of both Lewes and Eliot may be found in Richard Stang, *The Theory of the Novel in England 1850–1870* (New York: Columbia University Press, 1959), *passim*. Stang discusses the two writers separately. Gordon S. Haight asserts their intellectual independence of one another in "George Eliot's Theory of Fiction," *Victorian Newsletter*, 10 (1956), 1–3.

14. These details are from Stang, pp. 148–49. See also Raymond Williams, *Keywords*, rev. ed. (London: Fontana, 1983), pp. 257–62, for a history of the word *realism* in English.

15. See Stang, p. 149. George Levine includes an extended discussion of Thackeray in *The Realistic Imagination* (Chicago and London: University of Chicago Press, 1981), pp. 131–80.

16. Levine, *The Realistic Imagination*, p. 15.

17. Levine, *The Realistic Imagination*, pp. 15–18.

18. "Realism in Art: Recent German Fiction," *Westminster Review* (1858), rpt. in *A Victorian Art of Fiction*, ed. John Charles Olmsted (New York and London: Garland, 1979), p. 392. Italics Lewes's.

19. Stang notes the frequency of these and other metaphors, p. 149.

20. Lewes, "The Novels of Jane Austen," *Blackwood's Magazine* (1859), rpt. in *A Victorian Art of Fiction*, p. 447.

21. Lewes, "Realism in Art," in *A Victorian Art of Fiction*, pp. 394–95.

22. *The Life and Works of Goethe* (1855; rpt. London: Dent, 1908), p. 53.

23. I have distinguished between "Positivism," the organized system, or religion, based on the writings of Comte, and "positivism," the belief that all ideas are capable of empirical verification. Obviously one cannot keep these two entirely separate, as Comte's Religion of Humanity had many Victorian fellow travellers who accepted only certain philosophical tenets from Comte's writings. For an excellent historical account of Positivism see T. R. Wright, *The Religion of Humanity* (Cambridge: Cambridge University Press, 1986).

24. See Nigel Cross, *The Common Writer* (Cambridge: Cambridge University Press, 1985), pp. 179–86.

25. Eliot had already decided to attempt to write fiction herself when she wrote "Silly Novels by Lady Novelists." See Thomas Pinney's headnote to the article (*Essays* 300–301).

26. Cross, *Common Writer*, pp. 182–83.

27. See Janice Carlisle, *The Sense of an Audience* (Brighton: Harvester, 1982), pp. 169–70, and generally pp. 166–86.

28. Carlisle, p. 20.

29. Introduction to *Scenes of Clerical Life*, by George Eliot (Harmondsworth: Penguin, 1973), p. 18.

30. Lodge, p. 18.

31. "Art and Belles Lettres," *Westminster Review*, 65 (April 1856), 626–27.

32. *Studies in European Realism*, trans. Edith Bone (London: Hillway, 1950), p. 6.

33. See James D. Benson, "'Sympathetic' Criticism: George Eliot's Response to Contemporary Reviewing," *Nineteenth-Century Fiction*, 29 (1975), 428–40.

34. "Ruskin and George Eliot's 'Realism,'" *Criticism*, 7 (1965), 204.

35. I am following the usual practice of regarding the narrator of the novels up to *The Mill on the Floss* as a male persona. After the publication of *The Mill* the identity of George Eliot was public knowledge, and Eliot no longer attempted to impersonate a Thackerayan voice.

36. See Michael McKeon's discussion of epistemological questions in relation to early fiction in the section of *The Origins of the English Novel* entitled "Questions of Truth," pp. 23–128.

37. The comparison of literary realism to Dutch painting is not original to George Eliot. For example, Scott had evoked the Flemish school of painting in a review of Jane Austen's *Emma* in 1815, and Stang notes that the comparison "was to be used for countless other novels in the course of the century" (p. 142).

38. See Hugh Witemeyer, *George Eliot and the Visual Arts* (New Haven and London: Yale University Press, 1979), pp. 22–25, for a correction of the common misconception that Eliot only liked genre paintings, or that she thought they were the highest kind of art.

39. *The Principles of Success in Literature*, 3rd ed., Fred N. Scott, ed. (Boston, 1891), p. 84.

40. Abrams, p. 50.

41. Stang, p. 149.

42. Witemeyer, p. 4.

43. Ian Adam, "The Structure of Realisms in *Adam Bede*," *Nineteenth-Century Fiction*, 30 (1975), 127–49, identifies three distinct types of realism: pictorial, analytical, and dramatic. They are distinguished by narrative perspective and tone.

44. *The Pastoral Novel* (Charlottesville: University Press of Virginia, 1974), pp. 53–85. See also Kenny Marotta, "*Adam Bede* as a Pastoral," *Genre*, 9 (1976), 59–72.

45. Squires, pp. 60–67.

46. Witemeyer, pp. 75–76.

47. Witemeyer, p. 115.

48. Witemeyer discusses the blurring of generic boundaries in Victorian art, p. 115.

49. Christopher Wood, *The Pre-Raphaelites* (London: Weidenfeld and Nicolson, 1981), p. 17. George Eliot's realism is compared to the Pre-Raphaelites by a contemporary reviewer as a means of attacking her. See Rev. J. C. Robertson, unsigned review article, *Quarterly Review*, 108 (October 1860), 485.

50. Ludwig Feuerbach, *The Essence of Christianity*, trans. George Eliot (New York: Harper, 1957), p. 60.

51. E.g., "'Come now,' he went on, bringing forward the bottle and the loaf, and pouring some wine into a cup, 'I must have a bit and a sup myself. Drink a drop with me, my lad—drink with me'" (*AB* 42;472); "Adam, with an air of quiet obedience, took up the cup, and drank a little" (p. 473); "'Take a bit, then, and another sup, Adam, for the love of me'" (p. 475).

For a summary of the relationship between *The Essence of Christianity* and *Adam Bede* see U. C. Knoepflmacher, *Religious Humanism and the Victorian Novel* (Princeton: Princeton University Press, 1965), pp. 55–59.

52. *Uncle Tom's Cabin* sold 150,000 copies within six months of publication; *Pickwick Papers* was selling 40,000 copies per issue by the time part 15 appeared; Reade's *It Is Never Too Late to Mend* sold 65,000 copies in seven years. Thackeray, on the other hand, sold no more than 7,000 of each monthly part of *Vanity Fair*. These figures are from Richard D. Altick, *The English Common Reader* (Chicago and London: University of Chicago Press, 1957), pp. 301, 383–86.

53. "Victorian Reviewers and Cultural Responsibility," in *1859: Entering an Age of Crisis*, ed. Philip Appleman et al. (Bloomington: Indiana University Press, 1959), pp. 269–89.

54. Wolff, p. 283.

55. *Toward an Aesthetic*, p. 37.

56. I am using this word in the sense which Jurij Tynjanov gave it in his essay, "On Literary Evolution." Tynjanov explains the "automatization" of a literary element as an "effacement" or change in function. The element which is automatized becomes auxiliary, so for example, "If the meter of a poem is 'effaced,' then the other signs of verse and the other elements of the work become more important in its place, and the meter takes on other functions." In *Readings in Russian Poetics*, ed. Ladislaw Matejka and Krystyna Pomorska (Cambridge, Mass.: MIT Press, 1971), p. 69.

57. See Cross, *Common Writer*, for an account of the workings of the Victorian Grub Street, especially chapter 5, "The Female Drudge," pp. 164–203.

58. See Roland F. Anderson, "George Eliot Provoked: John Blackwood and Chapter Seventeen of *Adam Bede*," *Modern Philology*, 71 (1973), 39–47, for a full discussion of Eliot's relations with Blackwood up to the writing of chapter 17 of *Adam Bede*.

59. Whitwell Elwin, "*The Newcomes*," *Quarterly Review*, 97 (September 1855), rpt. in *A Victorian Art of Fiction*, p. 173.

60. Elwin, in *A Victorian Art of Fiction*, p. 175.

61. Elwin, in *A Victorian Art of Fiction*, p. 176.

62. Stang, p. 51.

63. "W. M. Thackeray, Artist and Moralist," *National Review*, 2 (January 1856), rpt. in *A A Victorian Art of Fiction*, p. 228.

64. Roscoe, in *A Victorian Art of Fiction*, p. 247.

65. Roscoe, in *A Victorian Art of Fiction*, p. 258.

66. The "imaginative penetrative" is one of the three types of imagination Ruskin describes in *Modern Painters*, vol. 2, part 3, section 2 (1846).

67. Kenneth Graham, *English Criticism of the Novel 1865–1900* (Oxford: Clarendon Press, 1965), p. 71.

68. *The Virginians*, ed. George Saintsbury (London: Oxford University Press, n.d.), p. 604. Quoted in Carlisle, p. 185.

69. *The Historical Novel*, trans. Hannah and Stanley Mitchell (1962; rpt. Harmondsworth: Penguin, 1981), p. 32. An important exception to this generalization about Scott is *The Heart of Mid-Lothian*, which focuses on the peasant girl Jeanie Deans. It is interesting that this novel is often regarded as one of the major influences on *Adam Bede*.

70. *Henry Esmond*, ed. George Saintsbury (London: Oxford University Press, n.d.), p. 14.

71. The details of original publication of reviews quoted from David Carroll, ed., *George Eliot: The Critical Heritage* (London: Routledge & Kegan Paul), are given in section 2 of the bibliography: "Victorian Reviews of George Eliot."

72. Gordon S. Haight, *George Eliot: A Biography* (New York and Oxford: Oxford University Press, 1968), p. 272.

73. *Atlantic Monthly*, 4 (October 1859), 522.

74. *Edinburgh Review*, 110 (July 1859), 249. *The George Eliot Letters* (3:148) identifies the author of this review as John Forster, but the *Wellesley Index of Victorian Periodicals* says that it is by Caroline E. S. Norton. Since the *Wellesley Index* bases its attribution on the account books of the *Edinburgh Review*, it is more likely to be correct.

75. *Blackwood's*, 85 (April 1859), 504.

76. *Edinburgh Review*, 110 (July 1859), 229–30.

77. E.g., Anne Mozley writes in *Bentley's Quarterly Review* (*CH* 86) that novels, by becoming more realistic, have gained ground in spite of the protests of "utilitarianism, useful knowledge, and Puritanism."

78. *Literary Gazette*, 26 February 1859, p. 281.

79. *Literary Gazette*, 26 February 1859, p. 281.

80. *Dublin Review*, 47 (1859), 42.

81. R. H. Hutton, "The Novels of George Eliot," *National Review*, 11 (July 1860), rpt. in *A A Victorian Art of Fiction*, p. 473. The review is wrongly attributed to Walter Bagehot in this collection.

82. Haight, *George Eliot*, pp. 269, 278. See also Suzanne Graver, *George Eliot and Community* (Berkeley and Los Angeles: University of California Press, 1984), p. 259.

83. *Westminster Review*, 71 (1859), 502.

84. For two modern studies which treat Eliot in the same way see note 1 to this chapter.

85. Marghanita Laski, *George Eliot and Her World* (London: Thames and Hudson, 1973), p. 95.

86. Hutton, in *A Victorian Art of Fiction*, p. 468.

87. Hutton, in *A Victorian Art of Fiction*, p. 469.

88. Hutton, in *A Victorian Art of Fiction*, p. 485.

89. *The Athenaeum*, 7 April 1860, p. 468.

90. Elinor Shaffer, *"Kubla Khan" and the Fall of Jerusalem* (Cambridge: Cambridge University Press, 1975), makes a similar point, pp. 234, 248–49, 253.

91. Eliot's response to Dallas is contained in a letter to William Blackwood, 27 May 1860 (*Letters* 3:299).

92. *Quarterly Review*, 108 (October 1860), 475.

93. *Quarterly Review*, 108 (October 1860), 498.

94. Here I am thinking especially of Paul de Man's work, for example, the essay "Intentional Structure of the Romantic Image," in *The Rhetoric of Romanticism* (New York: Columbia University Press, 1984), pp. 1–17; and "The Rhetoric of Temporality," in *Blindness and Insight*, pp. 187–228.

95. Graver, p. 14.

96. *Dublin Review*, 47 (1859), 34.

97. See Joseph Butwin, "The Pacification of the Crowd: From 'Janet's Repentance' to *Felix Holt*," *Nineteenth-Century Fiction*, 35 (1980), 349–71.

98. Murray Krieger, "*Adam Bede* and the Cushioned Fall: The Extenuation of Extremity" in *The Classic Vision* (Baltimore and London: Johns Hopkins University Press, 1971), pp. 208–9.

99. *North British Review*, 30 (May 1859), 563.

100. *The Country and the City* (1973; rpt. St. Albans: Paladin, 1975), pp. 204–5.

101. John Goode, "*Adam Bede*," in *Critical Essays on George Eliot*, ed. Barbara Hardy (London: Routledge & Kegan Paul, 1970), p. 29.

102. Shuttleworth, p. 44.

103. Although I focus on different aspects of the novel, my account of its rhetoric is similar to that of Dianne F. Sadoff, who writes: "Although George Eliot renounced Evangelicalism in favor of Feuerbachianism more than a decade before writing *Adam Bede*, her yearning for the transcendental signified undercuts her religion of man throughout the novel, and creates a tension between transcendence and realism which cannot be resolved in the novel's overdetermined closure." "Nature's Language: Metaphor in the Text of *Adam Bede*," *Genre*, 11 (1978), 411.

104. This stock Victorian phrase was applied to Dinah by the reviewer in the *Literary Gazette*, 26 February 1859, p. 282.

105. *Toward an Aesthetic of Reception*, p. 185.

Chapter 3

1. Many reviewers recognized the radically different nature of *Daniel Deronda* from its predecessors. R. E. Francillon was the most unequivocal; he wrote in *Gentleman's Magazine* that "it is practically a first book by a new author, and must be judged accordingly" (*CH* 396).

2. *Macmillan's Magazine*, 14 (August 1866), 272.

3. *Macmillan's Magazine*, 14 (August 1866), 272.

4. W. J. Harvey, "Criticism of the Novel: Contemporary Reception," in *Middlemarch: Critical Approaches to the Novel*, ed. Barbara Hardy (London: Athlone, 1967), p. 143.

5. Harvey, pp. 130–31.

6. Harvey, pp. 128–29.

7. J. A. Sutherland, *Victorian Novelists and Publishers* (Chicago: University of Chicago Press, 1976), pp. 190–93. For a detailed account of the circumstances surrounding the first edition of *Middlemarch* see Sutherland's chapter, "Marketing *Middlemarch*," pp. 188–205.

8. Sutherland, *Victorian Novelists*, p. 199.

9. "One Round of a Long Ladder: Gender, Profession, and the Production of *Middlemarch*," *English Studies in Canada*, 12 (1986), 219.

10. Haight, *George Eliot*, p. 443.

11. Sutherland, *Victorian Novelists*, pp. 202–3.

12. *Fortnightly Review*, 26 (1 November 1876), 601.

13. *Edinburgh Review*, 144 (October 1876), 442.

14. *Edinburgh Review*, 144 (October 1876), 443.

15. *Edinburgh Review*, 144 (October 1876), 450.

16. See Feltes, "One Round of a Long Ladder."

17. Sutherland, *Victorian Novelists*, p. 76; for Dickens and Thackeray see pp. 76–78.

18. Sutherland, *Victorian Novelists*, p. 196.

19. Graham, p. 71.

20. *An Autobiography* (London,1883), 2: 67.

21. Trollope, 1: 95.

22. Quoted in J. W. Cross, ed., *George Eliot's Life as Related in Her Letters and Journals* (Edinburgh and London: Blackwood, 1885), 3: 42. Italics mine.

23. *The Athenaeum*, 8 September 1875, p. 372.

24. *The Athenaeum*, 27 November 1875, p. 709.

25. *Impressions of Theophrastus Such*, in vol. 10 of *The Works of George Eliot* (Edinburgh and London: Blackwood, 1901), p. 100.

26. See Sol Liptzin, "The English Reception of Heine," *Victorian Newsletter*, no. 11 (1957), pp. 14–16.

27. See McCobb, pp. 192–201.

28. Arnold's "Heinrich Heine" was first published in *The Cornhill Magazine* (August 1863), and reprinted in *Essays in Criticism: First Series* (1865). I have used the text in *Prose Works*, ed. R. H. Super (Ann Arbor: University of Michigan Press, 1962), 3: 108.

29. Arnold, 3: 112–13.

30. *The Examiner*, 29 January 1876, p. 124.

31. *Fortnightly Review*, 26 (1 November 1876), 602.

32. *Fortnightly Review*, 26 (1 November 1876), 608.

33. *Darwin's Plots* (London: Routledge & Kegan Paul, 1983), p. 200.

34. *The Athenaeum*, 29 April 1876, pp. 593–94.

35. Graham, p. 122.

36. "The Strong Side of 'Daniel Deronda,'" *The Spectator*, 29 July 1876, p. 948.

37. *The Athenaeum*, 29 January 1876, p. 160; "Gwendolen Harleth," *Spectator*, 29 January 1876, p. 139.

38. *Examiner*, 29 January 1876, p. 125; *Edinburgh Review*, 144 (October 1876), 451.

39. *The Athenaeum*, 1 July 1876, p. 14; 2 September 1876, p. 303.

40. *Jewish Chronicle*, 15 December 1876, p. 585.

41. "The Rev. Dr. Hermann Adler on 'Daniel Deronda,'" *Jewish Chronicle*, 15 December 1876, p. 586.

42. "Mordecai: A Protest against the Critics," *Macmillan's*, 36 (June 1877), 102.

43. *George Eliot and Judaism*, 2nd ed. (1888; rpt. New York: Haskell House, 1970), pp. 10; 90.

44. Kaufmann, p. 45.

45. Among the most important studies are the chapter by Elinor Shaffer; Cynthia Chase, "The Decomposition of the Elephants: Double-Reading *Daniel Deronda*," *PMLA*, 93 (1978), 215–27; Sara M. Putzell-Korab, "The Role of the Prophet: The Rationality of Daniel Deronda's Idealist Mission," *Nineteenth-Century Fiction*, 37 (1982), 170–87; and Mary Wilson Carpenter, "The Apocalypse of the Old Testament: *Daniel Deronda* and the Interpretation of Interpretation," *PMLA*, 99 (1984), 56–71. George Levine, in "George Eliot's Hypothesis of Reality," stresses Eliot's achievement in *Deronda*. There are chapter-length accounts of the novel in Beer, *Darwin's Plots*, and in Rachel M. Brownstein, *Becoming a Heroine* (Harmondsworth: Penguin, 1984), pp. 203–38.

46. *Edinburgh Review*, 144 (October 1876), 455.

47. *Edinburgh Review*, 144 (October 1876), 456.

48. *Edinburgh Review*, 144 (October 1876), 450.

49. Graver, p. 253.

50. Graver, p. 254.

51. Graver, pp. 254–55. She is quoting from Joseph Jacobs's review.

52. *The Examiner*, 29 January 1876, p. 125.

53. For example, by Ian Watt, *The Rise of the Novel* (London: Chatto & Windus, 1957); Altick, *The English Common Reader*; Sutherland, *Victorian Novels*; Cross, *The Common Writer*.

54. *Fiction and the Reading Public* (London: Chatto & Windus, 1932), p. 169.

55. Leavis, *Fiction and the Reading Public*, p. 63.

56. Leavis, *Fiction and the Reading Public*, p. 161.

57. For example, Leavis talks of "a drug addiction to fiction" (p. 152), and describes the personality of the "eighteenth-century novelist"—rather a large abstraction—as "a mature, discreet, well-balanced personality" (p. 157). Words like "mature" and "adult" occur repeatedly as honorific terms in the work.

58. Literacy among males increased in England from 67.3 percent in 1841 to 97.2 percent in 1900. Among females the increase in the same period was from 51.1 percent to 96.8 percent. Statistics from Altick, p. 171. For the effects of increased disposable income on working-class leisure activities see F. M. L. Thompson, *The Rise of Respectable Society* (London: Fontana, 1988), pp. 288–91. See also Raymond Williams, *The Long Revolution* (London: Chatto & Windus, 1961), pp. 166–72.

59. *The Closing of the American Mind* (New York: Simon and Schuster, 1987).

60. See Robert A. Colby, "'How It Strikes a Contemporary': The 'Spectator' as Critic," *Nineteenth-Century Fiction*, 11 (1956), 182–206. A more recent and much fuller account of Hutton as a critic is Malcolm Woodfield, *R. H. Hutton: Critic and Theologian* (Oxford: Clarendon Press, 1986).

61. "The Strong Side of 'Daniel Deronda,'" *Spectator*, 29 July 1876, p. 948.

62. *DD* 40;462. See Witemeyer, pp. 101–4.

63. Shaffer, p. 265.

64. Shaffer, p. 265.

65. See Shaffer, pp. 251–82.

66. Kaufmann, p. 26.

67. "'Daniel Deronda': George Eliot and Political Change," in Hardy, ed., *Critical Essays on George Eliot*, p. 149.

68. Shaffer, p. 267.

69. See "Gwendolen Harleth and 'The Girl of the Period,'" in *George Eliot*, ed. Anne Smith (London: Vision, 1980), pp. 196–217.

70. Shaffer, p. 289.

Chapter 4

1. *Literary Criticism*, ed. Leon Edel and Mark Wilson, 2 vols. (New York: Library of America, 1984). All quotations from James are from this edition and page references will be given in the text. The abbreviation *EL* refers to vol. 1 *Essays on Literature, American Writers, English Writers*; *FW* to vol. 2, *French Writers, Other European Writers, The Prefaces to the New York Edition*. Details of first publication of James's reviews of George Eliot are given in section 2 of the bibliography: "Victorian Reviews of George Eliot."

2. See F. R. Leavis, *The Great Tradition* (1948; rpt. Harmondsworth: Penguin, 1962), pp. 93–140.

3. Useful models for such a study would be found in two essays by Jauss: "Goethe and Valéry's Faust: On the Hermeneutics of Question and Answer," in *Toward an Aesthetic of Reception*, pp. 110–38 and "Racine und Goethe's *Iphigenie*."

4. Paul B. Armstrong considers Henry James in relation to phenomenology in *The Phenomenology of Henry James* (Chapel Hill and London: University of North Carolina Press, 1983). For the Geneva school see Sarah N. Lawall, *Critics of Consciousness* (Cambridge, Mass.: Harvard University Press, 1968).

5. Armstrong, p. 207.

6. Leon Edel, *1843–1870: The Untried Years*, vol. 1 of *Henry James* (Philadelphia and New York: J. B. Lippincott, 1953), p. 294.

7. For a discussion of Arnold's influence on James see Vivien Jones, *James the Critic* (London: Macmillan, 1985), pp. 6–14.

8. This is immediately obvious from the contrast between the wide range of modes of literature which Jauss identified in his essay on lyric poetry of the year 1857 and the relatively narrow range which my own study of the reception of *Adam Bede* in chapter 2 suggests was present in England in 1859.

9. Graham, p. 77.

10. Jones, p. 108.

11. See Armstrong's chapter on "The Art of Fiction," pp. 37–68.

12. Elizabeth Coleman, "Henry James Criticism: A Case Study in Critical Inquiry," *Nineteenth-Century Fiction*, 40 (1985), 327.

13. When James, in "The Art of Fiction," calls the novel "a personal, a direct impression of life" (*EL* 50), the emphasis should be placed on the word "impression" as much as on the word "life." Armstrong, in his discussion of "The Art of Fiction," compares James's notion of the "impression" with Husserl's theory of "aspects" (*Abschattungen*). See pp. 37–45. Coleman also makes much of the differences between James's essay and Stevenson's response to it in "A Humble Remonstrance." She totally ignores James's response to Stevenson in a letter which, according to Armstrong, shows that "at bottom they actually agree" (p. 58).

14. Henry James, *The Middle Years* (London: Collins, 1917), pp. 80–81.

15. James, *The Middle Years*, p. 83.

16. Haight, *George Eliot*, p. 514.

17. James, *The Middle Years*, pp. 84–85.

18. Joan Bennett, *George Eliot: Her Mind and Her Art* (Cambridge: Cambridge University Press, 1948); Barbara Hardy, *The Novels of George Eliot* (London: Athlone, 1959); W. J. Harvey, *The Art of George Eliot* (London: Chatto & Windus, 1961).

19. "George Eliot," in *Victorian Fiction*, ed. Lionel Stevenson (Cambridge, Mass.: Harvard University Press, 1964), p. 294.

20. The first professor of English was the Reverend Thomas Dale, whose brief tenure at University College, London University commenced in 1828. See Franklin E. Court, "The Social and Historical Significance of the First English Literature Professorship in England," *PMLA*, 103 (1988), 796–807. However, the discipline was not really established on a systematic or widespread basis until the late nineteenth century. See Chris Baldick, *The Social Mission of English Criticism 1848–1932* (Oxford: Clarendon, 1983) for an account of "the views taken by the founders of modern English Studies and literary critics regarding the wider social effects and aims of this activity" (p. 3). Gerald Graff provides an institutional history of English studies in the U.S.A. in *Professing Literature* (Chicago and London: University of Chicago Press, 1987).

21. Gordon Haight, in his edition of the *Letters*, notes a number of these deletions, among the most famous of which are the comment, in an early letter on the morality of fiction, that "I shall carry to my grave the mental diseases with which they [novels and romances] have

contaminated me" (*Letters* 1:22), and the sentence, from a letter in which she speculates on the effect on herself of her father's death, which reads "I had a horrid vision of myself last night becoming earthly sensual and devilish for want of that purifying restraining influence" (*Letters* 1:284).

22. Gordon S. Haight, ed., *A Century of George Eliot Criticism* (Boston: Houghton Mifflin, 1965), p. xii.

23. *George Eliot* (New York: Alfred A. Knopf, 1975), p. 21.

24. Harvey, "George Eliot," p. 301.

25. *The Letters of Virginia Woolf*, ed. Nigel Nicolson and Joanne Trautmann, vol. 2 (New York: Harcourt Brace Jovanovich, 1976), pp. 321–22.

26. Two accounts of Eliot's debt to Positivism are Martha S. Vogeler, "George Eliot and the Positivists," *Nineteenth-Century Fiction*, 35 (1980), 406–31; and T. R. Wright, "George Eliot and Positivism: A Reassessment," *Modern Language Review*, 76 (1981), 257–72. The former studies Eliot in relation to the organized movement of Positivism and shows that Eliot had little connection with it. Wright, however, suggests persuasively that Comte is often present in Eliot's fiction, although more often than not her use of him tends to be critical. For a detailed history of the English Positivists see Wright, *The Religion of Humanity*.

27. In Haight, ed., *A Century of George Eliot Criticism*, p. 161.

28. In Haight, ed., *A Century of George Eliot Criticism*, p. 162.

29. "George Eliot" in *Aspects and Impressions* (London: Cassell, 1922), p. 1.

30. Gosse, p. 15.

31. Gosse, p. 8.

32. Baldick, p. 59.

33. Graff, p. 58.

34. *The English Novel* (London: Dent, 1913), p. 249.

35. *A Short History of English Literature* (1898; rpt. London: Macmillan, 1913), p. 753.

36. *Corrected Impressions*, 2nd ed. (London: Heinemann, 1913), p. 166.

37. Sir A. W. Ward and A. R. Walker, eds., *The Nineteenth Century II*, vol. 13 of *The Cambridge History of English Literature* (Cambridge: Cambridge University Press, 1916), pp. 340–402.

38. *A Survey of English Literature, 1830–1880* (London, 1920), excerpted in Haight, ed., *A Century of George Eliot Criticism*, pp. 197, 192.

39. *English Literature: Modern* (London: Williams and Northgate, 1911), p. 229. The work was reprinted eleven times between 1914 and 1929.

40. "Other Novelists of the Mid-Century" in *A Literary History of England*, ed. Albert C. Baugh, 2nd ed. (New York: Appleton-Century-Crofts, 1967), p. 1378. The second edition is, apart from the bibliographies and supplements, identical with the 1948 edition.

41. See Robert Morss Lovett and Helen Sand Hughes, *The History of the Novel in England* (Boston: Houghton Mifflin, 1932), p. 300, for a contrast—originating with the French critic Brunetière—between French naturalism and English realism, which concludes that Eliot's is

the superior mode. See also Ernest A. Baker, *The History of the English Novel* (London: H. F. & G. Witherby, 1937), 8: 269, for the same point, and Baker's chapter on Eliot generally for the emphasis on her humour (pp. 221–73).

42. See Baldick, chapter 4, "Literary-Critical Consequences of the War," pp. 87–108; and Terry Eagleton, *Literary Theory* (Oxford: Blackwell, 1983), pp. 28–30. For similar tendencies in the U.S.A. see Graff, pp. 69–72, and 128–32.

43. See Baldick, pp. 87–108.

44. Eagleton, *The Function of Criticism* (London: Verso, 1984), p. 66.

45. *Cornhill*, 43 (February 1881), 152–68, reprinted in *CH*; "Cross, Mary Ann or Marian (1819–1880)," *DNB* (1888); *George Eliot* (London: Macmillan, 1902). Subsequent references to *George Eliot* are given in the text in parentheses.

46. Stephen, "Cross, Mary Ann," 5: 218.

47. Stephen, "Cross, Mary Ann," 5: 221.

48. *The Craft of Fiction* (1921; rpt. New York: Viking, 1957). References to the work are given in the text.

49. *The Rhetoric of Fiction* (Chicago: University of Chicago Press, 1961).

50. *Aspects of the Novel* (1927; rpt. Harmondsworth: Penguin, 1962), p. 16.

51. Forster, p. 136.

52. "The Novels of George Eliot," *Criterion*, 18 (October 1938), 56.

53. *Early Victorian Novelists* (London: Constable, 1934), n.p. Subsequent references are given in the text.

54. *The English Novel* (1954; rpt. Harmondsworth: Penguin, 1958), p. 222.

55. Allen, *The English Novel*, p. 234.

56. *George Eliot* (New York: Macmillan, 1964), p. 148.

57. "The Greening of Sister George," *Nineteenth-Century Fiction*, 35 (1980), 295.

58. Woolf's essays on the subject are collected in *Women and Writing*, ed. Michèle Barrett (Dunvegan, Ont.: Quadrant, 1984). All quotations from Woolf are from this edition unless otherwise noted.

59. *A Room of One's Own* (London: Hogarth Press, 1929), pp. 110–11.

60. Showalter, "The Greening of Sister George," p. 292.

Chapter 5

1. For a very effective attack on the early professors of English see Q. D. Leavis, "The Discipline of Letters," *Scrutiny*, 12 (1943), 12–46.

2. I will at times refer to both Leavises, since they worked together and were part of a wider circle who shared many assumptions and who produced *Scrutiny* as a joint effort. However, my primary focus is on F. R. Leavis, since he wrote the crucial study of George Eliot with which I am mainly concerned here.

3. Ronald Hayman, *Leavis* (London: Heinemann, 1976) is merely an enthusiastic summary of Leavis's ideas, a poor substitute for reading the original works. Robertson undertakes the promising task of studying both the Leavises in relation to the novel in *The Leavises on Fiction* (New York: St. Martin's, 1981), but his work is theoretically naive, attempting to be "objective" and thereby falling into precisely the "bloodless neutrality" he declares that he wants to avoid (p. xi). Bilan, *The Literary Criticism of F. R. Leavis* (Cambridge: Cambridge University Press, 1979), is much more substantial, and contains useful critiques of Leavis's criticism. However, Bilan is not at all rigorous in his account of "Leavis's View of Society," and his response to Marxist attacks on that view is to suggest that such positions "given their bias can hardly be accepted uncritically," implying that, unlike the work of Hill and Williams, Bilan's own work transcends the ideological altogether. See p. 12.

4. See Raymond Williams, *Culture and Society 1780–1950* (1958; rpt. Harmondsworth: Penguin, 1963), pp. 246–57, and *The Country and the City*, pp. 312–13; Terry Eagleton, *Criticism and Ideology* (London: Verso, 1978), pp. 11–43, *Literary Theory*, pp. 30–53, and *The Function of Criticism*, pp. 69–84. For another interesting Marxist account see Iain Wright, "F. R. Leavis, the *Scrutiny* Movement and the Thirties," in *Culture and Crisis in Britain in the Thirties*, ed. Jon Clark et al. (London: Lawrence & Wishart, 1979), pp. 37–65.

5. F. R. Leavis, "Criticism and Literary History," *Scrutiny*, 4 (1935), 96–100. Bateson's response and a rejoinder by Leavis are published in "Correspondence," *Scrutiny*, 4 (1935), 181–87. René Wellek, "Literary Criticism and Philosophy," *Scrutiny*, 5 (1937), 375–83; F. R. Leavis, "Literary Criticism and Philosophy: A Reply," *Scrutiny*, 6 (1937), 59–70.

6. For an excellent account of the New Critics as a response to the prevailing practices in American universities see Graff, pp. 145–61 and 183–94.

7. *The Common Pursuit* (London: Chatto & Windus, 1952), p. 114.

8. *The Great Tradition*, p. 40. Subsequent references to *The Great Tradition* will be given in the text; references to other works by Leavis are all contained in the notes.

9. "Re-Reading the Great Tradition," in *Re-Reading English*, ed. Peter Widdowson (London and New York: Methuen, 1982), p. 128.

10. *Culture and Environment* (London: Chatto & Windus, 1933), pp. 1–2.

11. *Culture and Environment*, p. 5. Italics mine.

12. *The Country and the City*, pp. 18–21.

13. *The Country and the City*, pp. 312–13.

14. See Baldick, pp. 175–86.

15. "F. R. Leavis," in *Language and Silence* (1962; rpt. New York: Atheneum, 1967), p. 229.

16. The discussion of George Eliot was first published in the following issues of *Scrutiny*: 13 (1945), 172–87; 13 (1945), 257-71; 14 (1946), 15–26; 14 (1946), 102–31.

17. For a good discussion of the problems involved see Bilan, pp. 137–48.

18. See the discussion of *Middlemarch* in Hardy's *The Novels of George Eliot*, passim.

19. In fairness, one must note that Leavis modified his position subsequently, and wrote "in the re-reading that preceded the present note, my already growing sense that the surgery of disjunction would be a less simple and satisfactory affair than I had thought has been reinforced. And I have here given my reasons for holding that the admirer of George Eliot's

genius, intent on a full appreciation, will demand the whole book that she wrote, and will be right." "George Eliot's Zionist Novel," *Commentary*, 30 (1960), 318.

20. Leavis uses Shelley as a point of reference in his denigration of Balzac in *The Great Tradition*, pp. 40–41n.

21. "*Scrutiny*: A Retrospect," included in the reprint of *Scrutiny* (Cambridge: Cambridge University Press, 1963), 20: 5.

22. "*Adam Bede*," in "*Anna Karenina*" *and Other Essays* (London: Chatto & Windus, 1967), p. 49.

23. "*Adam Bede*," p. 55.

24. "Fiction and the 'Matrix of Analogy,'" *Kenyon Review*, 11 (1949), 539–60.

25. Schorer, p. 539.

26. Schorer, p. 556.

27. Harvey, *The Art of George Eliot*, p. 49.

28. The following are works either on George Eliot or containing a chapter on George Eliot and written by, or edited by, Barbara Hardy: *The Novels of George Eliot: A Study in Form* (London: Athlone, 1959); *The Appropriate Form: An Essay on the Novel* (London: Athlone, 1964); *Middlemarch: Critical Approaches to the Novel*, ed. Barbara Hardy (London: Athlone 1967); *Critical Essays on George Eliot*, ed. Barbara Hardy (London: Routledge & Kegan Paul, 1970); *Particularities: Readings in George Eliot* (London: Peter Owen, 1982); *Forms of Feeling in Victorian Fiction* (London: Peter Owen, 1985).

29. *Particularities*, p. 37.

30. *The Appropriate Form*, p. 1.

31. *The Appropriate Form*, p. 3.

32. See *The Appropriate Form*, pp. 3–4.

33. *Critical Practice* (London and New York: Methuen, 1980), p. 8.

34. *The Novels of George Eliot*, p. 233.

35. In *Particularities*, pp. 147–73. The essay was originally delivered as a lecture at Princeton University in 1979.

36. *Particularities*, pp. 149–50.

37. *Particularities*, p. 150.

38. In *Particularities*, pp. 75–85. The essay was originally the W. D. Thomas Memorial Lecture, University College, Swansea, 1973.

39. *Particularities*, p. 83.

40. A good example of Leavis's straightforward assertiveness in matters of belief occurs when he takes exception to David Cecil's attack on George Eliot's "Puritanism": "I had better confess that I differ (apparently) from Lord David Cecil in sharing these beliefs, admirations, and disapprovals, so that the reader knows my bias at once. And they seem to me favourable to the production of great literature" (*The Great Tradition*, p. 23).

Chapter 6

1. *The Novels of George Eliot*, p. 236.

2. Eagleton, *Criticism and Ideology*, p. 21.

3. See *Writing in Society* (London: Verso, 1983), p. 197.

4. "Fiction and the Rising Industrial Classes," *Essays in Criticism*, 17 (1967), 64.

5. Craig, p. 67.

6. "*Felix Holt, the Radical*," in Hardy, ed., *Critical Essays on George Eliot*, p. 110.

7. Kettle, p. 107.

8. Kettle, p. 109.

9. Williams, *Culture and Society*, p. 119.

10. *The English Novel from Dickens to Lawrence* (1970; rpt. St Albans: Paladin, 1974), pp. 62–77; *The Country and the City*, pp. 202–21.

11. Williams, *The English Novel*, pp. 64, 21.

12. Williams, *The English Novel*, p. 70.

13. Eagleton, *Criticism and Ideology*, p. 36.

14. Eagleton, *Criticism and Ideology*, p. 33.

15. Eagleton's work attempts to transcend the traditional Marxist commitments to mimesis and realism. See also Frow, *Marxism and Literary History*, and Tony Bennett, *Formalism and Marxism* (London and New York: Methuen, 1979).

16. Williams, *The Country and the City*, p. 208.

17. Williams, *The Country and the City*, p. 220.

18. It is worth noting that in *The Function of Criticism*, Eagleton reconsiders Williams's work and his own "diversion" into structuralist Marxism. See pp. 108–15.

19. Eagleton, *Criticism and Ideology*, p. 111.

20. Eagleton, *Criticism and Ideology*, p. 113.

21. *Social Figures* (Minneapolis: University of Minnesota Press, 1987).

22. Cottom, p. xxi.

23. Cottom, p. xx.

24. Foreword to Cottom, pp. xvi-xvii.

25. Eagleton, *Criticism and Ideology*, p. 116.

26. "Lyric Poetry and Society," trans. Bruce Mayo, *Telos*, 20 (1974), 57–58.

27. *Toward an Aesthetic of Reception*, p. 45. Translation slightly altered.

28. See Sheets's excellent discussion of the novel: "*Felix Holt*: Language, the Bible, and the Problematic of Meaning," *Nineteenth-Century Fiction*, 37 (1982), 146–69.

29. Sheets, p. 156.

30. See Catherine Gallagher, *The Industrial Reformation of English Fiction* (Chicago and London: University of Chicago Press, 1985), pp. 219–67.

31. Gallagher, p. 237.

32. Felix Holt is generally regarded by critics as espousing a Positivist theory of social change. For example, see Fred C. Thomson, "Politics and Society in *Felix Holt*," in *The Classic British Novel*, ed. Howard M. Harper, Jr., and Charles Edge (Athens: University of Georgia Press, 1972), p. 104.

33. Gillian Beer, *George Eliot* (Bloomington: Indiana University Press, 1986), p. 138.

34. A rather different treatment of the relationship between law and a higher Law in *Felix Holt* can be found in Norman Vance, "Law, Religion, and the Unity of *Felix Holt*," in Smith, ed., *George Eliot*, pp. 103–23.

35. For a discussion of the genesis of the legal plot in Eliot's correspondence with Frederic Harrison see Fred C. Thomson, "The Legal Plot in *Felix Holt*," *Studies in English Literature*, 7 (1967), 691–704.

36. For Eliot's "unavowed utopias" see Shaffer, p. 229.

37. Beer, *George Eliot*, p. 136.

38. "*Felix Holt*: Society as Protagonist," *Nineteenth-Century Fiction*, 17 (1962), 239.

39. Sheets, p. 165.

Chapter 7

1. Leavis, *The Great Tradition*, p. 37.

2. Leavis, *The Great Tradition*, p. 51.

3. Woolf, *Women and Writing*, p. 155.

4. *Memoirs of a Dutiful Daughter*, trans. James Kirkup (1959; rpt. Harmondsworth: Penguin, 1963), p. 140.

5. "[Why] Are There No Great Women Critics? And What Difference Does It Make?" in *The Prism of Sex*, ed. Julia A. Sherman and Evelyn Torton Beck (Madison: University of Wisconsin Press, 1977), p. 87.

6. For an interesting reading of *The Mill on the Floss* in terms of its divergences from a Wordsworthian paradigm see Margaret Homans's excellent "Eliot, Wordsworth, and the Scenes of the Sisters' Instruction," in *Bearing the Word* (Chicago: University of Chicago Press, 1986), pp. 120–52.

7. Gayle Greene and Coppélia Kahn identify two tasks for feminist scholarship: the revision of "concepts previously thought universal but now seen as originating in particular cultures and serving particular purposes"; and the restoration of "a feminist perspective by extending knowledge about women's experience and contributions to culture." "Feminist Scholarship and the Social Construction of Women," in *Making a Difference* (London and New York: Methuen, 1985), p. 2. Elaine Showalter sees these tasks as having been undertaken in a roughly sequential order, naming the first "feminist critique" and the second "gynocritics." "Feminist Criticism in the Wilderness," in *Writing and Sexual Difference*, ed. Elizabeth Abel (Chicago: University of Chicago Press, 1982), pp. 10–17.

8. *Literary Women* (London: Women's Press, 1978), pp. 194–95.

9. "Why Feminist Critics Are Angry with George Eliot," *College English*, 37 (1976), 549–61. It should be noted that not all "feminist critique" was as unsympathetic to George Eliot. Two useful accounts of *The Mill on the Floss* which read the novel as a record of the effect of sexist stereotypes are Elizabeth Deeds Ermarth, "Maggie Tulliver's Long Suicide," *Studies in English Literature*, 14 (1974), 587–601, and Carla L. Peterson, "The Heroine as Reader in the Nineteenth-Century Novel: Emma Bovary and Maggie Tulliver," *Comparative Literature Studies*, 17 (1980), 168–83.

10. Showalter, "Feminist Criticism in the Wilderness," pp. 14–15.

11. *A Literature of Their Own*, rev. ed. (London: Virago, 1982), pp. 7, 10.

12. Showalter, *A Literature of Their Own*, p. 35.

13. See Toril Moi, *Sexual/Textual Politics* (London and New York: Methuen, 1985), pp. 1–18.

14. Showalter, *A Literature of Their Own*, p. 131. For Ermarth and Peterson see note 9 in this chapter.

15. Showalter, "The Greening of Sister George," p. 299.

16. Showalter, "The Greening of Sister George," p. 310.

17. *The Madwoman in the Attic* (New Haven and London: Yale University Press, 1979), p. xi. Italics mine. Subsequent references to this work are included parenthetically in the text.

18. See "The Power of Hunger: Demonism and Maggie Tulliver," *Nineteenth-Century Fiction*, 30 (1975), 150–71.

19. de Man, *Blindness and Insight*, p. 26.

20. Moi, p. 65.

21. See Beer, *George Eliot*, pp. 147–99, for a discussion of *Middlemarch* in the context of the women's movement of the 1860s, and specifically p. 180 for the rejection of Moers's assertion that George Eliot was no feminist. An earlier, but still valuable discussion of the same topic is Kathleen Blake, "*Middlemarch* and the Woman Question," *Nineteenth-Century Fiction*, 31 (1976), 285–312.

22. Moi, pp. 1–18.

23. Moi, p. 49.

24. The links between feminist and historicist literary studies are considered in Judith Newton, "History as Usual?: Feminism and the 'New Historicism,'" *Cultural Critique*, 9 (1988), 87–121, and Janet Todd, *Feminist Literary History* (New York: Routledge, 1988).

25. Nancy K. Miller, "Emphasis Added: Plots and Plausibilities in Women's Fiction," *PMLA*, 96 (1981), 36–48. See also Elizabeth Weed, "*The Mill on the Floss* or the Liquidation of Maggie Tulliver," *Genre*, 11 (1978), 427–44; and Mary Jacobus, "The Question of Language: Men of Maxims and *The Mill on the Floss*," in Abel, ed., *Writing and Sexual Difference*, pp. 37–52. Subsequent references to Miller's article are incorporated parenthetically in the text.

26. "J. Hillis Miller: The Other Victorian at Yale," in *The Yale Critics*, ed. Jonathan Arac et al. (Minneapolis: University of Minnesota Press, 1983), p. 75.

27. The phrase is Donald Martin's, in the introduction to Arac, ed., p. xxix.

28. "Narrative and History," *ELH*, 41 (1974), 459. Subsequent references are incorporated paren-
    thetically in the text.

29. "Optic and Semiotic in *Middlemarch*," in *The Worlds of Victorian Fiction*, ed. Jerome H.
    Buckley (Cambridge, Mass., and London: Harvard University Press, 1975), pp. 125–45.
    Subsequent references are incorporated parenthetically in the text.

30. Gilbert and Gubar, p. 530.

31. Miller himself argues this in a "Commentary" on chapter 85 of *Middlemarch*, which is part
    of Barbara Hardy, J. Hillis Miller, and Richard Poirier, "*Middlemarch*, Chapter 85: Three
    Commentaries," *Nineteenth-Century Fiction*, 35 (1980), 432–53. For Miller's contribution
    see pp. 441–48.

32. See Roland Barthes, *S/Z*, trans. Richard Miller (New York: Hill and Wang, 1974); Levine,
    The Realistic Imagination, pp. 3-22.

33. "Variations on Authority: Some Deconstructive Transformations of the New Criticism," in
    Arac, ed., p. 4.

34. Chase, p. 218.

35. See Christopher Norris, *Deconstruction* (London and New York: Methuen, 1982), pp. 133–
    35; Jonathan Culler, *The Pursuit of Signs* (Ithaca: Cornell University Press, 1981), pp.
    176–78.

36. Chase, p. 218.

37. Graff, p. 242.

38. Scholes, p. 33.

39. Newton, p. 90.

Bibliography

Part 1 of the Bibliography lists only works by George Eliot. Part 2 includes all reviews cited in the text, and gives details of first publication only. The abbreviation *CH* identifies those reviews which were quoted from *George Eliot: The Critical Heritage*, ed. David Carroll. Reviews by Henry James were quoted from the collected *Literary Criticism*, ed. Leon Edel and Mark Wilson. Most of the attributions of authorship of unsigned reviews are from either Carroll or from Constance Marie Fulmer, *George Eliot: A Reference Guide*. Since the latter is not an entirely reliable work I have tried to verify its attributions from other sources, but in some cases that was not possible. Part 3 lists all other works cited in the text.

1. Primary Sources

Eliot, George. *Adam Bede*. Ed. Stephen Gill. Harmondsworth: Penguin, 1980.
———. "Art and Belles Lettres." *Westminster Review*, 65 (April 1856), 625–50.
———. *Daniel Deronda*. Ed. Graham Handley. Oxford: Clarendon Press, 1984.
———. *Essays of George Eliot*. Ed. Thomas Pinney. London: Routledge & Kegan Paul, 1963.
———. *Felix Holt, the Radical*. Ed. Fred C. Thomson. Oxford: Clarendon Press, 1980.
———. *The George Eliot Letters*. Ed. Gordon S. Haight. 9 vols. New Haven: Yale University Press, 1954–78.
———. *Impressions of Theophrastus Such*. In Vol. 10 of *The Works of George Eliot: Library Edition*. Edinburgh and London: Blackwood, 1901.
———. *Middlemarch: A Study of Provincial Life*. Ed. David Carroll. Oxford: Clarendon Press, 1986.
———. *The Mill on the Floss*. Ed. Gordon S. Haight. Oxford: Clarendon Press, 1980.
———. *Romola*. Ed. Andrew Sanders. Harmondsworth: Penguin, 1980.
———. *Scenes of Clerical Life*. Ed. Thomas A. Noble. Oxford: Clarendon Press, 1985.
———. *Silas Marner: The Weaver of Raveloe*. Ed. Q. D. Leavis. Harmondsworth: Penguin, 1967.

2. Victorian Reviews of George Eliot

Review Articles on Several Novels

Hutton, R. H. "The Novels of George Eliot." *National Review*, 11 (July 1860), 191–219.
James, Henry. "The Novels of George Eliot." *Atlantic Monthly*, 18 (October 1866), 479–92.
———. Review of Cross's *Life* of George Eliot. *Atlantic Monthly*, 55 (May 1885), 668–78.
Morley, John. "George Eliot's Novels." *Macmillan's Magazine*, 14 (August 1866), 272–79.
Robertson, The Rev. J. C. Unsigned review of *Scenes of Clerical Life, Adam Bede, The Mill on the Floss*. *Quarterly Review*, 108 (October 1860), 469–99.

Simpson, Richard. "George Eliot's Novels." *Home and Foreign Review*, 3 (October 1863), 522–49. In *CH*.

Scenes of Clerical Life

Anon. *Saturday Review*, 29 May 1858, pp. 566–67. In *CH*.
Lucas, Samuel. Unsigned review. *The Times*, 2 January 1858, p. 9. In *CH*.

Adam Bede

Anon. *Atlantic Monthly*, 4 (October 1859), 521–22.
Anon. *Literary Gazette*, 26 February 1859, pp. 281–83.
Anon. *London Quarterly Review*, 16 (July 1861), 301–7. In *CH*.
Anon. *North British Review*, 30 (May 1859), 562–64.
Anon. *Saturday Review*, 26 February 1859, pp. 250–51. In *CH*.
Chapman, John. Unsigned review. *Westminster Review*, 71 (1859), 486–512.
Collins, W. L. Unsigned review. *Blackwood's Magazine*, 85 (April 1859), 490–504.
Mozley, Anne. Unsigned review. *Bentley's Quarterly Review*, 1 (July 1859), 433–56. In *CH*.
Norton, Caroline E. S. Unsigned review of *Adam Bede* and *Scenes of Clerical Life*. *Edinburgh Review*, 110 (July 1859), 223–46.
Taylor, Frances. Unsigned review. *Dublin Review*, 47 (1859), 33–42.

The Mill on the Floss

Anon. *Dublin University Magazine*, 57 (February 1861), 192–200. In *CH*.
Dallas, E. S. *The Times*, 19 May 1860, pp. 10–11. In *CH*.
Jewsbury, Geraldine. Unsigned review. *The Athenaeum*, 7 April 1860, pp. 467–68.

Felix Holt, the Radical

James, Henry. Unsigned review. *Nation*, 16 August 1866, pp. 127–28.

Middlemarch

James, Henry. Unsigned review. *Galaxy*, 15 (March 1873), 424–28.
Hutton, R. H. Unsigned review of book 1. *The Spectator*, 16 December 1871, pp. 1528–29. In *CH*.
———. "George Eliot's Moral Anatomy." Unsigned review of book 6. *The Spectator*, 5 October 1872, pp. 1262–64. In *CH*.
———. Unsigned review. *The Spectator*, 7 December 1872, pp. 1554–56. In *CH*

Daniel Deronda

Anon. *The Athenaeum*, 29 January 1876, p. 160.
Anon. *The Athenaeum*, 29 April 1876, pp. 593–94.
Anon. *The Athenaeum*, 1 July 1876, pp. 14–15.
Anon. *The Athenaeum*, 2 September 1876, p. 303.
Anon. *Edinburgh Review*, 144 (October 1876), 442–70.
Anon. "A New Novel by 'George Eliot.'" *The Examiner*, 29 January 1876, pp. 124–25.
Anon. *Jewish Chronicle*, 15 December 1876, p. 585.
Anon. "The Rev. Dr. Hermann Adler on 'Daniel Deronda.'" *Jewish Chronicle*, 15 December 1876, p. 586.

Anon. *Saturday Review*, 16 September 1876, pp. 356–58. In *CH*.

Colvin, Sidney. Unsigned review. *Fortnightly Review*, 26 (1 November 1876), 601–16.

Dicey, A. V. Unsigned review. *Nation*, 19 October 1876, pp. 245–46. In *CH*.

Dowden, Edward. "*Middlemarch* and *Daniel Deronda*." *Contemporary Review*, 29 (February 1877), 348–69. In *CH*.

Francillon, R. E. Review. *Gentleman's Magazine*, 17 (October 1876), 411–27. In *CH*.

Hutton, R. H. "Gwendolen Harleth." *The Spectator*, 29 January 1876, pp. 138–39.

––––––. "The Strong Side of 'Daniel Deronda.'" *The Spectator*, 29 July 1876, p. 948.

––––––. Unsigned review. *The Spectator*, 9 September 1876, pp. 1131–33. In *CH*.

Jacobs, Joseph. "Mordecai: A Protest against the Critics." *Macmillan's Magazine*, 36 (June 1877), 101–11.

James, Henry. "Daniel Deronda: A Conversation." *Atlantic Monthly*, 38 (December 1876), 684–94.

Kaufmann, David. *George Eliot and Judaism*. Edinburgh, 1877. (Translation of a three-part article in *Monatschrift für Geschichte und Wissenschaft*.)

Picciotto, James. Review. *Gentleman's Magazine*, 17 (November 1876), 593–603. In *CH*.

Saintsbury, George. Review. *Academy*, 9 September 1876, pp. 253–54. In *CH*.

3. Other Sources

Abel, Elizabeth, ed. *Writing and Sexual Difference*. Chicago: University of Chicago Press, 1982.

Abrams, M. H. *The Mirror and the Lamp: Romantic Theory and the Critical Tradition*. Oxford: Oxford University Press, 1953.

Adam, Ian. "The Structure of Realisms in *Adam Bede*." *Nineteenth-Century Fiction*, 30 (1975), 127–49.

Adorno, Theodor W. "Lyric Poetry and Society." Trans. Bruce Mayo. *Telos*, 20 (1974), 56–71.

Allen, Walter. *The English Novel: A Short Critical History*. 1954; rpt. Harmondsworth: Penguin, 1958.

––––––. *George Eliot*. New York: Macmillan, 1964.

Altick, Richard D. *The English Common Reader: A Social History of the Mass Reading Public 1800–1900*. Chicago and London: University of Chicago Press, 1957.

Anderson, Roland F. "George Eliot Provoked: John Blackwood and Chapter Seventeen of *Adam Bede*." *Modern Philology*, 71 (1973), 39–47.

Arac, Jonathan, et al., eds. *The Yale Critics: Deconstruction in America*. Theory and History of Literature 6. Minneapolis: University of Minnesota Press, 1983.

Armstrong, Paul B. *The Phenomenology of Henry James*. Chapel Hill and London: University of North Carolina Press, 1983.

Arnold, Matthew. *Essays in Criticism: First Series*. In *Lectures and Essays in Criticism*. Vol. 3 of *Complete Prose Works*. Ed. R. H. Super. Ann Arbor: University of Michigan Press, 1962.

Auerbach, Nina. "The Power of Hunger: Demonism and Maggie Tulliver." *Nineteenth-Century Fiction*, 30 (1975), 150–71.

Austen, Zelda. "Why Feminist Critics Are Angry with George Eliot." *College English*, 37 (1976), 549–61.

Baker, Ernest A. "George Eliot." In *The History of the English Novel*. London: H. F. & G. Witherby, 1937. 8: 221–73.

Baldick, Chris. *The Social Mission of English Criticism 1848–1932*. Oxford: Clarendon Press, 1983.

Barthes, Roland. *S/Z*. Trans. Richard Miller. New York: Hill and Wang, 1974.

Beauvoir, Simone de. *Memoirs of a Dutiful Daughter*. Trans. James Kirkup. 1959; rpt. Harmondsworth: Penguin, 1963.

Beer, Gillian. *Darwin's Plots: Evolutionary Narrative in Darwin, George Eliot, and Nineteenth-Century Fiction*. London: Routledge & Kegan Paul, 1983.

_____ . *George Eliot*. Bloomington: Indiana University Press, 1986.

Belsey, Catherine. *Critical Practice*. London and New York: Methuen, 1980.

_____ . "Re-Reading the Great Tradition." In *Re-Reading English*. Ed. Peter Widdowson. London and New York: Methuen, 1982, pp. 121–35.

Bennett, Joan. *George Eliot: Her Mind and Her Art*. Cambridge: Cambridge University Press, 1948.

Bennett, Tony. *Formalism and Marxism*. London and New York: Methuen, 1979.

Benson, James D. "'Sympathetic' Criticism: George Eliot's Response to Contemporary Reviewing." *Nineteenth-Century Fiction*, 29 (1975), 428–40.

Bethell, S. L. "The Novels of George Eliot." *Criterion*, 18 (October 1938), 39–57.

Bilan, R. P. *The Literary Criticism of F. R. Leavis*. Cambridge: Cambridge University Press, 1979.

Blake, Kathleen. "*Middlemarch* and the Woman Question." *Nineteenth-Century Fiction*, 31 (1976), 285–312.

Bloom, Allan. *The Closing of the American Mind: How Higher Education Has Failed Democracy and Impoverished the Souls of Today's Students*. New York: Simon and Schuster, 1987.

Booth, Wayne. *The Rhetoric of Fiction*. Chicago: University of Chicago Press, 1961.

Bové, Paul A. "Variations on Authority: Some Deconstructive Transformations of the New Criticism." In *The Yale Critics: Deconstruction in America*. Ed. Jonathan Arac et al. Theory and History of Literature 6. Minneapolis: University of Minnesota Press, 1983, pp. 3–19.

Brownstein, Rachel M. *Becoming a Heroine: Reading about Women in Novels*. Harmondsworth: Penguin, 1984.

Butwin, Joseph. "The Pacification of the Crowd: From 'Janet's Repentance' to *Felix Holt*." *Nineteenth-Century Fiction*, 35 (1980), 349–71.

Carlisle, Janice. *The Sense of an Audience: Dickens, Thackeray, and George Eliot at Mid-Century*. Brighton: Harvester, 1982.

Carpenter, Mary Wilson. "The Apocalypse of the Old Testament: *Daniel Deronda* and the Interpretation of Interpretation." *PMLA*, 99 (1984), 56–71.

Carroll, David R. "*Felix Holt*: Society as Protagonist." *Nineteenth-Century Fiction*, 17 (1962), 237–52.

_____ . *George Eliot: The Critical Heritage*. London: Routledge & Kegan Paul, 1971.

Cecil, Lord David. *Early Victorian Novelists: Essays in Revaluation*. London: Constable, 1934.

Chase, Cynthia. "The Decomposition of the Elephants: Double-Reading *Daniel Deronda*." *PMLA*, 93 (1978), 215–27.

Chew, Samuel C. "Other Novelists of the Mid-Century." In *A Literary History of England*. Ed. Albert C. Baugh. 2nd ed. New York: Appleton-Century-Crofts, 1967, pp. 1364–81.

Colby, Robert A. "'How It Strikes a Contemporary': The 'Spectator' as Critic." *Nineteenth-Century Fiction*, 11 (1956), 182–206.

Coleman, Elizabeth. "Henry James Criticism: A Case Study in Critical Inquiry." *Nineteenth-Century Fiction*, 40 (1985), 327–44.

Cottom, Daniel. *Social Figures: George Eliot, Social History, and Literary Representation*. Theory and History of Literature 44. Minneapolis: University of Minnesota Press, 1987.

Court, Franklin E. "The Social and Historical Significance of the First English Literature Professorship in England." *PMLA*, 103 (1988), 796–807.

Craig, David. "Fiction and the Rising Industrial Classes." *Essays in Criticism*, 17 (1967), 64–74.

Cross, J. W., ed. *George Eliot's Life as Related in Her Letters and Journals*. 3 vols. Edinburgh and London: Blackwood, 1885.

Cross, Nigel. *The Common Writer: Life in Nineteenth-Century Grub Street*. Cambridge: Cambridge University Press, 1985.

Culler, Jonathan. *The Pursuit of Signs: Semiotics, Literature, Deconstruction*. Ithaca: Cornell University Press, 1981.

de Man, Paul. *Blindness and Insight: Essays in the Rhetoric of Contemporary Criticism.* 2nd ed. Theory and History of Literature 7. Minneapolis: University of Minnesota Press, 1983.

———. "Intentional Structure of the Romantic Image." In *The Rhetoric of Romanticism.* New York: Columbia University Press, 1984, pp. 1–17.

Dieckmann, Herbert, et al. "Interview/Hans R. Jauss." Trans. Marilyn Sibley Fries. *Diacritics,* 5, No. 1 (1975), 53–61.

Eagleton, Terry. *Criticism and Ideology: A Study in Marxist Literary Theory.* London: Verso, 1978.

———. *The Function of Criticism: From the Spectator to Post-Structuralism.* London: Verso, 1984.

———. *Literary Theory: An Introduction.* Oxford: Blackwell, 1983.

Edel, Leon. *1843–1870: The Untried Years.* Vol. 1 of *Henry James.* Philadelphia and New York: J. B. Lippincott, 1953.

Elton, Oliver. *A Survey of English Literature, 1830–1880.* 2 vols. London: Edward Arnold, 1920.

Elwin, Whitwell. "*The Newcomes.*" *Quarterly Review,* 97 (September 1855), 350–78.

Ermarth, Elizabeth Deeds. "Maggie Tulliver's Long Suicide." *Studies in English Literature,* 14 (1974), 587–601.

Feltes, N. N. *Modes of Production of Victorian Novels.* Chicago and London: University of Chicago Press, 1986.

———. "One Round of a Long Ladder: Gender, Profession, and the Production of *Middlemarch.*" *English Studies in Canada,* 12 (1986), 210–228.

Feuerbach, Ludwig. *The Essence of Christianity.* Trans. George Eliot. New York: Harper, 1957.

Forster, E. M. *Aspects of the Novel.* 1927; rpt. Harmondsworth: Penguin, 1962.

Frow, John. *Marxism and Literary History.* Cambridge, Mass.: Harvard University Press, 1986.

Fulmer, Constance Marie. *George Eliot: A Reference Guide.* Boston: G. K. Hall, 1977.

Gadamer, Hans-Georg. *Truth and Method.* No trans. 1975; rpt. New York: Crossroad, 1984.

———. *Wahrheit und Methode: Grundzüge einer philosophischen Hermeneutik.* 3rd ed. Tübingen: Mohn, 1972.

Gallagher, Catherine. *The Industrial Reformation of English Fiction: Social Discourse and Narrative Form 1832–1867.* Chicago and London: University of Chicago Press, 1985.

Gilbert, Sandra M., and Susan Gubar. *The Madwoman in the Attic: The Woman Writer and the Nineteenth-Century Literary Imagination.* New Haven and London: Yale University Press, 1979.

Goode, John. "*Adam Bede.*" In *Critical Essays on George Eliot.* Ed. Barbara Hardy. London: Routledge & Kegan Paul, 1970, pp. 19–41.

Gosse, Edmund. "George Eliot." In *Aspects and Impressions.* London: Cassell, 1922, pp. 1–16.

Graff, Gerald. *Professing Literature: An Institutional History.* Chicago and London: University of Chicago Press, 1987.

Graham, Kenneth. *English Criticism of the Novel 1865–1900.* Oxford: Clarendon Press, 1965.

Graver, Suzanne. *George Eliot and Community: A Study in Social Theory and Fictional Form.* Berkeley and Los Angeles: University of California Press, 1984.

Greene, Gayle, and Coppélia Kahn. *Making a Difference: Feminist Literary Criticism.* London and New York: Methuen, 1985.

Haight, Gordon S. *George Eliot: A Biography.* New York and Oxford: Oxford University Press, 1968.

———. "George Eliot's Theory of Fiction." *Victorian Newsletter,* 10 (1956), 1–3.

———, ed. *A Century of George Eliot Criticism.* Boston: Houghton Mifflin, 1965.

Hardy, Barbara. *The Appropriate Form: An Essay on the Novel.* London: Athlone, 1964.

———. *Forms of Feeling in Victorian Fiction.* London: Peter Owen, 1985.

———. *The Novels of George Eliot: A Study in Form.* London: Athlone, 1959.

———. *Particularities: Readings in George Eliot.* London: Peter Owen, 1982.

———, ed. *Critical Essays on George Eliot.* London: Routledge & Kegan Paul, 1970.

————. *Middlemarch: Critical Approaches to the Novel*. London: Athlone, 1967.

Hardy, Barbara, J. Hillis Miller, and Richard Poirier. "*Middlemarch*, Chapter 85: Three Commentaries." *Nineteenth-Century Fiction*, 35 (1980), 432–53.

Harvey, W. J. *The Art of George Eliot*. London: Chatto & Windus, 1961.

————. "Criticism of the Novel: Contemporary Reception." In *Middlemarch: Critical Approaches to the Novel*. Ed. Barbara Hardy. London: Athlone, 1967, pp. 125–47.

————. "George Eliot." In *Victorian Fiction: A Guide to Research*. Ed. Lionel Stevenson. Cambridge, Mass.: Harvard University Press, 1964, pp. 294–323.

Hayman, Ronald. *Leavis*. London: Heinemann, 1976.

Hirsch, Jr., E. D. *Validity in Interpretation*. New Haven and London: Yale University Press, 1967.

Hohendahl, Peter Uwe. *The Institution of Criticism*. Ithaca: Cornell University Press, 1982.

————. "Introduction to Reception Aesthetics." Trans. Marc Silberman. *New German Critique*, 10 (1977), 29–63.

————, ed. *Sozialgeschichte und Wirkungsästhetik: Dokumente zur empirischen und marxistischen Rezeptionsforschung*. Frankfurt: Athenäum, 1974.

Holloway, John. *The Victorian Sage: Studies in Argument*. London: Macmillan, 1953.

Holub, Robert C. *Reception Theory: A Critical Introduction*. London and New York: Methuen, 1984.

Homans, Margaret. *Bearing the Word: Language and Female Experience in Nineteenth-Century Women's Writing*. Chicago and London: University of Chicago Press, 1986.

Jacobus, Mary. "The Question of Language: Men of Maxims and *The Mill on the Floss*." In *Writing and Sexual Difference*. Ed. Elizabeth Abel. Chicago: University of Chicago Press, 1982, pp. 37–52.

James, Henry. *Literary Criticism*. Ed. Leon Eden and Mark Wilson. 2 vols. Vol. 1 *Essays on Literature, American Writers, English Writers*. Vol. 2 *French Writers, Other European Writers, The Prefaces to the New York Edition*. Library of America 22 and 23. New York: Library of America, 1984.

————. *The Middle Years*. London: Collins, 1917.

Jameson, Fredric. *The Political Unconscious: Narrative as a Socially Symbolic Act*. Ithaca: Cornell University Press, 1981.

Jauss, Hans Robert. *Aesthetic Experience and Literary Hermeneutics*. Trans. Michael Shaw. Theory and History of Literature 3. Minneapolis: University of Minnesota Press, 1982.

————. *Alterität und Modernitat der mittelalterliche Literatur: Gesammelte Aufsätze 1956–1976*. München: Fink, 1977.

————. "The Alterity and Modernity of Medieval Literature." Trans. Timothy Bahti. *New Literary History*, 10 (1979), 181–229.

————. *Ästhetische Erfahrung und literarische Hermeneutik I*. München: Fink, 1977.

————. *Ästhetische Erfahrung und literarische Hermeneutik*. Rev. ed. Frankfurt: Suhrkamp, 1982.

————. "The Idealist Embarrassment: Observations on Marxist Aesthetics." Trans. Peter Heath. *New Literary History*, 7 (1975), 191–208.

————. "The Identity of the Poetic Text in the Changing Horizon of Understanding." In *Identity of the Literary Text*. Ed. Mario J. Valdés and Owen Miller. Toronto: University of Toronto Press, 1985, pp. 146–74.

————. *Literaturgeschichte als Provokation*. Frankfurt: Suhrkamp, 1970.

————. *Literaturgeschichte als Provokation der Literaturwissenschaft*. Konstanzer Universitätsreden 3. Konstanz: Universitätsverlag, 1967.

————. "Paradigmawechsel in der Literaturwissenschaft." *Linguistische Berichte*, No. 3 (1969), 44–56.

————. "Racine und Goethes *Iphigenie*—Mit einem Nachwort über die Partialität der rezeptionsästhetischen Methode." *Neue Hefte für Philosophie*, 4 (1973), 1–46. Rpt. in *Rezeptionsästhetik: Theorie und Praxis*. Ed. Rainer Warning. München: Fink, 1975, pp. 353–400.

———— . "Theses on the Transition from the Aesthetics of Literary Works to a Theory of Aesthetic Experience." In *Interpretation of Narrative*. Ed. Mario J. Valdés and Owen Miller. Toronto: University of Toronto Press, 1978, pp. 137–47.

———— . *Toward an Aesthetic of Reception*. Trans. Timothy Bahti. Theory and History of Literature 2. Minneapolis: University of Minnesota Press, 1982.

Johnson, Pauline. "An Aesthetics of Negativity/An Aesthetics of Reception: Jauss's Dispute with Adorno." *New German Critique*, 42 (1987), 51–70.

Jones, Vivien. *James the Critic*. London: Macmillan, 1985.

Kettle, Arnold. "*Felix Holt, the Radical*." In *Critical Essays on George Eliot*. Ed. Barbara Hardy. London: Routledge & Kegan Paul, 1970, pp. 99–115.

Knoepflmacher, U. C. *George Eliot's Early Fiction: The Limits of Realism*. Berkeley and Los Angeles: University of California Press, 1968.

———— . *Religious Humanism and the Victorian Novel: George Eliot, Walter Pater, and Samuel Butler*. Princeton: Princeton University Press, 1965.

Krieger, Murray. "*Adam Bede* and the Cushioned Fall: The Extenuation of Extremity." In *The Classic Vision: The Retreat from Extremity in Modern Literature*. Baltimore and London: Johns Hopkins University Press, 1971, pp. 197–220.

Lanser, Susan Sniader, and Evelyn Torton Beck. "[Why] Are There No Great Women Critics? And What Difference Does It Make?" In *The Prism of Sex: Essays in the Sociology of Knowledge*. Ed. Julia A. Sherman and Evelyn Torton Beck. Madison: University of Wisconsin Press, 1977, pp. 79–91.

Laski, Marghanita. *George Eliot and Her World*. London: Thames and Hudson, 1973.

Lawall, Sarah N. *Critics of Consciousness: The Existential Structures of Literature*. Cambridge, Mass.: Harvard University Press, 1968.

Leavis, F. R. "*Adam Bede*." In "*Anna Karenina*" *and Other Essays*. London: Chatto & Windus, 1967, pp. 49–58.

———— . *The Common Pursuit*. London: Chatto & Windus, 1952.

———— . "Criticism and Literary History." Review of *English Poetry and the English Language* by F. W. Bateson. *Scrutiny*, 4 (1935), 96–100.

———— . "George Eliot's Zionist Novel." *Commentary*, 30 (1960), 317–25.

———— . *The Great Tradition: George Eliot, Henry James, Joseph Conrad*. 1948; rpt. Harmondsworth: Penguin, 1962.

———— . "Literary Criticism and Philosophy: A Reply." *Scrutiny*, 6 (1937), 59–70.

———— . "*Scrutiny*: A Retrospect." In *Scrutiny*. Rpt. Cambridge: Cambridge University Press, 1963, 20, 1–24.

Leavis, F. R., and Denys Thompson. *Culture and Environment*. London: Chatto & Windus, 1933.

Leavis, Q. D. "The Discipline of Letters." *Scrutiny*, 12 (1943), 12–46.

———— . *Fiction and the Reading Public*. London: Chatto & Windus, 1932.

Levine, George. "George Eliot's Hypothesis of Reality." *Nineteenth-Century Fiction*, 35 (1980), 1–28.

———— . *The Realistic Imagination: English Fiction from Frankenstein to Lady Chatterly*. Chicago and London: University of Chicago Press, 1981.

Lewes, George Henry. "Hegel's Aesthetics: Philosophy of Art." *The British and Foreign Review*, 13 (1842), 1–49.

———— . *The Life and Works of Goethe*. 1855; rpt. London: Dent, 1908.

———— . "The Novels of Jane Austen." *Blackwood's*, 86 (July 1859), 99–113.

———— . *The Principles of Success in Literature*. 3rd. ed. Ed. Fred N. Scott. Boston, 1891.

———— . "Realism in Art: Recent German Fiction." *Westminster Review*, 70 (October 1858), 488–518.

Liptzin, Sol. "The English Reception of Heine." *Victorian Newsletter*, No. 11 (1957), pp. 14–16.

Lodge, David. Introduction to *Scenes of Clerical Life*. By George Eliot. Harmondsworth: Penguin, 1973, pp. 7–32.

Lovett, Robert Morss, and Helen Sand Hughes. *The History of the Novel in England*. Boston: Houghton Mifflin, 1932.

Lubbock, Percy. *The Craft of Fiction*. 1921; rpt. New York: Viking, 1957.

Lukács, Georg. *The Historical Novel*. Trans. Hannah and Stanley Mitchell. 1962; rpt. Harmondsworth, Penguin, 1981.

————. *Studies in European Realism: A Sociological Survey of the Writings of Balzac, Stendhal, Zola, Tolstoy, Gorki and Others*. Trans. Edith Bone. London: Hillway, 1950.

Mair, G. H. *English Literature: Modern*. London: Williams and Northgate, 1911.

Mansell, Jr., Darrel. "A Note on Hegel and George Eliot." *Victorian Newsletter*, 27 (1965), 12–15.

————. "Ruskin and George Eliot's 'Realism.'" *Criticism*, 7 (1965), 203–16.

Marotta, Kenny. "*Adam Bede* as a Pastoral." *Genre*, 9 (1976), 59–72.

Martin, Graham. "*Daniel Deronda*: George Eliot and Political Change." In *Critical Essays on George Eliot*. Ed. Barbara Hardy. London: Routledge & Kegan Paul, 1970, pp. 133–50.

McCobb, Anthony. *George Eliot's Knowledge of German Life and Letters*. Romantic Reassessment 102:2. Salzburg: Universität Salzburg, 1982.

McGann, Jerome J. *A Critique of Modern Textual Criticism*. Chicago and London: University of Chicago Press, 1983.

McKeon, Michael. *The Origins of the English Novel 1600–1740*. Baltimore and London: Johns Hopkins University Press, 1987.

Miller, J. Hillis. "Narrative and History." *ELH*, 41 (1974), 455–73.

————. "Optic and Semiotic in *Middlemarch*." In *The Worlds of Victorian Fiction*. Ed. Jerome H. Buckley. Harvard English Studies 6. Cambridge, Mass. and London: Harvard University Press, 1975, pp. 125–45.

Miller, Nancy K. "Emphasis Added: Plots and Plausibilities in Women's Fiction." *PMLA*, 96 (1981), 36–48.

Millett, Kate. *Sexual Politics*. Garden City, N.Y.: Doubleday, 1970.

Moers, Ellen. *Literary Women*. London: Women's Press, 1978.

Moi, Toril. *Sexual/Textual Politics: Feminist Literary Theory*. London and New York: Methuen, 1985.

Naumann, Manfred. "Literary Production and Reception." Trans. Peter Heath. *New Literary History*, 8 (1976), 107–26.

————, et al. *Gesellschaft, Literatur, Lesen: Literaturrezeption in Theoretischer Sicht*. Berlin and Weimar: Aufbau-Verlag, 1973.

Newton, Judith. "History as Usual?: Feminism and the 'New Historicism.'" *Cultural Critique*, 9 (1988): 87–121.

Norris, Christopher. *Deconstruction: Theory and Practice*. London and New York: Methuen, 1982.

Pease, Donald. "J. Hillis Miller: The Other Victorian at Yale." In *The Yale Critics: Deconstruction in America*. Ed. Jonathan Arac et al. Theory and History of Literature 6. Minneapolis: University of Minnesota Press, 1983, pp. 66–89.

Pechter, Edward. "The New Historicism and Its Discontents: Politicizing Renaissance Drama." *PMLA*, 102 (1987), 292–303.

Perloff, Marjorie. "Ca(n)non to the Right of Us, Ca(n)non to the Left of Us: A Plea for Difference." *New Literary History*, 18 (1987), 633–56.

Peterson, Carla L. "The Heroine as Reader in the Nineteenth-Century Novel: Emma Bovary and Maggie Tulliver." *Comparative Literature Studies*, 17 (1980), 168–83.

Putzell-Korab, Sara M. "The Role of the Prophet: The Rationality of Daniel Deronda's Idealist Mission." *Nineteenth-Century Fiction*, 37 (1982), 170–87.

Redinger, Ruby V. *George Eliot: The Emergent Self.* New York: Alfred A. Knopf, 1975.

Robertson, P. J. M. *The Leavises on Fiction: An Historic Partnership.* New York: St. Martin's, 1981.

Roscoe, William Caldwell. "W. M. Thackeray, Artist and Moralist." *National Review*, 2 (January 1856), 177–213.

Ruskin, John. *Modern Painters.* Vol. 2. *Containing Part III, Sections 1 and 2. Of the Imaginative and Theoretic Faculties.* London, 1846.

Sadoff, Dianne F. "Nature's.Language: Metaphor in the Text of *Adam Bede.*" *Genre*, 11 (1978), 411–26.

Saintsbury, George. *Corrected Impressions: Essays on Victorian Writers.* 2nd ed. London: Heinemann, 1895.

———. *The English Novel.* London: Dent, 1913.

———. *A Short History of English Literature.* 1898; rpt. London: Macmillan, 1913.

Sartre, Jean-Paul. *What Is Literature?* Trans. Bernard Frechtman. New York: Harper & Row, 1949.

Schiller, Friedrich. "Was heisst und zu welchem Ende studiert man Universalsgeschichte?—Eine akademische Antrittsrede." In *Historische Schriften.* Vol. 4 of *Sämtliche Werke.* Ed. Gerhard Fricke et al. München: Carl Hanser, 1962, pp. 749–67.

Scholes, Robert. *Textual Power: Literary Theory and the Teaching of English.* New Haven and London: Yale University Press, 1985.

Schorer, Mark. "Fiction and the 'Matrix of Analogy.'" *Kenyon Review*, 11 (1949), 539–60.

Segers, Rien T. "An Interview with Hans Robert Jauss." Trans. Timothy Bahti. *New Literary History*, 11 (1979), 83–95.

Shaffer, Elinor S. *"Kubla Khan" and the Fall of Jerusalem: The Mythological School in Biblical Criticism and Secular Literature 1770–1880.* Cambridge: Cambridge University Press, 1975.

Sheets, Robin. "*Felix Holt*: Language, the Bible, and the Problematic of Meaning." *Nineteenth-Century Fiction*, 37 (1982), 146–69.

Showalter, Elaine. "Feminist Criticism in the Wilderness." In *Writing and Sexual Difference.* Ed. Elizabeth Abel. Chicago: University of Chicago Press, 1982, pp. 9–35.

———. "The Greening of Sister George." *Nineteenth-Century Fiction*, 35 (1980), 292–311.

———. *A Literature of Their Own: British Women Novelists from Brontë to Lessing.* Rev. ed. London: Virago, 1982.

Shuttleworth, Sally. *George Eliot and Nineteenth-Century Science: The Make-Believe of a Beginning.* Cambridge: Cambridge University Press, 1984.

Simpson, David. "Literary Criticism and the Return to 'History.'" *Critical Inquiry*, 14 (1988), 721–47.

Smith, Anne, ed. *George Eliot: Centenary Essays and an Unpublished Fragment.* London: Vision, 1980.

Squires, Michael. *The Pastoral Novel: Studies in George Eliot, Thomas Hardy and D. H. Lawrence.* Charlottesville: University Press of Virginia, 1974.

Stang, Richard. *The Theory of the Novel in England 1850–1870.* New York: Columbia University Press, 1959.

Steiner, George. "F. R. Leavis." In *Language and Silence.* 1962; rpt. New York: Atheneum, 1967, pp. 221–38.

Stephen, Sir Leslie. "Cross, Mary Ann or Marian (1819–1880)." *Dictionary of National Biography* (1888).

———. *George Eliot.* London: Macmillan, 1902.

———. Unsigned obituary article. *Cornhill*, 43 (February 1881), 152–68. In *CH.*

Suleiman, Susan R., and Inge Crosman, eds. *The Reader in the Text: Essays on Audience and Interpretation.* Princeton: Princeton University Press, 1980.

Sutherland, John A. "Publishing History: A Hole at the Centre of Literary Sociology," *Critical Inquiry*, 14 (1988), 574–89.

————. *Victorian Novelists and Publishers*. Chicago: University of Chicago Press, 1976.

Thackeray, William Makepeace. *The History of Henry Esmond, Esq*. Ed. George Saintsbury. London: Oxford University Press, n.d.

————. *The Virginians: A Tale of the Last Century*. Ed. George Saintsbury. London: Oxford University Press, n.d.

Thompson, F. M. L. *The Rise of Respectable Society: A Social History of Victorian Britain, 1830–1900*. London: Fontana, 1988.

Thomson, Fred. C. "The Legal Plot in *Felix Holt*." *Studies in English Literature*, 7 (1967), 691–704.

————. "Politics and Society in *Felix Holt*." In *The Classic British Novel*. Ed. Howard M. Harper, Jr., and Charles Edge. Athens: University of Georgia Press, 1972, pp. 103–20.

Todd, Janet. *Feminist Literary History*. New York: Routledge, 1988.

Tompkins, Jane P., ed. *Reader-Response Criticism: From Formalism to Post-Structuralism*. Baltimore and London: Johns Hopkins University Press, 1980.

Trollope, Anthony. *An Autobiography*. 2 vols. London, 1883.

Tynjanov, Jurij. "On Literary Evolution." In *Readings in Russian Poetics: Formalist and Structuralist Views*. Ed. Ladislaw Matejka and Krystyna Pomorska. Cambridge, Mass.: MIT Press, 1971, pp. 66–78.

Valdés, Mario J. *Phenomenological Hermeneutics and the Study of Literature*. Toronto: University of Toronto Press, 1987.

Vance, Norman. "Law, Religion, and the Unity of *Felix Holt*." In *George Eliot: Centenary Essays and an Unpublished Fragment*. Ed. Anne Smith. London: Vision, 1980, pp. 103–23.

A Victorian Art of Fiction: Essays on the Novel in British Periodicals 1851–1869. Ed. John Charles Olmsted. New York and London: Garland, 1979.

Vogeler, Martha S. "George Eliot and the Positivists." *Nineteenth-Century Fiction*, 35 (1980), 406–31.

Ward, Sir A. W. and A. R. Walker, eds. *The Nineteenth Century II*. Vol. 13 of *The Cambridge History of English Literature*. Cambridge: Cambridge University Press, 1916.

Warneken, Bernd Jürgen. "Zu Hans Robert Jauss' Programm einer Rezeptionsästhetik." In *Sozialgeschichte und Wirkungsästhetik: Dokumente zur empirischen und marxistischen Rezeptionsforschung*. Ed. Peter Uwe Hohendahl. Frankfurt: Athenäum, 1974, pp. 290–96.

Warning, Rainer, ed. *Rezeptionsästhetik: Theorie und Praxis*. München: Fink, 1975.

Watt, Ian. *The Rise of the Novel: Studies in Defoe, Richardson, and Fielding*. London: Chatto & Windus, 1957.

Weed, Elizabeth. "*The Mill on the Floss* or the Liquidation of Maggie Tulliver." *Genre*, 11 (1978), 427–44.

Weimann, Robert. "'Reception Aesthetics' and the Crisis in Literary History." Trans. Charles Spencer. *Clio*, 5 (1975), 3–35.

Wellek, René. "The Fall of Literary History." In *The Attack on Literature and Other Essays*. Chapel Hill: University of North Carolina Press, 1982, pp. 64–77.

————. "Literary Criticism and Philosophy." *Scrutiny*, 5 (1937), 375–83.

————. "Zur methodischen Aporie einer Rezeptionsgeschichte." In *Geschichte: Ereignis und Erzählung*. Ed. Reinhart Koselleck and Wolf-Dieter Stempel. Poetik und Hermeneutik 5. München: Fink, 1973, pp. 515–17.

Willey, Basil. *Nineteenth-Century Studies: Coleridge to Matthew Arnold*. 1949; rpt. Harmondsworth: Penguin, 1964.

Williams, Raymond. *The Country and the City*. 1973; rpt. St. Albans: Paladin, 1975.

————. *Culture and Society 1780–1950*. 1958; rpt. Harmondsworth: Penguin, 1963.

————. *The English Novel from Dickens to Lawrence*. 1970; rpt. St. Albans: Paladin, 1974.

————. *Keywords: A Vocabulary of Culture and Society*. Rev. ed. London: Fontana, 1983.

————. *The Long Revolution*. London: Chatto & Windus, 1961.

_____ . *Writing in Society*. London: Verso, 1983.

Witemeyer, Hugh. *George Eliot and the Visual Arts*. New Haven and London: Yale University Press, 1979.

Wolff, Michael. "Victorian Reviewers and Cultural Responsibility." In *1859: Entering an Age of Crisis*. Ed. Philip Appleman et al. Bloomington: Indiana University Press, 1959, pp. 269–89.

Wood, Christopher. *The Pre-Raphaelites*. London: Weidenfeld and Nicolson, 1981.

Woodfield, Malcolm. *R. H. Hutton, Critic and Theologian: The Writings of R. H. Hutton on Newman, Arnold, Tennyson, Wordsworth, and George Eliot*. Oxford: Clarendon Press, 1986.

Woolf, Virginia. *The Letters of Virginia Woolf*. Ed. Nigel Nicolson and Joanne Trautmann. Vol. 2. New York: Harcourt Brace Jovanovich, 1976.

_____ . *A Room of One's Own*. London: Hogarth Press, 1929.

_____ . *Women and Writing*. Ed. Michèle Barrett. Dunvegan, Ont.: Quadrant, 1984.

Wordsworth, William. "Preface to *Lyrical Ballads*." In *Fnglish Critical Texts*. Ed. D. J. Enright and Ernst de Chickera. London: Oxford University Press, 1962, pp. 162–89.

Wright, Iain. "F. R. Leavis, the *Scrutiny* Movement and the Thirties." In *Culture and Crisis in Britain in the Thirties*. Ed. Jon Clark et al. London: Lawrence & Wishart, 1979, pp. 37–65.

Wright, T. R. "George Eliot and Positivism: A Reassessment." *Modern Language Review*, 76 (1981), 257–72.

_____ . *The Religion of Humanity: The Impact of Comtean Positivism on Victorian Britain*. Cambridge: Cambridge University Press, 1986.

Zimmerman, Bonnie. "Gwendolen Harleth and 'The Girl of the Period.'" In *George Eliot: Centenary Essays and an Unpublished Fragment*. Ed. Anne Smith. London: Vision, 1980, pp. 196–217.

Index